AN INTRODUCTION
TO
CHRISTIAN
MISSIONS

by
HAROLD R. COOK

MOODY PRESS • CHICAGO

To My Wife,
faithful missionary helpmate,
whose love for Christ
and the missionary cause
has never flagged.

©1954
Fifteenth edition, revised, ©1971 by
THE MOODY BIBLE INSTITUTE
OF CHICAGO

Original Title: An Introduction to the Study of
Christian Missions

Sixteenth Printing, 1972

ISBN: 0-8024-4132-7

Printed in the United States of America

CONTENTS

Chapters		Pages
	Preface	5
1	Three Basic Questions	7
2	The New Testament and Missions (I)	18
3	The New Testament and Missions (II)	33
4	The New Testament and Missions (III)	43
5	The Old Testament and Missions (I)	49
6	The Old Testament and Missions (II)	59
7	Motives and Aims of Missions	65
8	Whose Responsibility?	71
9	The Christian's Responsibility—The Missionary Call	78
10	The Missionary Call—Testimonies	92
11	Missionary Qualifications—Essential	102
12	Missionary Qualifications—Physical and Educational	109
13	Missionary Qualifications—Personal Characteristics	118
14	Missionary Preparation—The Indispensables	127
15	Missionary Preparation—Special Subjects	138
16	Why Mission Boards?	152
17	Types of Mission Boards	160
18	How to Choose a Mission	170
19	Independent Missionaries	178
20	What a Missionary Does—Preliminary Tasks	187
21	What a Missionary Does—Major Activities (I)	197
22	What a Missionary Does—Major Activities (II)	209
23	A Church Missionary Program—How to Create Interest (I)	222
24	A Church Missionary Program—How to Create Interest (II)	238
25	A Church Missionary Program—Keeping Informed	244
26	A Church Missionary Program—Missionary Support	250
27	A Church Missionary Program—Personnel and Training	261
28	A Church Missionary Program—Organization	275
	Index	284

Preface to the Revised Edition

EVEN THOUGH THIS BOOK has continued to be widely used as an elementary text, it has seemed to the author that a revision was long overdue. Not that any radical restructuring of the book has been called for. After all, much of it deals with principles that change very slowly if at all. But the world is constantly changing, and the missionary scene is also in a state of flux. In addition there were some subjects not treated in the first edition that missions teachers say they would like to see included. So the whole work has been subjected to a thorough review.

Some of the changes are minor—perhaps scarcely noticeable. Such are the changes in style or expression. They are intended to produce greater smoothness, strength, or clarity. Geographical designations that are outdated have been changed; also such terms as "streetcar conductor" that belong to a slightly earlier day.

For the benefit of students, the underlying outline of the work is now much more clearly indicated. This may also be useful to teachers of the subject.

Here and there the reader will find some enlargement of the original material. At the close of chapter 1 is a brief reference to the new idea of "mission" as opposed to the older "missions." In chapter 2 appears a rather extended treatment of the question, Are the heathen really lost? Chapter 6 adds a brief study of missionary purpose in the Old Testament as revealed in Psalms. The study of motivation in chapter 7 adds a section on the love of Christ. This is basic, though not clearly stated in the original. In chapter 17 it seemed wise to add some explanatory material on the changing financial policies of the faith missions, especially in view of Internal Revenue Service rulings.

But the major changes are in the chapters on the church's missionary program. Besides rather extensive modifications of the text, the latter part of chapter 25 is now included in chapter 26. The former chapters 27 and 28 are now combined in one chapter, while a new chapter 28 is added to deal with the organization of the church's missionary program.

One noticeable omission is the list of suggested books for a church missionary library. So many new books are constantly appearing that such a list is out of date even before it is published. In its place it seemed advisable to tell how to go about locating the best books for the purpose.

All in all, it is the hope of the author that this revised edition will be even more useful than the one it supersedes. He has tried to maintain the same informal and simple style, even at the risk of oversimplification. The aim is not to impress scholars but to provide a useful tool for those who are just beginning to get acquainted with the vast enterprise of Christian missions.

HAROLD R. COOK

1

THREE BASIC QUESTIONS

WHAT PICTURE comes to your mind when people talk about missions? Is it a vision of a man in shorts and sun helmet talking to a bunch of naked savages? That's what it is to many people. And we can hardly blame them. What if it isn't a true picture of most missionary work today? After all, it is hard to put a spiritual enterprise like missions into a picture. And maybe that picture can serve as well as any other to tell the story of Christian missions.

What story does the picture tell you? You know, we often say that "a picture is worth a thousand words," and "good pictures tell the story." But really a picture tells a different story to everyone who looks at it. It depends on our background and experience. The picture of a mountain lake attracts the artist for its beauty. The fisherman sees it and right away wonders how the fishing would be there. But there may be a parent who shudders when he sees it. He remembers a son who was drowned trying to swim in the frigid waters of such a lake. The story is in the viewer as much as in the picture.

What story, then, does your vision of the missionary tell you? Why is he there? What is he talking about? Would you like to be in his shoes? Or do you think the whole thing is rather silly and presumptuous? Does the strangeness of the scene attract you? The romance? Or are you looking beneath the surface? What is your idea of missions?

Now let me give you mine. Perhaps I ought rather to say, let me give you the view of the man in the picture, the missionary. What does he think about it? What does missions mean to him? And to that basic question let us add a couple of others that are related to it. What is the difference between "home" missions and "foreign" missions? And why do some people oppose missions?

WHAT DOES MISSIONS MEAN?

To the Christian missionary and those who send him out, *missions is the Christian church trying to win others to the Christian faith, especially through a group of selected workers called missionaries.* This is the traditional definition. Now let us look at it in detail.

First, we have said that missions is the job of the Christian church. We are not talking here about denominations or local churches. We are talking about the great body of believers in Christ who make up His church. Missions can never be just a private affair. It always involves the church. That is true even of missions carried on by those whom we call "independent missionaries." They may be independent of control by any mission society, but almost always they are sent out and supported by one or more groups of Christians. Besides, they always think of themselves as carrying out a task that Christ gave to the whole church.

Second, we have said that missions is the Christian church trying to win others. In other words, missions calls for serious effort. It is true that some people come into the Christian faith without any person's deliberately trying to win them. But we do not usually count them as the fruit of missions. In this, missions is like selling. You are not a salesman when you simply hand over an item the customer asks for and take his money. You are just a clerk. In the same way missions is not simply making the Christian gospel available. It is not just saying, "Here it is; you can have it if you want it." It means a job of selling, getting people to want it enough to pay the price to get it. The missionary knows this is not easy.

Third, in missions the church is trying to win others to the Christian faith. Here is where we'll find some today who disagree with our definition, for this means, first of all, evangelism. It is evangelism in its historic sense of winning individuals to a faith in Christ. But what is evangelism to the evangelical Christian is proselytism to many others. They look at it as a sort of "sheep-stealing" or "cultural aggression."

For example, there are nonchristian countries today, such as India, that appreciate many of the social services of Christian missions, such as doctors and hospitals. But they object to evangelism. They don't want the people to be converted to the Christian faith. And this is quite understandable.

What is harder to understand is those *Christians* who try to separate the two things. How can you separate Christian service to humanity from the love of Christ that inspires it? Such people seem like those who would help a famished people by giving them food, but neglect to give them seed. The food does help to meet the physical need of the moment, but that is all. It is no permanent solution to the basic problems that create the need. It is using salve to relieve the symptoms without doing anything to cure the disease.

But we shall not take time to discuss these objections further. Without a doubt, Christian missions in the minds of most people still means a serious attempt to spread the Christian faith. It is not only the popular view, it is the only view supported by the Christian Scriptures.

Fourth, the work of missions is normally carried on through a group of selected workers called missionaries. True, there is a vast amount of missionary work carried on voluntarily by members of the Christian church. But they don't often think of themselves as missionaries. They are just personal witnesses to the transforming power of the gospel of Christ. The work of missions could hardly be carried on without the aid of these voluntary workers.

Without question we ought to use them more systematically and effectively than we do. Yet when we speak of missions we think primarily in terms of full-time missionaries.

Notice the word *selected*. For the purpose of our definition the method of selection is not important. The fact is. Even those who argue against the careful choosing of missionaries by a mission board do set up their own standards of selection. Maybe they will simply insist that the missionary be sure that God is calling him to the work. But added to that he will have to be able to persuade a number of Christians to provide his support. The important thing is that in one way or another missionaries are selected workers, selected for the job of missions. To a large extent the success of missions depends on the wisdom with which they are selected.

"Home" and "Foreign" Missions

Perhaps you noticed in our definition that we didn't make any distinction between "home missions" and "foreign missions." There is a good reason for it. We don't find any such distinction in the Scriptures. Really they are just two different phases of the same task. The different denominations don't even agree on where home missions ends and foreign missions begins. At least two or three of them carry on their missionary work in Mexico and Central America under a home missions board. Others look at this work as a part of foreign missions.

But we are not ready to give up the distinction altogether. Maybe it isn't basic, and we can't find a clear pattern for it in the Scriptures; but it is not contrary to Scripture, and it is practical. It has its real values. Business houses take notice of those values when they have many customers abroad. They usually set up a separate "export division" to take care of the foreign trade. Why? Simply because it brings up a lot of problems that are not found in the home market.

In the same way foreign missions faces many problems abroad that are not met at home. Let us define home missions simply as *missions carried on within the national boundaries.* Then we can see how this is so. For instance, at home we don't often face the problem of a different language. Nearly everybody speaks our language. There may be some differences in the customs of the people, but in the United States it is remarkable how much similarity you will find all the way from California to New York. So we don't have much of a problem of adjustment in this matter. Then we don't have the problems with the government that missionaries face in other lands. It is our own government and we are reasonably familiar with its operation. Also we know how to live in this climate, and almost everywhere we have access to doctors, dentists and other material assistance. We can even use older people as missionaries without much hesitation. It doesn't cost much to put them on the field, so if their term of service turns out to be short it doesn't mean such a big loss as it would abroad.· Finally, we don't have such serious problems in starting a church and helping people to find their place in it. It is already a familiar organization.

So the distinction between home and foreign missions is simply a practical one. Foreign missions calls for missionaries with different qualifications from those at home. They will have to use some different methods of work. The range of their activities will often be much broader. Their spirit and their message will be the same, but to be effective they will have to learn and follow different rules of practice.

This is why in these lessons we deal chiefly with foreign missions. To try to deal with both at the same time would in many cases lead to confusion. Some of the principles apply equally well to both home and foreign missions, as you will readily see. But from this point on, when we speak of missions we are thinking primarily of missions overseas.

WHY PEOPLE OPPOSE MISSIONS

Of course you can expect people who are not Christians to oppose missions. It would be strange if they approved. After all, no one believes in propagating what he thinks is not true. He may not mention his disbelief when he is arguing against missions, but it can't help being the main factor. So we are not going to bother with this kind of opposition.

What does concern us is the opposition from those who claim to be Christians. These are the people who say they believe the Christian message but oppose trying to win other people to the same faith. Why?

When we try to find the reasons, we run into some arguments that are really *excuses* instead of *reasons*. We could call them "camouflage reasons" because they only serve to cover up the real reasons. You will usually hear them expressed with catchwords or phrases picked up from somebody else and glibly repeated. "Charity begins at home" is probably the most common. (As if that meant that charity ought never to leave home!) "Officious meddling" is another term we hear, and sometimes "useless extravagance." It is seldom worthwhile to refute such objections. They are not the real reasons. But there are at least four basic reasons why many nominally Christian people oppose missions. We ought to give them some attention.

The first and perhaps the chief reason is one that you would have a hard time getting the objector to admit. It is the lack of a personal and vital experience of Christ. It is safe to say that a large part of the members of our churches in the homeland have never had a deep religious experience. Their parents were members of the church, and at the proper age they too joined. There was no deep conviction about it; it was just the thing to do. Many of them rarely attend church services, but they still count themselves Christians. Others are very faithful in attendance at the church, very active in its affairs, just as they would be in a club. But it means little more to them than that.

Now such people find it hard to understand missions. Christianity is good, they will admit. It is presumably superior to other religions. But why try to force our religion on other people? It is rather silly to get so wrought up about religion, anyway. Who knows but what for them their religion may be better than ours?

Naturally the one who looks at the church as he would at a club will not be deeply concerned about spreading its ministry to the ends of the earth. Oh, he may be proud of it and speak of it every now and then to friends and acquaintances. Maybe you can even persuade him to give a little help in a membership campaign. But that would be just for the local chapter. After all, membership in the club is nice, but it isn't a life-and-death affair.

How can such people comprehend those young men and women who are ready to bury themselves in out-of-the-way places and give their very lives to win others to Christ? They think it absurd. They speak of it depreciatively as "pietistic." They fail to realize that *the measure of Christ's importance to us is the extent to which we will go to make Him known to others.* So we can only conclude that many are not interested in missions because their own faith doesn't mean much to them. Of course it wouldn't mean much to others either.

A second reason for opposing missions is a preoccupation with self. Bluntly put, it is selfishness. It is not the grasping sort of selfishness that tries to seize all the best for oneself. It is a more passive type that we might call self-centeredness. It is the kind that becomes so absorbed in its own affairs that it is blind to the needs of others.

Some of those who oppose missions are more than just nominal Christians. They have had a deep religious experience. They are seriously concerned about spiritual needs that affect them personally or touch the local church to which they belong. But when it comes to missions, they say they "just can't see it."

Such a statement is more accurate than they realize. Indeed, they "can't see it." The difficulty is the lack of vision in themselves. They see well at short range only. The needs of people beyond their range of sight do not concern them. Nor can they understand why others should feel concerned.

A third reason is ignorance of actual conditions in other parts of the world. It is strange that we are always objecting that foreigners get a false picture of life in our land from the movies they see. Yet many of these movies have been made right here in this country by our own countrymen. At the same time we are quite willing to glean our ideas of life in other lands from the movies. This in spite of the fact that many of them are made by our own people and shot on locations right here at home. Some of them are highly imaginary and about as far from real life in those lands as they can be.

Of course some people don't get their ideas from the pictures but from books. Then it depends on the book. If it is fiction, the setting may be just as fictional, just as artificial as the plot. If it is a travel book, it may still be fiction. Some travelers are excellent storytellers. Their books are absorbing reading—but not always true. They write to entertain. They are often able to fill two or three hundred pages with the hastily plucked fruits of a two- or three-week excursion. They don't know the language, so of course they don't really know the people. But they can give you their impressions, and they can tell a lot of tales they have picked up here and there—tales that are full of color, even though the colors are false.

The usual author will do one of two things when he writes about the nationals of other lands. He may picture them as good-natured, contented, childlike people upon whom he looks with good-natured condescension. His servants and helpers he calls his "boys." Or else he may picture them as altogether vicious, unprincipled rogues, who need to be treated like the villains they are.

With the first picture the author succeeds in giving the impression that missions to such people are actually harmful. The native leads a carefree, happy-go-lucky life until the missionary comes to change his way of living and spoil his Garden of Eden. A young journalist in the South Pacific had such an idea. He saw some young Papuans with black bands around their sleeves and at once condemned the missionaries for teaching the natives "our rotten idea of wearing crape." But he spoke in ignorance. He didn't know that their former practice when a relative died had been to lop off a joint of a finger. This was one of the "charming native customs" that the missionaries had changed.

The second picture makes the natives out as hopeless and the missionaries as useless. The converts are only clever rascals who impose on the missionary's gullibility. A well-known traveler in Korea some years ago was particularly vicious in his printed attack on the American missionaries. He blamed the missionaries for the disturbances that had taken place in the Orient and urged the government to restrict what he called the "violence" of the missionary enterprise.

In that same book he says of the Korean, "He has neither initiative nor the capacity for work, while he combines intemperance, immorality and laziness in varying degrees." Then he goes on, "There is, however, an antidote for this state of things. If sufficient point be put into the argument, and the demonstration be further enforced by an occasional kick, as circumstances may require, it is possible to convert a first-class, sun-loving wastrel into a willing, if unintelligent servant. Under any conditions, his dishonesty will be incorrigible."

Would you be surprised to learn that this traveler nearly lost his life at the hands of the Koreans? His harsh tactics stirred up a riot among his servants. Before it was over he was seriously wounded and barely escaped with his life. Yet many still consult his book and accept its account.

During World War II many Christian soldiers served in what we often call mission lands and saw missions in operation. Wartime was not the best time to view their activities, but the men were amazed at the real accomplishments they saw. They had not expected to see such things. A firsthand view corrected many of the false ideas they had before. A large number of them became enthusiastic in their support of missions. Many became missionaries themselves after the war was over.

A *fourth* reason for opposing missions is one that, at least in its older form, no longer bears much weight. I suppose it is because people no longer show much interest in questions of theology. For the reason is theological.

There are two types of theology that are not friendly to missions. The older one is a type we sometimes call *hyper-Calvinism*. In its extreme form it emphasizes the sovereignty of God to such an extent that man seems to be nothing more than a puppet. Its classical expression of opposition to missions is in a statement an elderly minister is said to have made to William Carey, back in the eighteenth century: "When God wants to convert the heathen, He'll do it without your help or mine!" Almost no one would hold this view today.

But there is also a modern type of theology that opposes missions, at least in the sense of our definition. It is a theology that many call *liberal*. This term, however, is not very precise. It covers a variety of systems that call into question many parts of the historic Christian faith.

According to one view, Christianity is not unique. It is not *the* true religion; it is only one of many. And religion is only man's attempt to find God. Other religions are just other roads to the same end. So missionary work in our sense is wrong. The religion of other peoples may not suit us, but it fits them. Why unsettle them by trying to get them to worship our way? At most we can only join them in a mutual search for the ultimate truth.

We can only remark that if this be called Christianity, it is certainly not the Christianity of the New Testament. Neither is it the Christianity of the historic church.

But there is also another point of view that blunts the cutting edge of missions. It has changed the word *missions* to *mission*. *Mission* is the total responsibility of the church to all men in all phases of life, but particularly in the area of social concern. It cares very little for the expansion of the faith among those who do not know the Saviour. Its primary emphasis is on social action, on trying to get the church involved in shaping the affairs of this world.

So far is the divine dimension forgotten that many young people, influenced by this view, are saying, "Missions are irrelevant. We have to win the battle against racism, poverty, militarism, etc., in our own country before we have any right to preach to others." Given a theology that puts man at the center, they are right. But the gospel of humanism is not the gospel of our Lord and Saviour Jesus Christ.

2

THE NEW TESTAMENT AND MISSIONS (I)

How did foreign missions get started? Was it a part of Christianity at the beginning? Or did it come later? Did Christ Himself have anything to say about it? Is it a necessary part of the faith?

The only way we can answer questions like these is by turning to the New Testament itself. In its pages the Christian finds his rule of faith and practice. It is God's final revelation through our Lord and Saviour Jesus Christ. Also in it we find the earliest records of Christian missionary work. So we must see what the New Testament has to say.

But in looking at the New Testament there is one error we want to avoid. We don't want to choose just a few scattered texts to prove our point. This proof-text method does have some values. But it is also open to serious objections. It is all too easy for one to take a text out of its setting and make it teach something it was never meant to teach.

So instead we are going to consider the broad sweep of New Testament teaching. When we do refer to one specific passage or another, it will be simply to illustrate the general truth we present. In most cases you won't need the proof of chapter and verse. A general acquaintance with the New Testament derived from an open-minded reading of its words will be enough. The conclusion will be inescapable. You will see that in the New Testament missions is not something open to question. It is rather *the normal expression of a vital Christianity.*

Of course in these few pages we don't expect to cover all that the New Testament teaches about missions. That is too broad a field. What we are concerned with here is simply to show something of the place that missions occupied in New Testament Christianity.

CHRISTIANITY IS BY NATURE MISSIONARY

The New Testament pictures for us a faith that is by its very 'nature missionary. In other words, Christianity, if it is real Christianity, must of necessity be missionary. It is strange that so many fail to see this. That is, it is strange until we realize that many people's ideas of Christianity have only a remote connection with the New Testament.

NOT A MATTER OF PRIVATE CONCERN

Many have a false idea about religion. They think that religion is a purely private concern. It is something like a taste in literature. Some people like serious books, some prefer novels, while others prefer mystery stories and the daily paper. Each one is free to read what he wants, but not to tell others what to read. It is a purely personal matter.

The truth is that religion can seldom be a purely personal matter. Many primitive peoples recognize this when they make their religous allegiance a matter for community decision. The Christian religion, more than many others, goes beyond the purely personal. We grant that faith in Christ has to be personal. It is true, too, that some religious exercises, such as prayer and Bible reading, can be carried on privately. But these are not the whole of religion nor of the Christian faith.

Some countries, such as Spain, have pretended to believe that they are. They have professed to grant religious liberty to minority groups like the Protestants. They have said that everyone is free to believe as he chooses and, in the privacy of his own home, to worship as he pleases. But he may not make any public or even semi-public show of his faith. Neither may he speak of his faith to others so as to win them. This they call religious freedom. But obviously it is not the sort of freedom claimed for the established religion of the country.

Actually there are few if any religions that one can profess and practice privately. Such a religion would have to be mostly a matter of ritual, like some lodge ceremonies. It could not change the daily conduct of the worshiper. If it did it would affect others. Besides, if his religion changed a thief into an honest man, he would have to explain how it happened. Nor could a private religion aim at any changes in society, good or bad. It would have to be a religion content with things as they are. As a religion it would be a sham. (I wonder if some so-called Christians have reached that place?)

But this is far from true of New Testament Christianity. It has a great deal to do with personal conduct. It aims to transform lives. And through transformed lives it tries to work changes in society, sometimes revolutionary changes. That is why Christ said that He came "not to send peace, but a sword" (Mt 10:34).

NOT A MATTER OF COUNTRY OR RACE

There are many people, too, who have the false notion that religion is a matter of country or race or temperament. The idea is not a new one. The Syrians expressed it in Old Testament times in 1 Kings 20:23. They said about the Israelites, "Their gods are gods of the hills; therefore they were stronger than we; but let us fight against them in the plain, and surely we shall be stronger than they."

We don't express it quite so crudely today. But we do often say about those in other lands, "Their religion fits them." Several writers on Latin America in past years have solemnly affirmed that Protestantism could never take root there because it is "not congenial to the Latin culture." (Strangely enough, a recent census has revealed more than three million Protestants in the one Latin American country of Brazil.)

Now it is perfectly true that some religions by their very nature are limited to one country or people. An example would be Shintoism in Japan. But this is far from true of all. Buddhism is a small minority movement in India, the land of its origin. Its greatest successes have been in other parts of Asia. Islam has fewer followers in Arabia than in lands that Muhammad never saw. It is sometimes called a desert religion; but Indonesia, one of the two largest Muhammadan nations, is as far from desert as it is possible to be.

When it comes to Christianity, we have a strange phenomenon. It began among the Jews, but most of the Jews have never accepted it. It began in the Orient, but its strongest centers today are in the West. Its Scriptures are very little read in the original languages, but they are read around the world in more than a thousand other tongues.

No, Christianity cannot be simply a matter of private concern. Neither can it be limited to one country, one race, one type of culture. At least not the Christianity revealed in the pages of the New Testament.

TWO MAJOR MISSIONARY ELEMENTS

There are at least two major things that make Christianity missionary by nature: (1) its exclusive claims; and (2) its view of mankind.

First, its exclusive claims. The Romans of the early centuries and the unbelievers of today both have resented Christianity's claim to be the one true religion. The Romans would have been willing to grant it a place among the many religions of the empire. Others would do the same today. They will admit that it is, on the whole, a good religion in many ways. But they all object to the exclusiveness of the Christian faith. They resent its saying that other religions are false.

However, there can be no doubt that the New Testament claims exclusiveness for the Christian message. It doesn't present God as *a* god; He is *the only* God. Paul says, "We know that an idol is nothing in the world, and that there is none other God but one" (1 Co 8:4). Further, it doesn't present Jesus Christ as *a* savior; He is *the only* Saviour of men. As Peter said, "There is none other name under heaven given among men, whereby we must be saved" (Ac 4:12). This is the witness of the whole New Testament.

How does this make Christianity missionary? In just this way. If Christianity is *a* religion and Christ is *a* savior, then my obligation to tell people about Christ and His salvation is relatively small. After all, there are other ways of salvation open to them.

But if Christianity is *the only* true religion; if Christ is *the only* Saviour; if the gospel is *the only* message that can offer men eternal life, then how can I keep quiet? Can I rejoice in my own salvation, knowing that others are dying without that salvation? Must I not feel as Paul did when he wrote to the Romans, "I am debtor . . . to preach the gospel to you" (Ro 1:14-15)?

Second, the matter of Christianity's view of mankind. When we talk about salvation we mean salvation from sin and from the results of sin. Here we find the second reason why Christianity must be missionary. According to the New Testament, mankind is lost, condemned by God because of its sin. "All have sinned" (Ro 3:23).

Now, *sin* is not a very popular or meaningful word among most people today. To many the New Testament idea of sin is completely foreign. The pagan or the Muhammadan may indeed be familiar with the word. He may even willingly confess that he is a sinner. But it means very little because, to him, as likely as not, sin is just a matter of ceremonial impurity or it is inevitable. He has violated one of the arbitrary rules of his god. So he will have to pay some sort of forfeit to get back into good standing.

Such a person is likely to view the whole matter of sin rather lightly. After all, who could possibly keep all the rules of the game without a mistake? Especially when he is not really sure just what all the rules are. Sure, I am a sinner. So what? Aren't we all?

The idea of sin as moral iniquity, as something that defiles and degrades the soul of the sinner, is not common outside of Christianity. That sin is something that ought not to be, entirely apart from any divine command, is a new idea to most unbelievers. Even where they confess that they are sinners, the sense of the "sinfulness of sin" is lacking.

Our civilized pagans are not much better. They are acquainted with the words *crime, delinquency* and *error.* But to them *sin* is only a theological term used by old-fashioned preachers and straitlaced killjoys. No one is really a sinner and hence responsible for his sins. The criminal is just the product of a bad environment, or the victim of an undiagnosed illness.

Yet, unquestionably sin is a major theme of the New Testament—sin and salvation from sin. Sin has alienated the whole world from God. Sin has corrupted the nature of man. Sin has brought condemnation and death. No one is free from it; no one can save himself from it. Yet we are all held responsible for it before God. Only in Christ is there salvation, a salvation provided by God Himself. This is the essence of the New Testament message.

If we deny the New Testament view of man and his sin, we do not need to be missionary. If men, after all, are fundamentally good, though they do make mistakes; if sin is not the desperate thing the New Testament makes it out to be; if its results are not so disastrous; or even if we can plead that ignorance of the gospel relieves people from guilt and condemnation; then missions is not imperative. But no man can fully believe the New Testament picture of mankind apart from Christ and remain indifferent. If he really believes it, he cannot help feeling constrained to make the message of salvation known—known to lost men everywhere.

ARE THEY REALLY LOST?

We suggested above that some may plead that ignorance of the gospel relieves people from guilt and condemnation. This is not at all an uncommon idea. The reasoning goes something like this. First, God is and must be fair. Then, since it would be obviously unfair to condemn people who have never had a chance to hear the gospel, God certainly will not do it.

People who hold this view are usually sincere. It is the one explanation that seems to satisfy their own sense of fairness in the matter. But there are two things they fail to do. They fail to carry their reasoning to its logical culmination. And they fail to investigate or believe what the Scripture actually says.

Let us look at the implications of such a belief. It means that the gospel is the standard by which men are judged. No man can be condemned, then, however vile his life, if he is not aware of this standard of judgment. It means, moreover, that it is no kindness to give the gospel to the world. We know from experience that only a minority of those who hear the gospel ever accept it. So our missionary work that is intended to bring life to the people turns out rather to bring condemnation and death. What a bleak prospect!

But some will object that this isn't exactly what they are thinking of. What they really mean is that there are two standards. Only those who have had the chance to hear and accept the gospel will be judged by that standard. The others will be judged by how well they have lived up to such light as they have had.

The implications of this view are scarcely less serious.

What of the man who has heard the gospel but hasn't fully understood it? By what standard will he be judged? And where can you find the man who has completely followed the light he has had? If no one has, then how far short can a man fall and still be saved? How big a sinner do you need to be to be lost? What is the ground of salvation? Is it man's good works? Then why did Christ die? If man can be saved apart from Christ's sacrifice, is there any benefit at all in the gospel?

But most devastating of all to such a view is the fact that there is no scriptural basis for it. It is born of our own cogitations, divorced from any objective study of what the Bible has to say. The Scripture presents to us a quite different picture. Let us look at four of the most basic teachings of the New Testament.

First, every man is a sinner before God. (See Ro 3:23; 5:12.) He may be a likeable person; he may be a good friend, a considerate husband, and a kind father. Yet in his relation to God he is a rebel, one who perversely insists on following his own good pleasure and disregards what God has revealed to him as good and right. It is not a matter of breaking a few specific rules or commandments. It is not disobedience that comes from ignorance of what is right. Paul makes this clear in the first two chapters of his epistle to the Romans. In 3:9-12 he summarizes the matter by saying:

> We have before proved . . . that they are all under sin; as it is written, There is none righteous, no, not one: there is none that understandeth, there is none that seeketh after God. They are all gone out of the way, they are together become unprofitable; there is none that doeth good, no, not one.

Second, it is our sins that have separated us from God. We are "dead in sins" (Eph 2:1, 5). Sin is not a light thing in God's sight, like the unintentional breaking of a rule of a game. It is rather the expression of a corrupt nature that is unfit for fellowship with a holy God. You will hear some quote John 3:18 and say that men are condemned simply because they have "not believed in the . . . only begotten Son of God." This is wresting the verse out of its context. The next verse makes it clear that this has nothing to do with those who never heard of Christ. God would obviously be unjust if he condemned men for not believing in one of whom they have never heard. But He doesn't. He condemns men because they are sinners. It is their sin that separates them from Him (Is 59:2).

But third, God in His infinite mercy has provided a way of salvation in Jesus Christ. This, as you know, is the theme of the whole New Testament, so we don't need to go into detail. It was the whole purpose of Christ's coming. It was the one objective He had in dying on the cross. It was a sacrifice adequate to rescue a whole world from the blight of sin.

Fourth, however, God has prescribed only one means by which this salvation can be made effective. There is only one way in which those who are dead in sin can be reborn to new life. It is the way of faith (Heb 11). It is the faith that accepts the salvation God offers in Christ and trusts Him to make it effective in our lives (Ac 15:9).

Then what about those who have never heard the gospel? How can they have faith, how can they accept this salvation if they never hear about it? This is the rub. They can't. So they remain under the condemnation. They remain dead in their sins.

"But it's not right!" you may object. "Maybe some would believe if they only heard. Why should God condemn them because they haven't received the word?"

He doesn't! God never condemns a man for not doing what he has no opportunity to do. He only holds us guilty for not doing what we know we ought to do. He has condemned those who haven't heard, as well as us who have, simply because we are all sinners. We are all dead in sins. We need to be born again to new life. And there is only one way this can take place: through faith in Jesus Christ (Ac 4:12).

God Himself has done what He could. At infinite cost He has provided the salvation. It is sufficient for all men who will accept it. But in His divine wisdom, which we have no right to challenge, He has charged those of us who already know the good news with the responsibility of spreading it to others. They are, as we were, dead in their sins; and because of their sins "they are without excuse," just as we were. They can never blame God for condemning them.

There is a possibility that some of them—perhaps only a minority—will accept God's offer of new life if someone only tells them of it. But that puts the burden on us. We who have already been born to new life are the only ones who can open the door to others. We have the keys. How are we using them?

There is still one question for which I do not know the answer. It has not been revealed. It is hidden in the inscrutable counsels of God's own good pleasure. It is this: Why did God in His mercy allow me to hear the message of life in Christ Jesus and accept it, while many others have never heard? Obviously I am no better than they. Then why?

Only one answer can be given. The God of the Bible is sovereign as well as just. In His justice He has condemned us all for our sins. In His mercy He has provided a way of salvation. But since that mercy is completely undeserved, no one can question His right to reveal it first to whomever He pleases. I may rejoice that He made it known to me. But I cannot rejoice in it selfishly. If the news of His salvation comes to me first, I know that it is so that I may pass it on to others. If they never learn of it, it is not His fault but mine.

JESUS CHRIST AND MISSIONS

Jesus Christ taught missions. This was not only at the beginning, when He called His first disciples and said to them, "Follow me, and I will make you fishers of men" (Mt 4:19). Nor was it just at the end of His earthly ministry when He urged, "Go ye into all the world, and preach the gospel to every creature" (Mk 16:15). Rather, the whole tenor of His life and ministry was missionary.

LOOK AT THE PURPOSE OF CHRIST'S COMING

Sometimes we hear people say that Paul was "the greatest missionary of all time." Among those who have followed Christ that is probably true. But greater yet was the Lord Jesus Christ Himself.

The New Testament leaves us in no doubt about the missionary purpose of His coming into the world. In fact, this is one thing that makes it different from the birth of any other man. His coming was voluntary, and it had a definite, clear-cut purpose.

The Lord Himself told of that purpose when He said, "The Son of man is come to seek and to save that which was lost" (Lk 19:10). Again He said, "I came down from heaven, not to do mine own will, but the will of him that sent me" (Jn 6:38). And John wrote much later that "God sent his only begotten Son into the world, that we might live through him" (1 Jn 4:9).

Jesus Christ, then, was a missionary, a "sent one." He was sent with a purpose. And that purpose was the same as that of His missionaries today. It was to save those who were lost—those who were "dead in trespasses and sins."

LOOK, TOO, AT THE CHARACTER OF CHRIST'S LIFE

The character of the life of Christ was missionary in a very real sense. You see, a missionary, like an ambassador, is sent to represent someone else. He has an individuality, but he is expected to suppress it as much as possible. He is not allowed to have a private life. His every act is viewed as the act of the one who sent him. His speeches are not private expressions of opinion but official statements. He is expected to stand in the place of the one who sent him.

Of course missionaries, like ambassadors, forget this once in a while. But Jesus Christ never forgot it. One of the most outstanding characteristics of His life was its *utter selflessness*. He told His followers that He came "not to be ministered unto, but to minister, and to give his life" (Mt 20:28). And when Paul wanted to back up his exhortation for each believer to "please his neighbour for his good to edification," he reminded them that "even Christ pleased not himself" (Ro 15:2-3).

Even when Christ says, "I am the way, the truth, and the life," He says it without boasting or egotism. In fact, in that very statement He exalts the Father, for He adds, "No man cometh unto the Father, but by me" (Jn 14:6). The same is true when He says, "He that hath seen me hath seen the Father" (Jn 14:9). Actually this last verse is a clear statement of His missionary character—He stood before them in the place of the Father.

THEN CONSIDER THE OBJECTIVE OF CHRIST'S EARTHLY MINISTRY

Some might think that Christ's ministry was anything but missionary. That is, He limited it almost exclusively to those of His own nation, the Jews. On one occasion He actually told a foreign woman that He was "not sent but unto the lost sheep of the house of Israel" (Mt 15:24). Though in answer to her humble faith He did condescend to grant her request. Moreoover, when He first sent out the twelve He told them not to go to Gentiles or Samaritans (Mt 10:5), though He Himself on one occasion ministered to the Samaritans (Jn 4:5-42).

However, we need to understand these passages in the light of the whole gospel narrative. Then we can see how they fit. Without entering into disputed matters of interpretation, we can see two things clearly.

First, Christ did dedicate His earthly ministry to His own people, the Jews. On rare occasions He might minis-

ter to Samaritans or Gentiles, but these were exceptions.

But, second, even while He was ministering to the
Jews He envisioned a worldwide ministry for His gospel.
We see this on numerous occasions during His ministry,
as well as at the end of His life.

For instance, in the early part of Matthew (8:5-13),
which is considered to be the most Jewish of the gospels,
we have the story of the Roman centurion's servant. In
that case Christ granted the centurion's request and praised
the faith of that Gentile soldier. Then He added, in a prophetic vein, "Many shall come from the east and west, and
shall sit down with Abraham, and Isaac, and Jacob, in the
kingdom of heaven." Also, near the end of His life, in the
prophecy of Matthew 24 He said, "This gospel of the kingdom shall be preached in all the world for a witness unto
all nations" (v.14).

So we conclude that while Christ's earthly ministry
was primarily to the Jews, He nevertheless taught and prepared His disciples for the day when they would take His
gospel to all nations.

FINALLY, GIVE ATTENTION TO CHRIST'S GREAT COMMISSION

We have purposely waited until last to consider the
so-called Great Commission. This is because so many seem
to think it is the one basis for missions in the New Testament. As a result, if critics could cast doubt on the authen-
ticity of the Great Commission, it would cause the whole
foundation for missions to crumble. However, we have
already seen that missions is a part of the very nature of
New Testament Christianity and that it is taught by Christ
Himself, even apart from the Great Commission.

Christ gave the Great Commission to His followers
after His resurrection and before His ascension. It was the
one great charge He gave to His church. There are several
accounts. In fact, it may well be that Christ repeated His
charge more than once. In view of its importance, it would

be strange if He didn't. All four gospels and the Acts give
it in one form or another.

The most often quoted of the gospel accounts are
those in Matthew and Mark. Matthew 28:18-20 says:

> And Jesus came and spake unto them, saying, All
> power is given unto me in heaven and in earth. Go ye there-
> fore, and teach all nations, baptizing them in the name of
> the Father, and of the Son, and of the Holy Ghost: teaching
> them to observe all things whatsoever I have commanded
> you: and, lo, I am with you alway, even unto the end of the
> world. Amen.

Mark 16:15-16 is shorter and slightly different:

> And he said unto them, Go ye into all the world, and
> preach the gospel to every creature. He that believeth and
> is baptized shall be saved; but he that believeth not shall
> be damned.

Through the years there has been considerable contro-
versy about the final portions of Matthew and Mark. These
are the very parts that contain the account of the Great
Commission. Critics have contended that they were not
originally a part of those gospels but were added later.

We shall not enter into the merits of this argument.
Even if true, it does not necessarily mean that those portions were not faithful accounts and divinely inspired. But
as far as the Great Commission is concerned, we are not
limited to Matthew and Mark. John also has something to
say on the subject. He tells us that when Christ first
appeared among His disciples after His resurrection, He
said, *"As my Father hath sent me, even so send I you"*
(Jn 20:21).

Luke also is not silent. He tells us that after His
resurrection, Christ joined two disciples as they walked
along the way to Emmaus. They did not recognize Him
until He sat down to eat with them. Then they rushed
back to Jerusalem to tell the others that they had seen the

Lord. But in the midst of their report, Jesus Himself appeared and spoke to them. In His talk He said:

> Thus it is written, and thus it behoved Christ to suffer, and to rise from the dead the third day: and that repentance and remission of sins should be *preached in his name among all nations,* beginning at Jerusalem. And *ye are witnesses of these things.* And, behold, I send the promise of my Father upon you: but tarry ye in the city of Jerusalem, until ye be endued with power from on high (Lk 24:46-49).

Again in Acts (1:8) we have another often quoted expression of the same Great Commission:

> But ye shall receive power, after that the Holy Ghost is come upon you: and ye shall be witnesses unto me both in Jerusalem, and in all Judea, and in Samaria, and unto the uttermost part of the earth.

In the face of this evidence we can hardly deny that Jesus Christ taught missions, that He wanted His followers to be missionary, that He wanted His gospel to be preached throughout the world.

3

THE NEW TESTAMENT AND MISSIONS (II)

THE HOLY SPIRIT AND MISSIONS

IN READING the New Testament we discover that sometimes the disciples did not remember what Jesus had taught them. This was true of His resurrection. Matthew alone tells us of four times when Jesus spoke of His resurrection in advance (16:21; 17:9, 23; 26:32). He also tells us that the Jewish religious leaders were aware of that teaching. When He was crucified they set a watch to make sure that He stayed in His grave. They didn't want His disciples to steal His body and then claim that He had risen. But they might have spared themselves the trouble. The disciples apparently had forgotten that teaching.

Besides this, they didn't fully understand some of His teachings. They showed it often while He was alive. Sometimes they asked Him for an explanation. But on at least one occasion they were afraid to ask (Mk 9:32). When He died, they clearly didn't understand the meaning of His death. That is, they didn't understand it until after His resurrection. Even then we may question whether they grasped its full significance.

Of course this is what any experienced teacher learns to expect. He knows that those he teaches will not get all that he tries to give them. And of what they do seem to get, they will retain only a part. This may be partly the fault of the teacher, but not chiefly. More often we can find the cause in the pupils themselves. Man's ability to pay full attention to what is spoken, to comprehend it and then to remember it, is quite limited.

Under such conditions we would normally expect that Christ's teachings would undergo considerable change after His departure. No one wrote them down at the time. It would hardly be surprising if some were forgotten, or that others should be twisted because of poor understanding or faulty recollection. We would also expect conflicting testimony about just what Christ did teach.

Some say that this actually must have happened. They know it is the usual thing. So if the New Testament writers agree very closely on any subject, they can only come to one conclusion. It must be because they depended on the same document or source of information. Only when they disagree do they represent an independent tradition. So they emphasize strongly the differences between the gospel of John and the other three, the "Synoptics." They like to draw contrasts between the theology of Paul and the theology of Peter or James.

This is not the place to deal with the arguments they use. But one thing we can say. To the unprejudiced observer the remarkable harmony between the various writings that make up the new Testament is far more noteworthy than the apparent discrepancies. That such a varied group of writers, with no official board to check their writings, should present such a unified picture of Christ and His gospel is astounding. It is this remarkable harmony that calls for explanation. How could it have come about?

Of course Christ's disciples had imbibed much from simply being with Him during His ministry. Some might say that they had "caught the spirit of Christ." But as an explanation of the harmony in the New Testament, this falls far short. Those who have "caught the spirit" of a great man don't wait long after his death to differ among themselves. Just look at the followers of any of our modern "great men."

Rather, what the New Testament itself shows to be the controlling factor is a different kind of spirit. It is not an intangible, impersonal influence. It is the Holy Spirit of God. Jesus Himself had promised His coming before He died. In fact, Jesus went so far as to say that it was best for Him to leave so that the Holy Spirit would come. He said that He would send Him (Jn 16:7). He had already told His disciples that part of the task of the Holy Spirit would be to "teach you all things, and bring all things to your remembrance, whatsoever I have said unto you" (Jn 14:26).

Not only did Jesus Himself emphasize the importance of the coming of the Holy Spirit. The disciples did the same thing after He had come. In the book of the Acts the Holy Spirit is given such prominence that long ago it was said that the book should not be called "the Acts of the Apostles" but "the Acts of the Holy Spirit." In the rest of the New Testament, too, although He doesn't glorify Himself, the Holy Spirit clearly stands out as *the One who directed and controlled the growth of the church.*

FORESHADOWINGS OF FOREIGN MISSIONS

The New Testament, we say, presents the Holy Spirit both as the Initiator and as the one controlling factor in the expansion of Christianity. Even in what we may call the foreshadowings of that foreign missionary activity He stands out. There were at least two such foreshadowings in the early chapters of the Acts.

The first is in Acts 2, where we have the account of the coming of the Spirit upon the believers after Christ's ascension. It is significant that the Spirit came on the day of Pentecost. Pentecost was the feast which, perhaps more than others, brought Jews to Jerusalem from "every nation under heaven." It was as if the Spirit wanted to make it clear that the gospel they began to preach that day should reach all nations.

Again in chapter 8 is a most unusual account. We call it the story of Philip and the Ethiopian eunuch. Philip, one of the first deacons of the church, had preached the gospel in Samaria with remarkable effect. But now the angel of the Lord told him to leave that work and go down to the desert road that led from Jerusalem to Gaza. Here he saw a chariot to which the Spirit directed him. The man in the chariot was a foreigner. By birth and residence he was an Ethiopian, but apparently he had been converted to Judaism. Philip led him to faith in Christ and baptized him.

In both these cases we see foreshadowings of a work to come in other lands and among other peoples who had never professed the Jewish faith. But they were only fore-shadowings. The real work among the Gentiles had not yet begun. But even in the foreshadowings it was the Holy Spirit who directed what was done.

FIVE SPIRIT—DIRECTED STEPS

In spite of Christ's teaching, the church did not at first see that the whole world was to be its field. It had to be led out, step by step, into its worldwide missionary ministry. In the New Testament we can distinguish five such steps. They are represented by five crucial acts in which the Holy Spirit played a leading part. We suggest that you read them for yourself in the book of the Acts. Before the first step was taken. Christianity was limited to Jews and Jewish converts. After the last step it was obvious that Christianity was for the whole world.

STEP ONE: PETER PREACHES TO CORNELIUS (AC 10)

The first time the gospel was preached to a purely Gentile group was when Peter preached in the home of the Roman centurion Cornelius. Peter had not wanted to do it. His prejudices as a Jew kept him back. It took three divine acts to convince him that Gentiles also could have a part in the gospel.

The first act was the heavenly vision the Lord gave him in Joppa. Three times in the vision the Lord told him to kill the animals he saw for food. Three times he refused. To a Jew they were unclean animals. And three times the Lord insisted, "What God hath cleansed, that call not thou common."

On the heels of this vision came the men sent by Cornelius. Cornelius, too, had had a vision in which he was told to send for Peter. Before Peter ever saw the men, the Holy Spirit ordered him, "Go with them, doubting nothing: for I have sent them." So after some hesitation he went.

But going to Cornelius was one thing, and admitting him to the blessings of the gospel was still another. You can still see Peter's reluctance in his asking why they had sent for him. Cornelius told of his own experience and Peter was partly persuaded, especially in the light of his own vision. But it took a third divine act to seal the whole thing. As Peter explained the gospel to the assembled group, the Holy Spirit came on them as He had on the disciples on the day of Pentecost.

This final act of the Spirit convinced Peter. He baptized those who had believed. Later, when the Jewish believers in Jerusalem called on him to explain, he justified himself on the ground that he had only acknowledged what the Spirit had already done (Ac 11:17).

This was an exceptional case. We never find it repeated in the New Testament. Some say that it was Peter's use of the keys to open the door of faith to the Gentiles. It was certainly a crucial act. Its full significance becomes even more evident later, when Paul and Barnabas were called to account for their ministry to the Gentiles (Ac 15:7-11). It was Peter who first opened the door. But it was others who were to bear the major burden of missions to the Gentiles. Peter became rather "the apostle of the circumcision," with his primary ministry to Jews.

STEP TWO: THE CHURCH IN GENTILE ANTIOCH (AC 11:19-26)

Cornelius lived in Judea. We might call it the home field. But Antioch was far beyond the borders even of the northern region of Galilee. It was a Gentile city of great importance in the eastern Mediterranean.

Refugees brought the gospel to Antioch. They had fled from the persecution that began in Jerusalem when Stephen was killed. Wherever the refugees went they spoke of Christ, and here in Antioch their witness brought into being a flourishing congregation. There may be some question as to whether any of the members were really Gentile converts. But there is no doubt that Antioch became the first major center for spreading the gospel among the Gentiles.

The church there began independently of the church in Jerusalem. But before long the Jerusalem church took a definite interest in it. It decided to look into the situation. So it sent to Antioch an official representative, Barnabas. Aside from having been born abroad, Barnabas' chief qualification seems to have been that "he was a good man, and *full of the Holy Ghost* and of faith."

Barnabas looked over the situation and rejoiced in the evident working of the Spirit. He decided he would stay and help. But he also thought of another helper who would probably fit in very well. Not far away, at Tarsus in Asia Minor, lived Saul, the man who later was called Paul. Barnabas had been the one to introduce Saul to the church at Jerusalem. Perhaps at that time Saul had told him how that at his conversion the Lord had told him he was to work among the Gentiles (Ac 9:15; 26:17-18). Also, when Saul had left Jerusalem the Lord had said, "Depart: for I will send thee far hence unto the Gentiles" (Ac 22:21). So Saul would be peculiarly fitted to work in a Gentile city like Antioch. Barnabas went to Tarsus and brought him. It was an important move.

STEP THREE: BARNABAS AND SAUL SENT FORTH (AC 13)

The Holy Spirit clearly dictated the third step. "Separate me Barnabas and Saul for the work whereunto I have called them," He said (v.2). "So they, being sent forth by the Holy Ghost, departed" (v.4). The Spirit had called the men before. Now the church at Antioch set them apart for this missionary task.

We must not misunderstand the significance of what took place in Antioch. The church there was not a modern missionary church. That is, it did not have a mission board or society. It did not set up standards of acceptance for missionary candidates, nor plan their training. It did not direct them where to go nor what to do. Neither did it promise them financial support on the field. Though that certainly does not mean that such things are wrong.

What the church did is this: It showed a real interest in missions. It not only heeded the instructions of the Spirit but it did not hesitate to commit to the task two of its most outstanding leaders and teachers. It went even farther. It identified itself with them and the work they were to do by a sort of commissioning service, the laying on of hands. These were not two individuals acting on their own responsibility. Obeying the Holy Spirit, the church sent them forth. And to the church they rendered their report when they returned.

STEP FOUR: THE JERUSALEM COUNCIL (AC 15)

This fourth step followed the first missionary journey of Barnabas and Paul. In fact, it was a direct result of that step and the preceding one. There were still many in the church who were not convinced that Gentiles could be Christians—at least not without becoming Jews. The issue came to a head in Antioch. Some who had come down there from Jerusalem were teaching that the converts had to become Jews in order to be Christians.

Some have called this the first really great crisis in early Christianity. It was a momentous one for Christian missions. To use Christ's own figure of speech, it was a case of "new wine in old bottles." It was an attempt to bottle up the new wine of the gospel in the old wineskins of Judaism.

What if the Judaizers had been successful? What if the converts had been required to become Jews in order to be Christians? It is conceivable that Christianity might still have been to some degree missionary. But its mission could not possibly have enjoyed much success. The gospel of Christ is a potent force. It has in it the power to revolutionize men and societies. But when its messengers are weighted down with all sorts of forms and conditions that they have to propagate along with the gospel itself, their task becomes almost impossible. Those Judaizing Pharisees were probably honest men and sincerely Christian—yet unenlightened by the Spirit. They did not see then what is so obvious today, that a Christianity of the sort they proposed, so closely attached to the Judaism of that day, could never win the world.

But while we may criticize them in the light of today, we need to look out lest we fall in the same sort of error. For it is all too common in missionary work today to insist that people accept not only the gospel but with it all the paraphernalia to be found in our churches at home. We may not be Judaizers but we do tend to become Americanizers or something of that sort.

A church council was called in Jerusalem to consider the problem. The turning point in its deliberations came when Peter reminded them of how the Spirit had worked in the case of Cornelius. Since God had accepted the Gentiles on the basis of simple faith in Christ, why should the church try to lay greater burdens on them? To this word was added the testimony of Barnabas and Paul. They told how the Spirit had worked among the Gentiles on their missionary journey.

Then the council gave its decision. The Judaizers were repudiated. The Gentiles should not be troubled in their new faith. The simple prohibitions that the council laid down were in no way a hindrance to further missionary work. Instead, the way was now clear for greater expansion.

It is important to note that when the council gave its decision it said, "It seemed good *to the Holy Ghost,* and to us" (v.28).

STEP FIVE: TO THE REGIONS BEYOND IN EUROPE (AC 16)

The fifth and final step was the one taken at Troas. Paul and his companions on the second missionary journey had gone clear across Asia Minor to the northwest. As they moved forward, the Spirit hemmed them in on the right hand and on the left until they came down to the sea. To go any farther would mean crossing over into Europe. That would be a big step.

This step too was guided by the Holy Spirit. Not only had He guided the missionaries to Troas but in Troas He gave Paul the well-known vision of the man of Macedonia. This was what determined the missionaries to go on over into Europe.

But what did this step mean? It was not the first time the gospel was proclaimed in Europe. There were probably believers already in Rome. In fact, Paul himself was soon to write a letter to them in anticipation of a personal visit.

It may have been an indication that Christianity was to turn westward and northward for its greatest successes— to Europe rather than Asia. But take note that the Asia mentioned in verse 6 is not the continent of Asia. It was a province of Asia Minor named Asia, with Ephesus as its chief city. Paul visited it later on this same journey. Perhaps we may say that this was the first *missionary* entrance of Europe—the first time men went there with the deliberate purpose of spreading the gospel. Other missionaries would soon be following. And Europe did later become the major center of Christendom.

But perhaps just as important is the fact that this was *Paul.* Not in vain was he called "the apostle of the Gentiles." Not for naught do modern writers call him "the greatest missionary." His work was dynamic and it took firm root. Even today we study his work in order to improve our own.

His work was intensive, yet it also became much more extensive than that of others. No man has left a greater mark on Christian missions than Paul.

Now Paul's ministry up to this time had been in western Asia, especially in Syria, Palestine, and Asia Minor. His original home was in southeastern Asia Minor. There were many Greeks in Asia Minor, but it was still different from Europe. A water barrier separated the two continents, but with it there seems to have been also a barrier in thinking.

At least in Paul's case this seems to have been true. When the Spirit led him to sail across to Macedonia, it appears that in his thinking the last barrier to a world ministry was passed. He didn't stop in Macedonia. On down into Greece he went. He conceived a great desire to go on to Rome. He wrote of this to the church at Rome. He even wrote that he would like them to help him on his way still farther west to Spain (Ro 15:23-24). In his day that was the western extremity of the world.

So we see that the first step toward a full proclamation of the gospel among the Gentiles was taken when Peter preached to Cornelius. The last decisive one was when Paul went to Macedonia. And at each step along the way it was the Holy Spirit who directed the movement.

4

THE NEW TESTAMENT AND MISSIONS (III)

WHO DID THE MISSIONARY WORK in New Testament days? Was it a select group of specially prepared believers? What information does the New Testament itself give us about them?

THE TWELVE

Let us begin with the apostles. That the twelve apostles were intended to be missionaries, and that most of them did become missionaries, is hardly open to question. Their very title *apostle* is nothing but the Greek form of the word *missionary*. They did stay around Jerusalem a long time, perhaps until the council described in Acts 15. In that chapter "apostles and elders" are mentioned. But by the time of Paul's last visit to Jerusalem, it appears that all the apostles had left the city. Acts 21:18 says only that "all the elders were present." Whether more than one of the apostles may have died by that time we have no way of knowing. Of course James, the brother of John, had long before been executed by Herod (Ac 12:2).

About Peter we do know a little. While Paul calls Peter "the apostle of the circumcision," that did not keep him from being a foreign missionary. Paul himself tells us of Peter's being in Antioch (Gal 2:11). He was even fellowshiping with the Gentile believers in that foreign city. In fact, Paul says he scolded him for withdrawing from the Gentiles when certain Jews came up from Jerusalem.

We can't be sure whether Peter ever visited Corinth in Greece. It doesn't seem very likely. Yet he did have an influence there. It was such an influence that, when the church began to split into several factions, one of the parties claimed to be Peter's party (1 Co 1:12).

Furthermore, Peter's first epistle implies that it was written from the foreign city of Babylon (1 Pe 5:13). This is not at all strange. Even though Peter ministered chiefly to Jews, we know that there were many Jews in that eastern region who never returned to Palestine after the captivity.

It is true that Roman Catholic writers claim that by "Babylon" Peter really meant Rome. This is largely because they want to find in Scripture some proof of their claim that he was the first bishop of Rome, the first pope. However, in either case he would be a foreign missionary. Also, though the tradition is much disputed, there is a story that he was martyred in Rome.

The Scripture gives us little information about the later ministry of John. It seems clear that he and Peter were both in Jerusalem until the time of the Jerusalem council (Gal 2:9). But after that we are not sure. The almost universal tradition is that he went to Ephesus, a mission field, where he ended his days. It also says that it was from Ephesus that he was exiled to the island of Patmos, where he received the Revelation.

If we have little information in the New Testament about the later ministry of Peter and John, we have even less about the rest of the twelve. The Syrian Christians of South India claim that Thomas went to India and established their church. The claim has enough basis to warrant serious consideration by historians. There is also a tradition that Matthew went to Egypt and Ethiopia. And there are other traditions concerning others of the twelve. Some of the traditions are plausible; others are later inventions and are obviously false.

From all the evidence we have, the most that we can say is that all of the apostles except James appear to have become foreign missionaries.

But, besides the twelve, there are also other missionaries mentioned by name in the New Testament.

Paul and His Companions

Whenever we talk about missionaries in the New Testament, people think immediately of Paul and his companions. This is only natural. Paul is the one they have read most about. His work is the most familiar to us. Not only do we have a long section of the Acts devoted to it, but we also have a collection of his own letters. On the other hand we really know very little about the missionary work of others.

Because we have relatively so much information about Paul, and so little about the others, we often tend to disregard the others, as if their work were not important. This is a serious mistake. We need only to look at the rapid expansion of Christianity in the first century in so many different areas to realize that no one man could have been responsible for it all. Yes, not even a single group of men.

Yet Paul's work was important. Not only did he pioneer new areas in Asia Minor and Greece. He made a strong impact in Rome. He inspired others to enter the work and guided them in it. He laid down principles of operation that men have studied from that day to this. And all this apart from his unique contributions to Christian theology.

Paul was not one of the twelve. Yet none of them had his background in the study of the Jewish religion. His call to missionary service was simultaneous with his remarkable conversion (Ac 26:16-18). But a number of years were to pass before he could carry it out fully. He was forced to flee from both Damascus and Jerusalem and return home to Tarsus. Not until Barnabas took him to Antioch did the door begin to open for his greatest ministry.

On the first missionary tour of Cyprus and southern Asia Minor it was Barnabas who took the lead rather than Paul. But then Paul came into his own. A second tour, which he headed, took him as far as Macedonia and down into Greece as far south as Corinth. Later there was a third tour of some of the same places, with more or less lengthy stays in several strategic centers.

His voyage to Rome was in one sense involuntary,

since he went as a prisoner. Yet it fitted into his missionary purpose admirably. Whether he won his appeal and was released from this imprisonment we are not sure. If he did he may have visited Spain before being imprisoned once more. It seems certain that he was finally martyred in Rome.

As for Paul's companions, we have already said something about Barnabas. He occupies a very prominent place at the beginning. It is interesting to note that in Acts 14:14 he is called an apostle. Barnabas parted company with Paul after an argument about taking Mark along on a second trip. Barnabas may have been influenced by the fact that Mark was a relative. Yet later results seem to show that his judgment was sound. Paul himself, toward the end of his life, wrote to Timothy, "Take Mark, and bring him with thee: for he is profitable to me for the ministry" (2 Ti 4:11). Of Barnabas' later ministry, however, all we know is that he returned to Cyprus.

Silas we know as Paul's second partner on his missionary journeys. Timothy and Titus were younger men whom Paul associated with him in his missionary work. The letters he wrote to them might be called "letters to younger missionaries." They tell us a little about these men, and also something about the missionary principles and methods in which Paul instructed them.

Luke, a physician, accompanied Paul for a time. Just how often or how long we don't know. But his greatest service was in his writing. He wrote one of the four gospel accounts. In addition, he became the first missionary historian by writing the book of the Acts.

Paul and Luke both tell us of others who did missionary work, such as Apollos, Aquila and Priscilla, Demas and Tychicus. But we get only fragmentary glimpses of them. We wish we knew more.

UNNAMED MISSIONARIES

Of this we are sure: The missionaries whose names we know are only a tiny portion of a great company of missionaries who, in New Testament times, carried the gospel to a large part of the Roman Empire and even beyond. Who first preached the gospel in Rome itself? We don't know. Who established the church in Alexandria, the metropolis of Egypt? We have no idea. What were the names of those who began the work in Antioch? They are not given. Yet these were the three principal cities of the empire.

It is clear that there were many Christians engaged in spreading their faith to other lands. A large part were humble witnesses whom circumstances had taken to those lands. There was a vitality to their faith that made them proclaim it wherever they went. There were others who, whether on their own initiative or under commission from a church, devoted their lives to this task of missions. And, as in the case of any good work, there were even some false missionaries. Paul found it necessary to warn against them on at least one occasion (2 Co 11:13).

CONCLUSION

In conclusion to this whole section we may state that it is abundantly clear that the New Testament is a distinctively missionary book. All the authors of its various parts were missionaries, with the possible exception of James and Jude. In fact, all the books appear to have been written in a foreign language—Greek. In only one or two cases has it been seriously suggested that a book may have been written originally in Aramaic, the language of the Jews of that day. As far as our earliest copies are concerned, they are all in Greek.

The epistles of Paul were all written to missionary churches or to younger missionaries. The single exception is the one to Philemon, who was a member of a missionary church. James and Peter both wrote to Jews, but to the Jews abroad. Revelation was written for the comfort and encouragement of missionary churches. And of course Acts is primarily a missionary account. Luke's previous book, the gospel, was addressed to Theophilus, whose name is Greek, whether he is a real person or only stands for the Greek-speaking believers.

All in all, we cannot escape the conclusion that New Testament Christianity was essentially and intentionally missionary.

5

THE OLD TESTAMENT AND
MISSIONS (I)

WHEN A MISSIONARY wants to give a people the Word of God in their own tongue, he begins by translating some part of the New Testament. This is only to be expected. It is in the New Testament that we have the message of Jesus Christ our Saviour. He is the culmination of God's revelation to man. And these are the books that tell us of Him and of the salvation that He wrought. So then, although missionaries have translated some parts of the Bible into well over a thousand languages, most of these have only the New Testament or a part of it.

Now the missionaries do not mean to indicate by this that we should neglect the Old Testament. Doubtless none of them would be willing to contend that the Old Testament is any less the Word of God than the New. If they were able to give the people the whole Bible, they would not withhold any bit of it. They would do this even when the people's reading of the Old Testament might raise some questions difficult to explain.

Probably none of them would go as far as did Ulfilas, the great missionary to the Goths in the fourth century. Ulfilas made the first translation of the Bible into any Germanic tongue for these Goths. But he refused to translate the books of the Kings. His Goths were already too inclined to warlike deeds. He was not going to provide them with any further encouragement or excuse from the Bible if he could help it.

But most missionaries today do not shun to declare to the people "the whole counsel of God," insofar as they are able. They even make it possible for polygamous Africans to read the accounts of polygamy in the Old Testament. Still it is true that missionaries, as well as preachers in the homeland, tend to dwell much in the pages of the New Testament, with their rich exposition of the life that is ours in Christ.

Even when we choose a text for a missionary message to the folks at home, a text that often serves only to give a sort of biblical introduction to our story of life and Christian service in another land, we usually turn to such passages as Acts 1:8 or Romans 10:14-15. Only occasionally do we refer to some passage in the Old Testament. Why? Is it that the Old Testament has no missionary character? Not at all. It just doesn't have so many brief, to-the-point texts that we can readily use to introduce a missionary talk. Its missionary character is readily apparent to those who become familiar with its message.

Now, in studying the missionary character of the Old Testament, there is one thing we want to avoid as far as possible. It is the same as with our study of the New Testament. We don't want to choose certain proof texts from here and there, pulling them out of their context and arbitrarily putting them together to prove our thesis. We want to seek honestly for the message that the Old Testament itself has to give us.

Three questions stand out for which we shall want answers. Let us state them here briefly to begin with, and then come back to deal with each one in detail. First is the question, *Does the Old Testament have a missionary message?* That is, for whom is its message important? Is it just for the Jewish people and for the age in which it was written? Or does it also concern other peoples and other ages? Does its message have a vital significance for us today? Does it concern peoples whose cultures differ as widely as those of the Russians and the Japanese?

Our second question is this: *Does the Old Testament show a missionary purpose?* That is, does it show that it was God's intention to have its message known among other peoples besides the Jews? It is not always easy to show intent. God doesn't always reveal clearly just what His ultimate purpose may be in any specific case. But we shall see if He has given us in the Old Testament any revelation of a purpose that we could call distinctly missionary.

For the last question we would ask, *Does the Old Testament reveal any missionary activity?* That is, was there before the time of Christ any attempt to bring the blessings of the Old Testament revelation of God to other people than the Jews? We can readily understand that the Jewish nation as a whole might overlook its missionary responsibility. Hasn't the Christian church done the same thing for long periods of its history? In fact, aren't there many Christians today, in spite of the clear injunctions of the New Testament, who say they don't believe in missions? But our question is, Was there any comprehension of a missionary responsibility among those who had the Old Testament revelation? And was there any attempt to fulfill this responsibility, whether by direct evangelism or in some other way?

Now let us return to our first question:

DOES THE OLD TESTAMENT HAVE A MISSIONARY MESSAGE?

What is a missionary message? Very simply, *it is a message that one has and another needs.* It is a message that by its very nature ought to be propagated, ought to be spread abroad.

Let us look at the basic message of the Old Testament. What is it? Clearly it is more than just history and law and poetry and prophecy. These are what one might call the "literary values" of the Old Testament. But the greatest value is the message it tries to convey to us. It is a message from God Himself. The author of the epistle to the Hebrews is referring to the Old Testament when he writes in his opening words, "God . . . hath . . . spoken." Then about what has He spoken?

FIRST OF ALL, HE HAS SPOKEN ABOUT HIMSELF, THE BEGINNING
AND THE END.

Just what is the Old Testament message about God?
Here some unbelievers will say that there is more than one.
They will object that the God of the prophets is not the
same as the God of the law. They try to reconstruct the
development of the idea of God in the Old Testament
according to their own notions. Jehovah was at first a tribal
deity of a wandering group of Bedouins, they say. Then,
as the Jewish nation emerged and grew, they needed a
broader concept. So their crude, harsh and primitive ideas
gave way to the more advanced views of a later day. This
is simply the older evolutionary hypothesis carried over
from the field of biology to religion.

We are not going to follow these fanciful reconstruc-
tions. Rather, we are going to try to see in broad terms
just what the book itself has to say.

*In the Old Testament the first picture of God is that
of the Creator of the universe.* This is a concept so familiar
to us that we fail to grasp its significance for others. We
think it rather trite.

Now it is true that many heathen do have a more or
less vague idea of a creator. But others do not. It is worth
noting how Paul began his famous sermon on Mars Hill
in Athens. Even though he was addressing a cultured Greek
audience, he saw fit to begin with, "God that made the
world and all things therein" (Ac 17:24). He knew that
Greek religion had no such creator.

What a missionary message this is to the millions today
who still fear the spirits of rivers and trees, mountains
and lakes, animals, birds, and other creatures! "There
is an almighty God over all, a God who created all these
things!" "The heavens declare the glory of God; and the
firmament sheweth his handywork" (Ps 19:1). Is not this
a missionary message?

*Closely allied with this picture of God as Creator is
that of His oneness.* God is one. This uniqueness of God
is the substratum of the whole Old Testament from the
law through the prophets.

Interestingly enough, it is on this basis that Muham-madan missionary work has been carried on and has enjoyed great success among the pagans. "There is no God but God" is one of the two basic elements of their creed.

Man in his rebellion against God has invented for himself a multiplicity of gods. But then he groans to be delivered from these demons of his own creation. What a missionary message, to be able to assure men that they do not need to' placate a horde of capricious, evil-working spirits. There is one God, one only. He is the one who created all things.

Third, the Old Testament pictures God as righteous. Again there are some who think this is trite. "Of course God is righteous," they say; "otherwise He wouldn't be God!" But this is only an indication of what effect the Bible has had on their thinking. Even those who profess unbelief are affected by its teachings. For where did they get the idea that God is righteous?

Certainly not from heathenism. The heathen gods are not generally righteous. That is, they are not righteous in any moral sense. They can only be considered righteous if we admit that anything a god does is right simply because the god does it. Pagan gods are usually deceitful, immoral, licentious creatures whose only law is their own caprice.

There are many in our day who speak of the stern justice of the God of the Old Testament as if it were unat-tractive and unbecoming. They would prefer a milder and more permissive God. They do not realize that even stern justice would be a great relief to the followers of pagan gods. The pagan gods are like Oriental despots. Their very whims are laws, and what is right today may be wrong tomorrow. "How can you know?" their followers ask. "How can you be sure what the god wants?" What a relief to worship a God whose demands are always right and just!

But, in the fourth place, God is also merciful and compassionate. All through the Old Testament His justice is balanced with mercy and compassion. We see it even in close association with His judgment. We see it in the cov-enant He made with Noah and all mankind right after the flood (Gen 9:15-17). We see it in the law, "shewing mercy unto thousands" (Ex 20:6). We see it in the Psalms and in the prophets (Ps 119:64; Mic 7:18). How the world needs this mercy and compassion!

Finally, the Old Testament shows us a God who is sincerely interested in His creatures, especially in man. There is nothing farther from the Old Testament view of God than the idea that He created the world, established its laws, "set it going and then went fishing."

It is not only in such New Testament passages as John 3:16 that we find God's concern expressed for mankind. It is found throughout the Old Testament. Even in the special covenant He made with Abraham (Gen 12:3; 18:18; 22:18) and repeated later to Jacob (Gen 28:14), He did not fail to mention the blessing it would bring to all the world.

SECOND, GOD HAS SPOKEN ABOUT MAN

The Greek philosopher who urged, "Know thyself," expressed a deep truth. We don't know ourselves, but we need to. We need to know our capabilities and our weaknesses. We need to know wherein we are like others and wherein we differ. We need to know what can be expected of man—what forces move him.

The first thing the Old Testament tells us about man is that he was made in God's image (Gen 1:26-27). There are unbelievers who scoff at this. They laughingly say instead that "man made God in his own image." False as their statement is, it is still not so ridiculous as one might think. For if a man had to invent a god, how could he do better than make him in the image of man? After all, what higher nature has he ever known? With all his weaknesses and his failures, man is still the crown of creation. He is the only creature who has been able to bring much of the rest of creation under a measure of personal control. No wonder the psalmist wrote, "Ye are gods; and all of you are children of the most High" (Ps 82:6).

Now it is not easy for us who look on the outward appearance to see God's image in man. Sometimes we find it particularly hard. There are some in whom that image seems to be more disfigured than usual. We ourselves fall far short of God's perfection, yet we tend to despise those who seem to be a little farther away from it than we. We magnify their inferiority to us, forgetting the old adage about "the pot calling the kettle black."

We talk about racial superiority. We used to speak of "the white man's burden." We are like those Latin Americans who look down on the Indians as inferior creatures and proudly speak of themselves as *racionales*—rational beings. We even talk sometimes about the uselessness of missionary work among backward peoples. I have such a letter in my files from a highly educated American. And all because we refuse to believe the truth we find at the beginning of the Old Testament: that man, as man, was made in God's image.

Closely related to this first teaching about man is the Old Testament doctrine of the unity of the human race. The Old Testament does at times distinguish between families and tribes and nations. But our modern racial discrimination based on color is completely foreign to it. It is true that some do try to justify their racial attitudes by an appeal to the Old Testament. There are a few who still call attention to the curse Noah pronounced against Canaan, the son of Ham (Gen 9:25). They contend that because of that curse all Negroes must forever be servants. This in spite of the fact that Canaan was certainly not a black man.

Such teachings do not come from a study of the Old Testament. Instead they are born of our prejudices. And because we want to believe them, we try to find some basis for them in Holy Writ. In all honesty we ought to acknowledge that they are rationalizations.

What the Old Testament really does teach is the unity of the human race. We all have a common ancestor. In him we all were made in God's image. By descent from him we all are brethren. Each has followed his own willful way, and some have prospered more than others, but in nature we are one—one even in our sins.

Men have always resisted this idea of the unity of mankind. Partly it is because of pride, the sort of pride that makes a prosperous man deny his poor relations. But even more it is because it means responsibility. If all mankind is one, then every ruler is responsible to his people, the noble to the commoner, the privileged to the less privileged. We are all of the same stuff. Then, too, those in foreign lands who don't have the blessings we enjoy in Christ do have a just claim on us. It doesn't matter that their race and culture are different from ours. They are still of the same blood.

But the Old Testament is also a message about man's sin. Like a great mirror, the Old Testament reveals to us our hearts. And what we see there is not altogether pleasant. It is not a cause for pride. Even the best of us are guilty. Sin has corrupted all of mankind.

The heathen gods are nearly always arbitrary and capricious. Their commands are seldom based on what is of itself right and good. As a result, sin among the heathen comes to be not much more than ceremonial defilement. It is not impurity of heart but of body; not violation of conscience but of rules.

But in the Old Testament sin is revealed as moral iniquity. Before the law was ever given, in the days before the flood, "the imagination of the heart of man" was evil, and God condemned him. Sin existed apart from the law. It was not the law that made it sinful. The law merely pointed it out and condemned it.

Now the law did establish for the Israelites certain forms and ceremonies. But they were never intended to be an end in themselves. Isaiah 1:11-17 shows how useless God held them to be by themselves: "To what purpose is the multitude of your sacrifices unto me? saith the LORD .... Wash you, make you clean; put away the evil of your doings from before mine eyes; cease to do evil; learn to do well."

Not only among the heathen but in all the world today this message is needed. Even in Roman days it had a great attraction for pagan idolators. The Old Testament told of a standard of righteousness that was unchangeable, a righteousness that was in the very nature of things. So numerous Romans and Greeks became converts to Judaism. They felt the need of such a message.

Besides this, the Old Testament pictures sin as universal among men. No one is free from its contamination. All are sinners and need to be redeemed from sin. How strangely this contrasts to the idea that many hold today, the notion that primitive peoples lead a happy, childlike existence, unaware of sin until the missionary comes. Not only is this far from the Old Testament teaching, it is the most absurd sort of fiction. Only overromantic Americans, ignorant of the realities of heathenism, could imagine such things. For however perverted his ideas of sin may be, the heathen is always conscious of its presence.

Also the Old Testament reveals sin as that which separates men from God (Ps 14:2-3). That is the real burden of its message: sin separating man from the source of life; God seeking to reconcile man to Himself that he may live again. This indeed is a message that is needed—a missionary message.

But again, the Old Testament message is also a message of salvation and hope. From the entrance of sin, in Genesis 3, to such wonderful prophetic utterances as Isaiah 1:18, this message is repeated in innumerable ways. "Though your sins be as scarlet, they shall be as white as snow."

Who could keep such a message to himself? Who could believe the reality of such a hope and not make it known to others?

We could go on and show other details of the Old Testament message that are missionary. We find, for example, that the Old Testament is concerned with the *fundamental problems of all mankind,* and not just those of one group. Its appeal is so universal that people everywhere forget that its leading characters were Jewish. They think of them in terms of their own race and nation. This universality of appeal makes it a missionary book.

Then, too, there is no question about the missionary character of its *prophetic message.* The prophets often

forgot national boundaries as they carried out their ministry. It was too big, too vital to be limited to one people,
even the "chosen people."

But we don't believe it is necessary to go farther. The
message of the Old Testament clearly has a missionary
character.

6

THE OLD TESTAMENT AND MISSIONS (II)

DOES THE OLD TESTAMENT SHOW A MISSIONARY PURPOSE?

WE HAVE SPENT a great deal of time with the missionary *message* of the Old Testament. If the message itself is missionary, then it is hardly necessary for us to get other evidence to prove that the Old Testament also has a missionary *purpose*. Yet we can plainly show that, too, from its own words. God's revelation in the Old Testament was to be for *all* people.

GENESIS

Look at the opening chapters of Genesis. Man sinned, and immediately God made known what was to be the channel of his redemption. But as we read the story in chapter 3 we realize that this is not to be the redemption of just one man, nor even of a single family or nation. God's plan embraces the whole of humanity. He purposed to provide a salvation sufficient for all mankind.

Again, in chapter 4 we have the account of the first murder. But with it we have the foundation for that very sense of missionary responsibility that Paul expresses so forcefully in Romans 1:14. When God questioned Cain about his brother, Cain burst out rather petulantly, "Am I my brother's keeper?" Many a modern follower of Cain has tried to shrug off responsibility for others in the same way. But God still thrusts aside that flimsy excuse. He still wants to hear from us the acknowledgment, "I am debtor both to the Greeks, and to the Barbarians; both to the wise, and to the unwise. So, as much as in me is, I am ready to preach the gospel"—I am ready to tell everyone the good news of God's redemption.

The first eleven chapters of Genesis have to do with the whole of mankind. It is not until chapter 12 that the scope becomes more limited. Then we have God choosing one man, Abram, and his descendants to stand in a special relationship to Himself. The Hebrew people are to be the channel of His revelation and of the salvation He is going to bring to the world.

But even in choosing Abram, and in making a special covenant with him, God did not lessen His vital interest in all men. Look at the way He states His promise to this man of faith. Every time He repeats it He mentions that He purposes in this way to bring blessing to the whole world. "In thee shall all families of the earth be blessed" (Gen 12:3); "all the nations of the earth shall be blessed in him" (Gen 18:18); "in thy seed shall all the nations of the earth be blessed" (Gen 22:18). When He renews the promise to Jacob, He says the same thing, "In thee and in thy seed shall all the families of the earth be blessed" (Gen 28:14).

EXODUS

In the book of Exodus we have the beginning of God's special dealings with the Hebrew people, as He tries to make them into a nation to fulfill His purposes. We see Him called "the God of the Hebrews," as if He were a purely national deity. His great final purpose in choosing them is nearly lost to sight. It is subordinated to the immediate program of welding them into a nation and bringing them into possession of the promised land. When He gave the law to the people at Mount Sinai, the Ten Commandments did begin with a reminder that the God who was speaking was the same one who had created the universe. But the law itself and the covenant were given to them as a people distinct from the rest of mankind.

LAW

Still, even in the law we don't entirely lose sight of the final worldwide objective. In Numbers 14:21 God says, "As truly as I live, *all the earth* shall be filled with the glory of the LORD." Again in Deuteronomy 10:14-19 He reminds the Israelites, "Behold, the heaven and the heaven of heavens is the LORD'S thy God, the earth also, with all that therein is. Only the LORD had a delight in thy fathers to love them, and he chose their seed after them, even you above all people, as it is this day . . . . For the LORD your God is God of gods, and Lord of lords." And lest they should get haughty because of this great privilege, He adds, "Love ye therefore the stranger: for ye were strangers in the land of Egypt."

PSALMS

As we move on to Psalms, we encounter even more very clear evidences of God's missionary purpose. Many of the psalms are devotional and personal. Others have to do primarily with the people of Israel. But scattered through them here and there are glimpses of a much wider horizon.

Sometimes they simply express God's dominion over all men everywhere. "The earth is the LORD'S, and the fulness thereof; the world, and they that dwell therein" (24:1).

At other times they exhort all peoples to worship Him: "Make a joyful noise unto God, all ye lands" (66:1). "O praise the LORD, all ye nations: praise him, all ye people" (117:1).

Often they prophesy that all peoples will come to Him: "Be still, and know that I am God: I will be exalted among the heathen, I will be exalted in the earth" (46:10). "O thou who hearest prayer, unto thee shall all flesh come" (65:2). "All nations whom thou hast made shall come and worship before thee, O Lord; and shall glorify thy name" (86:9). In one case the prophecy is very specific: "Ethiopia shall soon stretch out her hands unto God" (68:31).

At least two psalms tell those who know God to witness for Him: "Sing praises to the LORD, which dwelleth in Zion: declare among the peoples his doings" (9:11). "Make known his deeds among the people" (105:1).

And one expresses specifically a missionary purpose: "That thy way may be known upon earth, thy saving health among all nations" (67:2).

PROPHETS

Of course when we come to the prophets the consciousness of God's missionary purpose becomes very strong. Perhaps no one expresses it more beautifully than Isaiah. In chapter 49 v. 6, God speaks to His servant, the Messiah, and says, "It is a light thing that thou shouldest be my servant to raise up the tribes of Jacob, and to restore the preserved of Israel: I will also give thee for a light to the Gentiles, that thou mayest be my salvation *unto the end of the earth.*"

In another Messianic passage, 52:13-15, God says: "Behold, my servant shall deal prudently, he shall be exalted and extolled, and be very high. As many were astonied at thee; his visage was marred more than any man, and his form more than the sons of men: so shall he sprinkle *many nations;* the kings shall shut their mouths at him: for that which hath not been told them shall they see; and that which they had not heard shall they consider."

SUMMARY

To sum up, does the Old Testament show a missionary purpose? Who can doubt it? Even in the choosing of the Hebrew people that missionary purpose stood out. As one writer has put it,

> The choice of one race among many was not an antimissionary act on God's part, selecting one and letting others go by; it was rather among the most missionary of His acts, choosing one and filling it with a sense of His will and deep understanding of His nature so that it might

teach all mankind that nature and that will. *God's elections are always for the channeling of blessings. The favored group that forgets this will soon lose the favor.*

DOES THE OLD TESTAMENT REVEAL ANY MISSIONARY ACTIVITY?

This third question is an interesting one, and one that deserves more careful study and attention than we are going to be able to give it. Does the Old Testament reveal any missionary activity? Was there any attempt to bring the blessings of the Old Testament revelation to others? Did those who received the revelation comprehend its scope? Did they realize it was for all men? Were the descendants of Abram conscious of their God-given task?

It is very evident that a majority of the people did not have any such consciousness. In the minds of many the idea of the extension of the message was unquestionably tied in with the expansion of political Israel. The benefits to be had through a knowledge of the true God were for those who became Jews.

This is not a strange idea. In fact it is all too readily understood in the world today. A common accusation against the missionaries of Christ in many lands today is that they are tied up with their governments. They are held to be spies or advance agents of American or British imperialism, either politically or economically.

But if the Old Testament has a clear missionary message and purpose, there must have been *some* appreciation of the call to a more unselfish ministry. In some cases we know this was true. Whatever other lessons we may get from the book of Jonah, for example, we know that it is definitely a missionary book. The prophet's message was not a pleasant one. He was a very unwilling, and later a disgruntled, missionary. Yet a missionary he was, and that in the distant Assyrian city of Nineveh.

Still, such examples of missionary activity are comparatively rare in the Old Testament. Such men as Daniel did make God known in other lands. But little is said about any large-scale attempt to win others to His worship.

In spite of this lack of information about missionary activity in the Old Testament, we know that some was carried on before the time of Christ. Christ Himself speaks of the strenuous efforts of the Pharisees "to make one proselyte" (Mt 23:15). Also there were numerous proselytes or converts to the Jewish faith who came to the feasts at Jerusalem, as on the day of Pentecost (Ac 2:10). So there was some recognition of missionary responsibility, even though it was very little in comparison with the later Christian missionary enterprise.

For it is in Christianity that missions reaches its peak.

7

MOTIVES AND AIMS OF MISSIONS

BEFORE WE TALK about the particular motives and aims that we ought to have in missions, we need to understand our terms. We often confuse the two terms, *motives* and *aims,* both in our thinking and speaking. We use them to mean just the same thing.

Now a motive is something that prompts one to act. It is the force that impels us to do what we do. It may be considered as answering the question *Why?*

An aim is an objective, an end in view. It is what we expect to accomplish through our action. It may be regarded as answering the question *What?* or *To what end?*

What brings the two into such close association that they are hard to distinguish is this: sometimes the purpose to be accomplished by our action is so desirable in itself that it moves us to act. The motive force then is the force of attraction. It is the force of the magnet instead of that of the rocket. It is the sort of power that a prize has to make men exert themselves more than they ever would through a sense of duty. In this chapter, however, we are going to try to keep the two things distinct.

MOTIVES

To get at the motives, we need to ask, Why do people want to be foreign missionaries? What reasons impel them to offer their lives for Christian service in foreign lands? Notice that we are going to keep it on this personal level, which is basic, rather than enter into the church's motives.

We need to answer these questions. In one way or another every young person who volunteers to serve Christ in the foreign field has met them or is sure to do so. Sometimes those who ask the questions are the scoffers, those who have no real comprehension of Christianity and can't be expected to understand its world ministry. But just as often they are professing Christians, some of whom would sincerely like to know. Then sometimes, too, it is the candidate's own heart that wants a clear-cut answer.

If you are thinking of foreign missionary service, you want to evaluate your motives carefully. There is perhaps no other type of work where your motives will have so much to do with your success. Romantic notions, the desire to travel, the "lure of the exotic," the purely emotional response to a stirring missionary message—all these are motives. They may even be strong enough to get some young people out to the field. But their weakness usually shows up as soon as the young missionary comes face to face with actual conditions in an unfavorable, even actively hostile, environment. They can't keep him going.

A Chinese writer, now teaching in an American university, once commented on the ineffectiveness of many modern missionaries to China. He wrote to the effect that missionaries today don't have the strong motivation that marked the earlier missionaries. This is one of the main reasons why they have been so ineffectual. The early missionaries had their faults. They sometimes used wrong methods. They may even have aroused unnecessary antagonisms. But they had an overpowering sense of divine mission that overcame many such handicaps.

There are some today who, with their vaunted superior knowledge, presume to criticize and even ridicule those early missionaries. They call attention to the mistakes they made. They tell us that their theology is outmoded. They accuse them of attacking the pagan faiths indiscriminately and not appreciating the good features to be found in them. They criticize them for becoming dictatorial or paternalistic. And to some extent they are right.

Yet at the same time some of these critics, alarmed at the confusion, uncertainty and lack of real effectiveness today, have urgently called for a reexamination of the basis principles of missions. And of course that involves motivation. But any amount of scholarly investigation is not enough. Study can discover motives but it cannot generate them. For any missionary to be effective, he must have something fundamental, something deeply compelling to thrust him into the work — something similar to what Paul experienced when he wrote, "Woe is me if I preach not the gospel!"

In the experience of most successful missionaries we find two closely related motives that seem to stand out as more compelling than any others.

First is a keen realization of what we have in Christ. It is the consciousness that in Christ we have what the whole world desperately needs. We have a message and a life so eternally valuable that the whole world ought to have them.

When a man is sure that the way of Christ is not only a better way but is the *only* good way; when his experience of Christ has transformed and ennobled his own life; when he faces heathenism frankly, realizing its awfulness, but at the same time realizes that it can be changed by the same Saviour who changed his life; he cannot help feeling the constraint of missions. Such a motive, such an inner constraint, is not only enough to send him to the field. It will also sustain him in the midst of difficulties and discouragement.

The second motive, closely related to the first, is simply the command of Christ. Of course that command has no force for one who has never acknowledged the lordship of Christ. Neither is it very effective in the life of one who has never learned to obey. But the one who wholeheartedly has submitted to the authority of Christ, who finds pleasure in seeking to do His will, or even feels strongly the sense of duty to his Lord, finds that this motive is a strong one. It may even be sufficient of itself. No other reason is needed, such a one decides, for the Lord Himself has commanded and it is for His servant to obey.

These two motives have generally proved to be more compelling than any others. But if we look at them closely we find that they both have a common base. That base is the love of Christ. In 2 Corinthians 5:14-15 Paul affirms, "The love of Christ constraineth us; because we thus judge, that if one died for all, then were all dead: and that he died for all, that they which live should not henceforth live unto themselves, but unto him which died for them, and rose again."

If we, then, have experienced the love of Christ, and if we in turn have a real love for Him, we need no other motivation to make Him known. The life that we enjoy is the gift of His love. How can we ever repay Him? The commands He gives come from the one we love, so we gladly obey. We could hardly do anything else without denying that love. The love of Christ is the deepest motivation possible.

But we don't mean that there aren't other motives. There are many others. In fact it is doubtful if any of us can completely analyze his motives in all their complexities.

It is difficult to know, for example, just how much of the spirit of adventure enters into the decision of some young people to be missionaries. Others have been led to think that full surrender to the Lord necessarily means foreign missionary service. Then sometimes a young man wants to serve the Lord but doesn't think he can qualify as a preacher or teacher. So he thinks he may find in foreign service a place for the abilities that couldn't be used at home.

Where missions send out short-term missionaries for teaching, some may look at it as an opportunity for getting some experience while making a contribution to the Lord's work. In the case of missionaries' children, they sometimes simply follow in the footsteps of their parents, doing a work with which they are already somewhat familiar. And we might add that many young people are moved by an appeal to youthful idealism and by an altruistic desire to help humanity. Look at the enthusiasm for the Peace Corps. Young people are still idealists.

These and many other motives may or may not play a part in sending a missionary to the field. Even where they do, they need not be condemned. What we need to recognize is that they are inferior motives. They don't have the powerful drive or the sustaining force of the two principal motives. At best their place is secondary.

AIMS

Now, it is the motives that determine the aims of foreign missions. The man who is moved solely by compassion for human suffering will feel that his ministry is done when he relieves that suffering. His aim is to heal sick bodies, to feed the hungry, to give shelter to the homeless, to stop unjust oppression. But the one who is moved by a sense of obligation to make known the gospel goes much deeper. It has meant life to him. His aim is to see that gospel bring the same life to others in other lands.

In greater detail we may say that the true missionary of Christ has but one great aim, in two phases. It is to witness to Christ in such a way that (1) men will put their faith in Him, and that (2) the church of Christ will be established and built up. This aim is entirely spiritual, as it should be. Did not Christ say, "Seek ye first the kingdom of God, and his righteousness; and all these things shall be added unto you" (Mt 6:33)? This aim includes both evangelism and teaching.

Notice that we do not say that the one aim is "to preach the gospel." Such a statement is as shallow as it is inaccurate. The missionary cannot "deliver his soul" by the simple act of delivering the message, without regard to the results. He is more than a herald who merely repeats the words he is told to repeat. The missionary is a witness—a witness who is deeply concerned that others believe his testimony and render a favorable verdict.

Preaching is important in missionary work. It is a prime way of presenting the message and seeking to persuade men to accept it. But the preaching must be in terms that the people addressed can understand. It must be with the sincerity that is born of experience. It must reveal a warm interest in those to whom it is directed. And preaching is only one way of witnessing. There are many others.

We have said that the true missionary has one great aim. This does not mean that he may not have many other related aims. It simply means that all the others will be subordinated to this one principal aim.

For instance, he will heal the sick and feed the hungry, but not as ends in themselves. They will be as expressions of the life of Christ that dwells in him. He will teach the illiterate so that they may come to a better understanding of Christ. He will introduce new ideas, new practices, and, perhaps in a few cases, a new civilization or way of life. But it won't be because he thinks that these things in themselves are of prime importance. It will be because they are necessary to the full expression of the life of the Saviour. All his purposes will center in the one great purpose, and from it they will all derive their significance.

Perhaps the greatest weakness in Christian missions today comes from a deviation from this one great aim. Our mission schools and colleges continue to bear the name of Christian long after they have lost sight of any distinctively Christian objective. Our social services become so involved in the physical and the economic that we neglect the spiritual. Or we become so interested in promoting *our* mission, *our* denomination, *our* movement, that we forget the Saviour and *His* church that *He* bought with *His* own blood. At times we content ourselves with making modest progress toward some minor objective, not noticing how far short we fall of the main goal. Even when we don't actually turn aside, we tie ourselves up with trivialities.

God grant us a clear vision of our objective!

8

WHOSE RESPONSIBILITY?

UPON WHOM does the responsibility for missionary work rest? Up to this point we have not considered such a question. We have not differentiated between the obligation of the individual and the obligation of the church.

But just who is responsible? Is missions the responsibility only of those individuals who feel a special interest in such a cause? Or should we consider missions the responsibility of the church as a whole? Sometimes we have acted as if it were the enterprise of just a select few, some of whom have gone out as missionaries, while the others volunteered to support them in their work. Is this as 'it should be?

This individualistic attitude is very prominent in some circles today. You can see it in the large number of independent missionaries who try to start and carry on a work unconnected with any denomination or church group. You can see it in the rapidly growing number of independent mission societies. They get their support from interested individuals in a large number of churches, but they are not in any way subject to the control of those churches.

You can see it too in the attitude of many young people who offer themselves for missionary service. They look on their action merely as the fulfilling of a personal obligation. They have no thought that they might be called to represent a larger fellowship—the church. In modern political terminology they think of themselves as "personal representatives" of Christ rather than "ambassadors" of Christ and His church. Are they right?

When we look to the New Testament for the answer,

we find two answers. Rather we should say that the Scriptures teach that both the individual and the church are responsible. And there is no clear marking out of the responsibility of each one. In a way it is like the responsibility of several men who have signed a note for a mutual friend. When the note is due, if the man can't pay it himself, the creditor can demand payment of all the signers jointly, or of any one of them individually. That is, they may all get together and pay the note, each one giving his share; or any one of them may be made to pay the full amount. Each one who signs the note makes himself liable for it all; though if they are all honest and able, each one will give his part.

Now when Christ gave His Great Commission, He didn't indicate exactly how it was to be carried out. He gave it to the group of disciples who met with Him after His resurrection, and it seems clear that He expected each one to feel his responsibility to witness for his Lord. Yet from the beginning the church as a body looked upon the extension of the work as a part of its corporate responsibility. So Philip preached first in Samaria on his own initiative. But the church in Jerusalem sent its representatives to confirm the work. In Antioch the Spirit had already called Barnabas and Saul to missionary service. But the church was instructed by the Holy Spirit to send them forth, and they reported to it on their return.

As Christians we have all been given a great task to perform by our Lord and Saviour. So long as that task has not been completed it is a lien against each one of us for which He may hold us personally accountable. Yet it is also a lien against the church. It is the church's task; but it is also yours and mine. We are all responsible.

THE CHURCH'S RESPONSIBILITY

In speaking of the church's responsibility, we want to focus our attention here on the local congregation.

Under present conditions of missionary work the local church, denominational or not, has certain rather clear obligations to fulfill.

It is just here that a very basic weakness in the missionary enterprise shows up. It is that the local church often is not aware of any such missionary obligations. Or if it is aware of them, it chooses to pay very little attention to them.

In a denominational church a quota is often assigned for the financial support of the missions of that denomination. But small as the quota may be, the church often fails to meet it. Independent churches do not have a mission board to assign them a quota. So the individual church may choose to do something about missions or not, just as it sees fit.

In either case what the church does will depend largely on its leadership. It is characteristic of our Protestant churches that their affairs are generally managed by a handful of people. This is true even when they are most democratically organized. The average church member seldom does more than attend some of the church services and make a small contribution. Only an inspiring and constructive leadership can get him to take a larger share in the church's business.

But local church leaders are not often well informed in missionary matters. Neither do they have much interest in affairs that are not under their own control. The pastor himself has usually had little training in the line of missions, even those of his own denomination. They don't usually present it to him in the seminary as an essential part of his ministry. It is one of the extras, something useful to engage in after the local needs are fully met. Even the Ladies' Missionary Society is often busy with other things besides missions, because it doesn't have strong missionary leadership.

Yet the world mission of witnessing to Christ among all people is the *one great charge* that the Saviour gave to His church after His resurrection. Apart from worship, the church really exists for just two purposes: witnessing and fellowship. We emphasize the second but all too often forget the first.

FOUR RESPONSIBILITIES

Let us present here four definite responsibilities that pertain to the local church.

First is the responsibility to recognize that missions is a part of the church's essential ministry. It is not a question of home missions or foreign missions. That doesn't enter into it. Instead it is a question of whether the church is going to minister to its own little group or extend its ministry to those who are outside. It is a question of a self-centered ministry as opposed to a ministry that looks beyond self to the needs of others.

We don't need to worry about the artificial distinction between home missions and foreign missions. The church that feels keenly the need to reach out and minister to the lost in its own community can never stop there. A compassionate interest in others isn't even stopped by national boundaries. Once we turn our look outward, "the field is the world."

The same thing is true about the church that is deeply concerned for foreign missions. It can't be blind to the needs on its own doorstep. That is, it can't if it is sincerely concerned for the souls of men and is not merely attracted to missions by the romance of strange lands and people.

This first responsibility is basic. It is to acknowledge that the church doesn't exist for itself. It is not a social club. It is not a haven of rest. If it is to fulfill its divine purpose it must be missionary. And the first step in fulfilling that purpose is to acknowledge it—to look at it as a duty that must be carried out.

When a church recognizes that missions is a part of its essential ministry, it is then responsible to give to missions the same careful, prayerful attention that it gives to any other part of its work. It should not relegate missions to some missionary society within the church as if it didn't concern the whole body of believers. It should plan for missions. It should bring missionary problems to the church prayer meeting and to the governing board. It should give to missions a definite place in the church budget.

Too many churches don't have a definite missionary program, even when they are "missionary-minded." One such church comes to mind, which often opened its doors to missionary speakers. The church always made a generous donation to each missionary speaker *at the time he spoke.* But in the several years of my acquaintance with it, the church never took on the regular support of any missionary or mission work. Under such circumstances missions comes to be looked on, not as a responsibility but as a pleasurable pastime.

We need to get down to business in missions. Our churches need to stop dabbling and start working. Only so can we meet our God-given responsibility.

Perhaps we ought to say another word about *praying* for missions. "Prayerful attention" means more than just praying, "God bless the missionaries." It means more than praying about how much to give. It means actually interceding for the work that is going on. It means praying for the specific problems of those who do the work. It means having such a real concern for it all that our concern expresses itself in intercessory prayer.

We don't need to go into the values of intercessory prayer. It is enough to realize that the missionaries themselves count heavily on it. They know that their efforts alone can never accomplish what they have to do. God must work. They know too that God is not reluctant to hear their own requests. But at the same time they know that God wants church and missionaries to be united in this task. Prayer is one way to express that spiritual union.

The third responsibility of the local church is the task of providing money and other material support for missions. It is the thing that most people think of first. Unfortunately too many of them seem to think of it as the only responsibility. It is an important task, but in carrying it out there are several errors the church needs to avoid. Let us list three of them.

1. First, spend the Lord's money for missions as carefully as you would for redecorating the church or for a new church organ. Many a church pays less attention to the distributing of its missionary funds than it does to the choice of a new hymnal. The church should know as much about the causes for which its missionary money goes as it would if each member were investing his personal funds. We should never be less careful of the Lord's money than our own.

2. Second, don't give *only* for the support of individual missionaries or special projects. Of course it is good to have personal contact with individual missionaries, expecially if they are from your church. It is good also to have at least a share in their personal support. The same thing applies to special projects. They do have a way of stimulating people to give. But don't stop there.

The reason is this: Who is going to pay the many other expenses of carrying on the work? Who will pay for the house the missionary lives in? Who will provide him with the literature and other supplies he needs? Who will pay for his travel, or even for the cost of getting his salary to him at his remote post? Who will pay for the scores of other expenses that are necessary for the carrying on of the mission? Don't forget these needs.

3. Third, when you do support a missionary, don't feel that your support entitles you to dictate his private life. Support him because you believe he is a faithful representative of the Lord, and do it as unto the Lord. Your stewardship ended when you gave the gift. His began. He is responsible to the Lord, not to you, for using the money wisely, just as you were responsible to the Lord while the money was in your hands.

A fourth and very important responsibility of the local church to missions is the provision of missionary candidates. Missionaries must come from the local churches. Actually missionary work in other lands is to a large degree a reflection of the spiritual life of the churches at home. To a large degree, we say, but not entirely. It sometimes happens that our missionaries got their deepest spiritual impressions away from the home church. It may have been in a Bible camp, a Christian youth group, a campus Christian organization or a Bible training school. But in general our foreign missions reflect the Christianity of the churches from which the missionaries come.

For this reason it is important for the local church to have a definite program of missionary education. In many of our churches there are untapped resources of manpower for missions, simply because the young people know nothing of the work and have never been faced with the challenge of giving their lives for Christ in a missionary way. It is the church's business to challenge them, to turn their hearts in this direction. That some churches have been doing this was revealed in a survey made of new missionaries. The survey showed that a majority had first become interested in missions in their home church. The home church has the key to the missionary personnel problem.

9

THE CHRISTIAN'S RESPONSIBILITY—
THE MISSIONARY CALL

As a member of the local church, every Christian has a share in the responsibilities of the church to missions. But there are some other responsibilities that are purely personal. In fact, each individual's participation in the missionary program of the church will depend on his personal response to the appeal of Christ.

The Christian's greatest responsibility is to do just what Saul did on the way to Damascus—to say, "Lord, what wilt thou have me to do?" Until you take this step, it is useless to talk about any other. You cannot ease a troubled conscience by offering to support a representative on the mission field if you ought to be there yourself. If you are not surrendered to go to the mission field for Christ, you are not surrendered to Christ!

But only a small part of those who do surrender will actually be sent. Not every volunteer is acceptable for this work. The requirements of missionary service are such that many of those who are willing to go will have to be ruled out. Still, it is the ones who have such a willing heart that Christ can use in every kind of Christian work. Many of our most effective Christian workers at home are those who once wanted to go out as missionaries but were prevented.

This brings up the matter of the missionary call.

The Missionary Call

When a young person asks about the missionary call,

he usually means, "How can I tell whether the Lord wants *me* on the foreign mission field?"

He may have some interest in scriptural and philosophical definitions of a call, but it is the answer to this personal question that he really wants. It is this answer that concerns him, his life and his actions. He will listen patiently to our generalizations if we can make him see just how they apply to his particular case. Otherwise he will turn away in disappointment and perhaps wonder if we really know the answer. Or he may wonder if there is any such thing as being sure of the Lord's will in the matter.

Perhaps his wondering is fully justified. I myself have heard explanations of the missionary call, and read others, that impressed me as being rationalizations. They seemed to be attempts to provide some sort of doctrinal basis for a course of action already taken, whose real explanation was only vaguely understood.

Sometimes the one doing the explaining has a fixed idea of what the missionary call *ought* to be. Then in the light of that idea he tries to view his own actions as a fulfillment of the call. He may have an uncomfortable feeling that his own call has not fully conformed to the pattern. Yet he hesitates to acknowledge it, even to himself. After all, it is not an easy matter to analyze our own experience in retrospect and avoid reading into it some of the things we think should have been there.

There are other explanations of the call that, while they do touch certain important aspects, usually leave the young Christian still unsatisfied. "A need, a consciousness of that need, and an ability to fill the need" is one such explanation. It is perhaps as good a definition as one can put in so few words. Yet it seems to imply that human need alone is the call. It leaves out the Lord Himself and His relation to the one who is called.

Neither does this explanation provide any basis for deciding which of many needs at home and abroad should have the prior claim. Even if we say, "Go where the need is greatest," the matter is still uncertain. Can we measure need just by the number of needy people? Can we say that the savages of New Guinea are spiritually more needy than the cultured Japanese? Are *all* foreign fields more needy than *any* home field?

Perhaps we may not succeed here any better than others in clarifying the matter. Yet what we say below is a sincere attempt to treat the matter objectively. We shall keep in mind the authority and the teachings of the Scriptures, while acknowledging at the same time the validity and the value of Christian experience.

THREE FALSE IDEAS

Before we can give a clear answer to the question, What is the missionary call? we must remove some false ideas that are obstructing the way. We don't know how some of these ideas got started, but they have been repeated so often and are so little challenged that people accept them almost as if they were axiomatic.

First is the idea that we must have some special divine call to go beyond the borders of our own country as Christ's witnesses to the lost. That is, we may hear Christ's call to devote our lives to Christian service, and so long as we don't leave the limits of our own country we are free to labor anywhere from Maine to California just as we see the need and find the opportunity. But let someone suggest that there is a greater need, and perhaps an open door, just beyond the national boundary, and we raise objections. Immediately we begin to talk about not having a "call" to foreign missionary service.

It is as if we thought the boundaries of the nations were established as limits by God. As if a special divine passport must be issued—or rather that a special divine command must be given—before we dare cross over to the other side with the gospel. We don't hesitate to move three thousand miles from Miami to Seattle at the invitation of a church; but to fly an hour or so across to Haiti we must first have a special "call"!

Merely to bring such an idea under scrutiny is to refute it. Where can we find any basis to support it? Certainly not in the Scriptures. There the whole world is presented as the field, with no division into "home" and "foreign" fields. Philip preached the gospel in Samaria, and the refugees from Jerusalem planted the church in Gentile Antioch, with no thought of waiting for a special call to those regions. The refugees were fleeing from the first wave of persecution, and wherever they went they spoke of the Saviour. The idea of a special divine call to minister outside the borders of Judea and Galilee does not seem to have entered into their heads. They were witnesses to everyone everywhere.

Of course those who first established the church in Antioch were not what we would call full-time workers today. So it may be well to take a look at those who took the leadership there later and gave full time to a Christian ministry.

First mentioned is Barnabas, who already was prominent in the work in Jerusalem. It was the Jerusalem church that sent Barnabas to Antioch. They had heard of the work there and apparently believed that Barnabas would be just the man to look into the situation and establish the new believers in the faith. Barnabas went, found a need for his services and decided to stay.

But Barnabas saw that another man could be used there too. He remembered Saul, the man he had first introduced to the believers in Jerusalem. He knew that Saul had gone home to Tarsus in Asia Minor. We don't know what Saul was doing at the time, but Tarsus was not far from Antioch. So Barnabas went there to get Saul and bring him to help out in the new church.

We may well assume that both Barnabas and Saul had waited on the Lord before agreeing to go to Antioch. But it is perfectly clear, and the Scriptures plainly state, that the initiative in both instances came from other men. The Jerusalem church "sent" Barnabas, and Barnabas "brought" Saul. Not a word, not even a hint, is given that any divine call, any unusual spiritual experience, was needed to overcome their reluctance to leave their own land as ministers of Christ. True, Barnabas was a native of Cyprus and Saul of Cilicia, but Antioch was still a foreign field to them both.

As for the other "prophets and teachers" in Antioch, "Simeon that was called Niger, and Lucius of Cyrene, and Manaen, which had been brought up with Herod the tetrarch," it is evident that at least Lucius and Manaen were not from Antioch and so could be called foreign missionaries. But there is no indication of the way in which they had come into the work there. They may have been among the refugees. Or they may have been among the prophets mentioned in Acts 11:27 who came down from Jerusalem at the same time as Agabus. At any rate, the fact that they were ministering in a foreign field didn't call for any special comment.

In all the New Testament account there is only one instance when a national or geographic boundary seemed to require a special call before the missionaries would decide to cross it. That was on Paul's second missionary journey, when he and his companions reached Troas. There they got a remarkable revelation of God's will that they should go on over into Europe.

This unusual experience, generally named the "Macedonian call," is often held to be the typical missionary call. Even some otherwise careful missionary writers and speakers have plainly called it such. They have tried to show how it applies to the situation young Christians face today when they are confronted with the challenge of foreign missionary service. They encourage young people to look for some such experience as Paul had, either explicitly or implicitly. And when the experience does not come, the young people become confused and discouraged.

THE CHRISTIAN'S RESPONSIBILITY

This is really the *second* of the false ideas that keep us from a proper understanding of the missionary call. We need to realize that *the "Macedonian call" was positively not the missionary call!* It wasn't even a typical call of any sort! It was an unusual experience, and all the more striking because it was so unusual. Perhaps it had to be striking to accomplish its purpose at that time and in the hearts of those men.

It is not at all unreasonable to suppose that on other occasions, even today, God may make use of such unusual means to call men to one task or another. Yet in the New Testament this case was the exception rather than the rule. And in Christian experience today such occurrences are still exceptional.

We have said that the "Macedonian call" was not the missionary call. Even a superficial reading of the preceding chapters in the Acts should make this abundantly clear. Paul was already a missionary; he had been a missionary for some years. Actually this incident took place in the midst of his second great missionary tour. He was already in a foreign land when the vision came. And it came, not to call him and his companions to missionary service, but to call them to extend their operations beyond Asia Minor to Europe. If we can remove from our thinking the idea that this was a typical call to foreign missionary service, we shall clear the way for a better understanding of what such a call really is.

A third misunderstanding that needs to be cleared up is the notion that the missionary call necessarily is associated with some definite field. Some young people are greatly perturbed because, while they are sure that the Lord wants them to go forth as foreign missionaries, they do not know the precise field. Here again the common idea is inconsistent with the scriptural examples.

When Barnabas and Saul started out on their first missionary journey together, they were sure of just one thing. They knew the work they were to do, for the Spirit had said to the church, "Separate me Barnabas and Saul for *the work whereunto I have called them.*" But it is doubtful that they knew just in what places they were to carry on this work. Note carefully their itinerary. Cyprus was nearby, it was unevangelized, and it was the homeland of Barnabas. What would be more natural than that they should go there first? From western Cyprus the next logical step was the mainland of Asia Minor. Here the evangelization continued until they reached the border of Paul's own province of Cilicia. Presumably he had carried on work there before going to Antioch. They now retraced their steps, establishing better the work they had begun, finally returning to Antioch with their mission completed. It is remotely possible that the whole trip had been planned ahead of time. But various details, such as Mark's leaving them when they entered Asia Minor, seem to show otherwise.

Whether or not they knew just where they were going on that first trip, Paul certainly didn't know in advance the itinerary of his second journey. He started out to revisit the churches Barnabas and he had established before. But soon he was trying other doors. Finding some of them temporarily closed, he pushed on in the only forward direction that was open, until he reached Troas. From there the Macedonian vision gave him a clear enough call to the next place. But Macedonia was only a stepping-stone. Without any other vision Paul continued on westward and southward into Greece until he came to Corinth.

On the return from Corinth, Paul visited the province of Asia, whose capital was Ephesus. The Lord had forbidden him to preach there earlier on this same tour. But now there was no hindrance. He spent only a brief time in Ephesus, but later he returned for a much more extended ministry.

Paul's great trip to Rome was not the result of any

vision or special revelation. In writing to the brethren there before he went, he said that he had desired for many years to make the trip and see them. Since his apostolic ministry had now been completed where he was, he would soon be ready to visit Rome on his way to Spain (Ro 15: 23-24). He went in a way he hadn't expected, as a prisoner, but he was still fulfilling a personal ambition.

So as we review the career of the great missionary to the Gentiles, we see that he seldom enjoyed a special revelation to direct his movements. Only twice after his conversion do we hear of such an experience. Once was when the Lord told him to leave Jerusalem, since his mission was to be to the Gentiles (Ac 22:17-21). He was told to leave but wasn't told where to go. The other occasion was when he received the Macedonian vision. There only the important initial step was revealed. In fact, he had only two alternatives—either to go on across to Europe or to go back along the road he had come. It was not a question of choice of field but of advance or consolidation. And the Lord directed advance.

To sum up: (1) a *special* divine call is not necessary to witness for Christ beyond the national border; (2) the striking vision that Paul received at Troas, the so-called "Macedonian call," was *not* his missionary call, nor is it typical of such a call; and (3) the call to missionary service is not *necessarily* associated with a definite field at home or abroad.

It might seem from this that we have completely ruled out the idea of a call. But this is not so. We have merely tried to clear the ground in order to construct a more scriptural and sound doctrine of the missionary call. The call is not lacking. In fact it is fundamental. No one should go into any mission field without a sense of call if he expects to enjoy God's blessing on his ministry. But to wait or look for an experience that at best is quite unusual is to open the way for disappointment and frustration.

POSITIVE ASPECTS OF THE CALL

There are two aspects of the missionary call, one general and one particular. For clearness of thinking we usually do well to distinguish the two. We must recognize also that the first is fundamental to the second.

GENERAL CALL

The *general missionary call* is synonymous with the Great Commission. It is expressed in various ways: "Go ye therefore and teach all nations. . . . Go ye into all the world and preach the gospel . . . . As my Father hath sent me, even so send I you. . . . Ye shall be witnesses unto me . . . unto the uttermost parts of the earth." But the message is the same. It is the call of Christ to those who follow Him to go out and witness for Him everywhere. It includes all of His disciples; not one is omitted from its scope. The Christian who fails to bear witness to his Saviour is disobedient to this call, which is meant for him.

This call is general because it includes all Christians as prospective missionaries. But it is also general because it includes all unbelievers as the missionary field. It is not a question of home missions or foreign missions, of city missions or missions on the frontier. This is a call to be Christ's ambassadors to lost sinners without regard to the places where they may be found.

There is no use trying to talk about a special call to the foreign mission field until the matter of this general missionary call is settled. It is just as useless as it would be to discuss the call to missionary service before the issue of putting one's faith in the Saviour has been settled. It has been well said that a trip across the ocean doesn't make a missionary. But neither does failure to go abroad keep a man from being a missionary.

Lest you be tempted to discount the importance of this general missionary call, take time to observe how similar it is to your call to salvation. In fact, if you look carefully through the New Testament you will find that the word *call* is most often used in connection with salvation rather than with service.

Note that the call to salvation is a general call issued to all sinners. It is a call to "whosoever will." Occasionally the Lord speaks to an individual and says, "Follow me"; but usually His invitation is, "Come unto me, *all* ye that labour and are heavy laden." Wasn't that the kind of call you answered when you came to Christ to receive His salvation? Wasn't it a general invitation you accepted, but one that you realized was sincerely intended to include you? Did you wait for a special divine invitation, an audible voice to call out your name? Did you wait to be drafted?

Clearly the call to salvation is enough when the sinner hears it and realizes it is meant for him. But the call is not complete, is not effectual, until the sinner responds, "Lord, I believe!" In the same way the general call to witness for Christ is enough when the believer hears it and realizes that it is meant for him. But to make it effectual he too must say, "Here am I, Lord; send me!" When God calls and man responds, then the divine call is complete.

Actually, for foreign missionary service, as for any other, it is not *essential* to have any other call than this general call. Christ's missionaries are those who have a deep and compelling sense of their obligation to obey His command and make known His salvation to all men.

Many missionaries are mentioned in the New Testament besides the apostles. Some are mentioned by name, as Titus and Apollos and Epaphras, and others anonymously, as the Thessalonian believers. But so far as we have information, the majority carried on their ministry in obedience to this general call. With the living Christ in their hearts, they were constrained to be His witnesses everywhere.

INDIVIDUAL ASPECT

Still there is an *individual aspect to the call,* and in some cases a *separate individual call.* We have spoken of the response to Christ's general commission. This of course is an individual response. No one can answer for another, not even a father for his son, much as he may want to. It is in this response that we see clearly the hand of the Holy Spirit. He who opens the eyes of sinners to behold the Saviour and moves them to accept His invitation to receive life in Him is the same one who illumines the understanding of the saints and opens their ears to the call to make the Saviour known in every land. The way in which He does this we may understand as little in the one case as in the other, but it is just as effectual. "Whereas I was blind, now I see" may be all the testimony we can give. But it is enough.

It is in this individual aspect of the missionary call that we run into the question of fields of service. Shall it be the foreign field or the home field? If the foreign field, which one? Such questions are constantly asked and should be answered. Hardly ever are they answered with a vision or some other such striking experience. We shouldn't think that this is impossible, but the normal way is otherwise.

In this matter friends may counsel and preachers exhort, and missionary speakers may even resort to scolding. But the final decision is between you and God. Sometimes, in order to see the matter in its proper relationships, we might do well to drop the word *call* and speak of this as a matter of guidance. There may be a special call. We are not ruling it out. But more often the young Christian is simply wanting to be shown *where* he is to serve.

The general principles of guidance certainly apply here: a recognition of the need for guidance, a willingness to be led, a deliberate renunciation of self-interest, a close walk with God so as to be sensitive to His wishes, as well as a constant use of the Word of God and earnest prayer.

Christ's own command to "look on the fields" should lead us to contemplate their needs and feel the compassion that such needs should inspire. A careful study of the fields, such as William Carey made, may open the way for God's guidance. Listening to missionaries from various fields is helpful. At first it may seem confusing because there are so many needs in so many places. But it often happens that after a time.one of those fields begins to stand out as the place where God can use you to the greatest advantage.

Consider carefully the question whether you should serve Christ in the home country or abroad. To think that unless God calls you specially to some foreign land you ought to take up Christian service at home is the worst possible attitude to take. There are too many Christian workers who have drifted into a position in the homeland simply because they have not had a special call to anything else.

How do you dare to stand in *any* pulpit as a minister of Christ without the clear conviction that He has called you there? The call of the pulpit committee or of the church is no substitute for Christ's call. What makes you think that it is any less necessary to feel an overpowering divine compulsion to give your life to a ministry in Middletown, U.S.A., than in a Congo forest? If a call is necessary for the one, it is just as necessary for the other.

Should you serve at home or abroad? Don't expect a satisfactory answer to this question until you have first answered a couple of others. Are you sure God wants you in full-time service for Him? Your answer to this question may mean service on the foreign field. It often does. But just as often the Lord calls a man to His ministry first. He may even give him a time of service at home. Then He sends him abroad as His messenger to other peoples. At all events it is essential to know whether you should be set apart exclusively for Christian service.

Too many of us take it for granted that full conse-cration necessarily means going into full-time Christian ministry. Such an idea tends in the same direction as the idea held in the Middle Ages that for a really devout life one had to withdraw from the world and enter some monas-tery. It may take out of the workaday world those very elements that it needs to keep it from ever increasing corruption. It fosters the all too common notion that "busi-ness and religion don't mix." As a matter of fact, there is no good reason why a laborer or a businessman may not be as earnest a Christian witness and as truly spiritual as any minister. Many are.

But even if you are sure that the Lord wants you in full-time service, there is still another question you must answer. Are you ready to surrender your own will to His? Will you gladly do whatever He wants you to do? Such surrender is not easy. Neither is it always as complete as we suppose at the moment. Yet is it right to expect God to lead you to the field of *His* choice, when you have already determined in your own heart where *you* want to go? If you honestly want His guidance, you will have to be ready to put yourself in His hands and gladly follow His directions, *wherever* He may lead.

Does selfish ambition enter into your plans? The desire for recognition and praise from other Christians? It is better to please God than men. It is even more satisfying to your own soul. Are you afraid of privations? Do you shrink from a venture that means a radical change in your way of living? Do you dread contact with strange, unfamil-iar people? Your Saviour has promised to be with you all the days until the end. But only *if you go!* That promise is connected with the command to go!

On the other hand, there are some for whom other fields always appear greener than those near at hand. For some there is a purely human attraction in strange lands and people. They need to ask themselves, Can I be happy to stay at home and minister in an unromantic field, if that is where Christ wants me most? For them the decision to stay may be fully as difficult as the decision to go is for others. But the call to stay may be just as definite and the results of obedience just as joyful.

Now if you have answered these two preliminary questions in the affirmative—if you are sure the Lord wants you to dedicate your whole life to His service and are confident that your greatest desire is to fulfill His will, whatever that will may be and wherever it may lead—the main question becomes much easier to answer. Not that anyone can answer it for you. You should not accept their answers even when they urge them on you. This is between you and God. It is He who must guide you.

But it may help you to know how He has led others. If the testimonies of those who have experienced *salvation* are honored of the Lord in leading others to enjoy that same experience, then the testimonies of those whom the Lord has called and blessed in *missionary service* may be used in revealing God's ways of guidance to other puzzled young Christians.

We give some of these testimonies in the next chapter.

10

THE MISSIONARY CALL—
TESTIMONIES

WE WISH WE KNEW about the missionary calls of all of our great missionaries. It would help us to see more clearly the many ways in which the Lord leads men into missionary service. But we don't. Only now and then do we get a clear picture of how the Lord dealt with one of them. Sometimes we have it in his own words. Sometimes we have to depend on the accuracy of his biographer.

In this chapter we talk about seven truly great missionaries. They all lived in the past century, so their works have stood the test of time. Four of them were British and three were American. (The day had not yet come when American missionaries would outnumber all others.) They went to several fields in Africa and the Orient. And the information we have about their calls is fairly clear. We give their own words when we can.

DAVID LIVINGSTONE

The very name Livingstone spells Africa. No missionary is better known today. Also, very few captured the imagination of their own day to such an extent as he.

Yet Livingstone did not at first intend to go to Africa. In fact, he didn't plan to be a missionary at all. Not that he was opposed to missions. He thought every Christian ought to be a soul-winner, that it ought to be his chief desire and aim. But when it came to foreign missions, Livingstone's idea was that he would give money for it. He would give everything he earned above what he needed to live.

But that wasn't God's idea. One day Livingstone read an item that changed his whole life purpose. Dr. Karl Gützlaff, brilliant and devout missionary pioneer, had traveled up and down the coasts of east Asia all the way from Siam to Korea. Now he was pleading for missionaries for the great empire of China. When Livingstone thought of those millions of Chinese without Christ, and of the lack of suitable workers to give them the gospel, he decided to prepare and offer himself.

For China, did we say? Then how did he get to Africa? The Opium War did it. Livingstone prepared to be a medical missionary in China, and the London Missionary Society accepted him. But before he could sail, the war closed the door. Now what should he do? They suggested the West Indies. But he didn't think his medical training would be so useful there.

At this point Robert Moffat entered the picture. The great South Africa missionary was at home in Britain speaking about the work in that dark land. Here is Moffat's own account:

> I had occasion to call for someone at Mrs. Sewell's, a boarding-house for young missionaries in Aldersgate street, where Livingstone lived. I observed soon that this young man was interested in my story, that he would sometimes come quietly and ask me a question or two, and that he was always desirous to know where I was to speak in public, and attended on these occasions.

> By-and-by he asked me whether he would do for Africa. I said I believed he would, if he would not go to an old station, but would advance to unoccupied ground, specifying the vast plain to the north, where I had sometimes seen, in the morning sun, the smoke of a thousand villages, where no missionary had ever been.

> At last Livingstone said, "What is the use of my waiting for the end of this abominable Opium War? I will go at once to Africa!" The Directors concurred, and Africa became his sphere.

John G. Paton

When an author wants to write a thrilling missionary story for young people, he is very likely to turn to the life of John G. Paton. Not many can be compared with it. Paton went to work among cannibals in the New Hebrides Islands of the South Pacific. He lived a long life and an exciting one. Also he found the time to tell about it.

Paton began as a city missionary in his native Scotland. He seemed to be doing well, but he says:

> Happy in my work as I felt, and successful by the blessing of God, yet I continually heard, and chiefly during my last years in the Divinity Hall, the wail of the perishing Heathen in the South Seas; and I saw that few were caring for them, while I well knew that many would be ready to take up my work in Calton and carry it forward perhaps with more efficiency than myself.
>
> Without revealing the state of my mind to any person, this was the supreme subject of my daily meditation and prayer; and this also led me to enter upon those medical studies, in which I purposed taking the full course; but at the close of my third year, an incident occurred, which led me at once to offer myself for the Foreign Mission field.
>
> The Reformed Presbyterian Church of Scotland, in which I had been brought up, had been advertising for another Missionary to join the Rev. John Inglis in his grand work in the New Hebrides. Dr. Bates, the excellent convener of the Heathen Missions Committee, was deeply grieved, because for two years their appeal had failed.
>
> At length, the Synod, after much prayer and consultation, felt the claims of the Heathen so urgently pressed upon them by the Lord's repeated calls, that they resolved to cast lots, to discover whether God would thus select any Minister to be relieved from his home-charge, and designated as a Missionary to the South Seas. Each member of the Synod, as I was informed, agreed to hand in, after solemn appeal to God, the names of the three best quali-

fied in his esteem for such a work, and he who had the clear majority was to be loosed from his congregation, and to proceed to the Mission field—or the first and second highest, if two could be secured.

Hearing this debate, and feeling an intense interest in these most unusual proceedings, I remember yet the hushed solemnity of the prayer before the names were handed in. I remember the strained silence that held the Assembly while the scrutinizers retired to examine the papers; and I remember how tears blinded my eyes when they returned to announce that the result was so indecisive, that it was clear that the Lord had not in that way provided a missionary. The cause was once again solemnly laid before God in prayer, and a cloud of sadness appeared to fall over all the Synod.

The Lord kept saying within me, "Since none better qualified can be got, rise and offer yourself!" Almost overpowering was the impulse to answer aloud, "Here am I, send me!" But I was dreadfully afraid of mistaking my own emotions for the will of God.

So I resolved to make it a subject of close deliberation and prayer for a few days longer, and to look at the proposal from every possible aspect.

From every aspect at which I could look the whole facts in the face, the voice within me sounded like a voice from God.

JAMES CHALMERS

"Tamate" the natives called him. "The Great Heart of New Guinea," said Robert Louis Stevenson. And certainly no one had a wilder field, nor one that called for a greater heart. His first ten years in the islands farther east were tame in comparison with the years on the southeast coast of New Guinea. He lived continually in the shadow of death. A man's man. But unlike Paton, he was finally killed and eaten by the cannibals.

Chalmers says that it was in his teens that he came to the great decision of his life:

I remember it well. Our Sunday school class had been held in the vestry as usual. The lesson was finished, and we had marched back into the chapel to sing, answer questions, and to listen to a short address.

I was sitting at the head of the seat, and can even now see Mr. Meikle taking from his breast-pocket a copy of the *United Presbyterian Record,* and hear him say that he was going to read an interesting letter to us from a missionary in Fiji.

The letter was read. It spoke of cannibalism, and of the power of the Gospel, and at the close of the reading, looking over his spectacles, and with wet eyes, he said, "I wonder if there is a boy here this afternoon who will yet become a missionary, and by-and-by bring the Gospel to cannibals? And the response of my heart was, "Yes, God helping me, and I will."

The unusual thing about Chalmers' call was that it came, as he says, several years before his conversion. He forgot his decision for a time and wandered far from Christ. Then came his conversion, his preparation for the ministry, and his city missionary work in Glasgow. He remembered his youthful vow and, after several talks with Dr. Turner of Samoa, he applied to be sent to the South Pacific.

ADONIRAM JUDSON

Every American Baptist knows Judson's name. Not only was he one of the first party of missionaries to go out from the United States, but he later inspired the beginning of the American Baptist Foreign Mission Society. Burma was his field. He could scarcely have hit upon a harder one. Yet he came to be called "the Apostle of Burma."

According to his son, two things moved Judson to go to the mission field. After his striking conversion, he had entered Andover Seminary to prepare for the ministry. There he came in touch with Samuel Mills and other missionary-minded students. They were just a small group, but deadly in earnest. And Judson soon became as zealous as the others for the starting of an American missionary society.

But it was not only the fellowship with these other students. It was also a sermon. He had already finished his first year at the seminary when he read it. The sermon had been preached in England by Dr. Claudius Buchanan, a chaplain of the British East India Company. It had for its title "The Star in the East" and spoke of the power and progress of the gospel in India. Judson's own son says that "this sermon fell like a spark into the tinder of Judson's soul." Six months later he made his final decision to serve Christ as a foreign missionary.

JOHN SCUDDER

John Scudder was the first American medical missionary to India. He went out under the earliest American society, the American Board of Commissioners for Foreign Missions. Later he was to open the Arcot field for the Reformed Church in America. He was also the head of one of the most remarkable missionary families in history. Its members through nearly half a dozen generations have served as missionaries on many fields.

Scudder wanted to be a minister. But when his father strongly opposed the idea, he turned to medicine. In this field he did such good work that he soon built up a good practice and began to prosper financially. Then one day the course of his life was suddenly changed.

In the course of his practice he went to attend a Christian woman who was ill. In her room he saw a tract, *The Conversion of the World, or the Claims of Six Hundred Millions.* He became interested and asked to borrow it. At home he read it over and over, until finally he fell to his knees, saying, "Lord, what wilt thou have me to do?" He didn't hear an audible voice, but in his heart he knew the answer was, "Go and preach the Gospel to the heathen."

However, Scudder couldn't make the final decision alone. He had a wife to think of. He said to himself, "I have one to consult whose interests are blended with my own, and whose happiness may be seriously affected by my decision. I will lay the subject before *her* mind as it lies before mine. If she say nay, I shall regard it as settling the question of duty."

"From love to Christ," he added, "and a sense of duty, she decided for the life of a missionary. That purpose never gave way. It never even faltered."

At about that time the American Board advertised for a doctor who would be willing to go as a missionary. Dr. Scudder applied and was sent out.

James M. Thoburn

James M. Thoburn, later Bishop Thoburn of the Methodist Episcopal Church in India, was one of the most illustrious missionaries of that church. No one ever did more to promote the expansion of his church in the Indian peninsula. And his efforts extended beyond India itself to other lands.

From shortly after his conversion, Thoburn says that he was repeatedly faced with the challenge of the mission field. He became a minister and was appointed to a circuit of churches. Then one day, after he had preached for about a year, the challenge came again with increased force. He had sat down to read his church paper and was struck by the leading editorial. It was an appeal for six young men to go to India. He writes:

> I was powerfully moved by the appeal, not so much by anything it contained as by a strong impression that I ought to be one of the six young men to go forth. I dropped the paper and fell upon my knees and promised God that I would accept the call if only He would make it clear that He was sending me. I asked for some token, for some definite indication that I was called from above, not only in a general way to become a missionary, but to that special field and at that special time.

Thoburn made up his mind to ask the advice of his

presiding elder as soon as he saw him. When they met, the elder, not knowing what was on the young preacher's mind, remarked, "I met Bishop Janes on the train this morning."

"Bishop Janes!" Thoburn replied. "What can he be doing out here?"

"He is on his way west, looking for missionaries for India. He wants six immediately."

Thoburn's heart leaped into his throat. But before he could reply, the elder continued, "James, how would you like to go?"

"It is very singular," the young preacher replied, "but I have come here with the special purpose of asking your advice about going to India."

"Well, I must tell you that you have been in my mind all morning. I incline to think you ought to go. I have felt so ever since the bishop told me his errand."

Going to a little "prophet-chamber," Thoburn prayed for guidance. He says:

> I did not receive any message, or realize any new conviction, or come down from my sacred audience with God feeling that the matter was forever settled, and yet that hour stands out in my life as the burning bush must have stood in the memory of Moses. It was my burning bush. It has followed me through all the years which have passed.

ALEXANDER M. MACKAY

It was once said that Uganda was "the brightest spot on the map of Africa." The man who first sowed the gospel in that central African kingdom was Alexander Mackay of the Church Missionary Society. He did not live to see the great harvest, but few tales of dauntless courage and persistence are more inspiring than his life.

Mackay prepared himself to be a civil engineer. Missions was not in his mind when he left Britain for Germany to continue his studies. But he was a sincere Christian, so he was not deaf to the Lord's call when it came. It came in a very unusual way. In a letter to his sister from Berlin he wrote:

> Well, it is through you, or what you wrote me on December 11 last, that what I now have to write you exists.
> You told me then that you had been at a social meeting of our Literary Association in Chalmers Memorial Church; that there you heard Dr. Burns Thomson . . . urge young men of the Association to give themselves to the work and go out as medical missionaries . . . to Madagascar . . . .
> Well, I am not a doctor, and therefore cannot go as such; but I am an engineer, and propose, if the Lord will, to go as an engineering missionary. Miserable chimera you will no doubt call such an idea. Yet immediately on the receipt of your letter I wrote Dr. Bonar, offering myself to such work, and asking his advice.

A couple of months later he wrote to his father:

> Man is a volent being, by virtue of what God has made him. Yet man is inwardly swayed by external circumstances.
> Now if to my ears or hands there comes the message, "Who will go to preach the gospel in Madagascar?" how can I, except in unbelief, say otherwise than that God caused that message to come to me? And if it is of God, must I not say, "Here am I; send me"?

The London Missionary Society was not able to use Mackay in Madagascar at the time. But in 1875 the Church Missionary Society appealed for a worker of Mackay's qualifications for East Africa near Mombasa. He saw the appeal and wrote home:

> Remembering that Duff first thought of Africa as a mission field, but was sent to India, and that Livingstone originally intended to evangelize China, but the Lord willed he should spend his life in Africa, so perhaps the Lord means me, after all, to turn my attention to the Dark Continent; accordingly I have offered my services to the C.M.S.—the greatest missionary society in the world—for Mombasa.

The C.M.S., however, had already engaged another man. Then a little later the *Daily Telegraph* published Stanley's letter about his visit to Mtesa, king of Uganda, in which he challenged Christians to send missionaries to that land. The C.M.S. took up the challenge and accepted Mackay for the work.

SUMMARY

These, then, were the missionary calls of seven really great missionaries of Christ. No one would question that they were truly called, though the circumstances of their calling were so different. In fact, one great lesson we can learn from their testimonies is the diversity of ways in which God may lead.

Notice well the following facts. Not one of these missionaries saw a vision, dreamed a dream, or heard an audible voice calling him to go. All of them were influenced by reading or hearing an appeal for willing workers. Yet the appeal was general. Only Thoburn had a personal appeal made to him, and it was just one of the confirmations of his call.

Most of these men, however, were in places where they could readily hear the call when it came. Paton, Thoburn, and Chalmers were ministering at home. Judson was studying for the ministry, and Scudder had wanted to do so. Judson was also influenced by missionary-minded companions.

In six of the seven cases the call had some connection with a definite field. Yet only three actually served in those fields. The others went elsewhere.

From this we can see that the missionary call is not likely to come in a miraculous way. Neither does it come to all people in the same way. Rather, if we wanted to define it we should probably have to say that *the missionary call is the Great Commission, plus the assurance in your heart, no matter how it comes, that God wants you to go as His witness to those who do not know the Saviour.*

11

MISSIONARY QUALIFICATIONS—
ESSENTIAL

WE SAID that the individual Christian's first responsibility to missions is to offer himself. However, we added that the requirements for a missionary are such as to rule out a great many who might like to serve as missionaries. They just wouldn't be able to qualify. In this chapter and the next two we talk about missionary qualifications, especially for foreign service.

HIGH DEMANDS

Just what qualifications does the foreign missionary need? In general, we may say, all the qualifications that make a good witness for Christ in the homeland, plus some others. Those others are made necessary because he does his witnessing in a foreign land, under unfavorable circumstances, and with a broader field of operations.

The requirements of an ambassador for Christ in a foreign land are very high. We would do wrong to minimize them. He must perform his ministry in unfamiliar surroundings. He does it through a new language or languages that he has to learn by dint of hard labor. He labors among people who are often hostile, and whose culture is quite different from his own. His message is open to suspicion, since he is a foreigner. As often as not he finds that the climate and living conditions hamper his work and sap his strength. Yet he has to carry on a broad ministry, and that with only a fraction of the equipment and helps that are available in the homeland.

Whatever the mission *boards* may require, the mission *field* demands men and women of the highest caliber and exacts the utmost from them.

102

Contrary to what many think, Christian piety alone is not enough for missionary service. Missionaries are not dreamy-eyed idealists, as the cartoonists like to picture them. By force of circumstances they have to be realists. They couldn't last long otherwise. Their work makes demands upon every faculty and most of the knowledge they possess, even among primitive peoples.

Yet it is true that the most essential qualifications for a good missionary are spiritual. Others are valuable, but the spiritual ones are basic. The ten we are going to discuss may not be exhaustive, but they are characteristics that mark every successful missionary of Christ. Do you have them?

THE ESSENTIAL QUALIFICATIONS

DEVOTION

Whole-hearted devotion to Christ and His gospel is a prime requisite. You can't do without it and be a missionary. You can't win others to Christ if your own allegiance is shaky. If you are uncertain about your faith, if you can't say with heartfelt assurance, "I *know* whom I have believed," you had better stay at home. Missionaries are those who are "sold" on their faith.

SPIRITUALITY

The missionary of Christ must be spiritually minded, as opposed to material minded. That is because his chief aims are spiritual. You don't reach spiritual ends by physical means. The missionary can't disregard the physical; it is a necessary part of his life and work. But he dare not let it take first place. The temptation to regard material things too highly is just as great on the field as it is at home, if not greater. So it is not easy, even for a missionary, to 'seek first the kingdom of God, and his righteousness." But it is essential to his ministry. The eternal value of the soul—of the things of the spirit—must occupy first place in the mind of Christ's messenger to the lost.

TRUST

Some missionaries are called "faith" missionaries. But they are not the only ones who have to live a life of faith. Every missionary learns by experience the meaning of faith. In a foreign country they are usually far from their accustomed means of human aid. At times funds and supplies fail. There are other times when illness strikes and no doctor or nurse is in ready reach. Or the authorities may be against them and the people suspicious and unfriendly. The powers of darkness seem almost overwhelming. Even in their own hearts they struggle with discouragement, and there are no Christian advisers to whom they can turn for comfort and encouragement. They come to realize that in themselves they can do nothing.

Have you learned to trust God for every need, material and spiritual? You will need to know that lesson to be a good missionary. Such trust doesn't spring up full-fledged in a time of crisis. You don't get it automatically when you reach the field as a missionary. Rather, it grows little by little as you look to God for even the small things and find Him faithful. There are plenty of chances to learn to trust Him, even in the life of a student. Then when the time of great need comes, if you have learned that lesson you will find your heart spontaneously turning to the one you already know can meet your every need.

LOVE

People expect the missionary to be the very embodiment of God's love to man. Isn't he some times the only representative of the Christian gospel in a place? And isn't the heart of the gospel the love of God? The love of God that sent His Son into the world to die for sinful men is the same love that sends the missionary to make that salvation known.

It is easy to love some people. It is not so easy to love others. But the missionary cannot choose to love just those who are loveable. The love of Christ is what has constrained the missionary to go forth, the love that poured itself out for all of us even when we were His enemies. It is that same love of Christ that the missionary aims to reveal as best he can when he pours out his own life in unselfish devotion to the people to whom he goes. He learns to think of them as "my people." Without that love he could hardly keep going. Without that love his labor would be fruitless.

MORAL COURAGE

We are not talking here about morality itself, either the "new morality" or some other kind. We are talking about having the courage of one's moral convictions. There are people whose standards of right and wrong are very flexible. They can be bent to fit almost any situation so as to offend no one. There are others who say they believe "right is right"; but they don't believe it very audibly. That is, they don't have the courage to stand up for what they believe. Both types are "easy to get along with." They never stir up arguments.

But such people do not make good missionaries. Firm standards of right and wrong are essential equipment for the missionary. And not only firm standards but the courage to make them known. He may be called narrow-minded. That is part of the price for having convictions. But it is the water in the narrow channel that flows with the greatest force.

Not that the missionary needs to be obnoxiously opinionated. We are talking only about right and wrong. Neither does he have to be overly harsh in denouncing sin. The Scripture advises "speaking the truth in love." But the truth must be spoken, sin must be faced frankly and openly, or the missionary has no ministry worth the name.

PURPOSE

There is an ailment afflicting many young people today that we might call lack of purpose. It is more prevalent than many of us realize. Those who are affected by it are not sure just what they want to do in life. They don't know what goal they ought to aim for. So they temporize. They hold back from making any definite decision, just waiting for circumstances to show them what is most likely to be to their immediate advantage. Sometimes they drift through high school and college, and graduate still uncertain about the course ahead.

Now a temporary uncertainty, especially in making a decision that will affect the whole course of your life, is not serious. After all, such a decision calls for long and careful deliberation. But if you always find it hard to make up your mind; if you habitually show a lack of eager purposefulness; if you don't know what it is to have one great aim to which you will bring all other interests into subjection; then you won't make much of a missionary.

A missionary must be a man of vision. His vision must be a high and worthy objective toward which he dedicates the whole course of his life. He needs to have a God-given vision. If you don't yet have it, ask Him to give it to you.

DISCERNMENT

What we mean here is what many would call "common sense." In this matter the missionary is quite different from his caricature. Actually he has to be a man of vision without being visionary. His vision often leads him to see beyond the present circumstances. But he dare not blind himself to things as they are. The very continuance of his ministry often depends on his practical discernment. He must be able to face up to unpleasant facts and discern the real issues at stake. He must be ready to acknowledge the problems with all their complexities and know that superficial answers won't do. Few missionaries could be called theoreticians. Their ministry calls for a greater balance of the theoretical with the practical.

ZEAL

A real missionary is rightly a zealot. His zeal doesn't have to be of that effervescent type that shows itself in vigorous demonstrations of emotion. It may be an intense, slow-burning but all-consuming type that drives him steadily on in spite of opposition. But a zealot he is. A lazy, indifferent missionary belies his name. There is just no place for him in the work. We can do better without him.

CONSTANCY

In every field there are disappointments and discouragements. Perhaps missionaries are more often disappointed with themselves than with any other one thing. The experiences of missionary work often show us just how weak we really are. When we come to realize this there comes a strong temptation to give up.

It is easy for others to say, "If you are sure the Lord sent you there, you won't give up." But there is more to it than that. All too readily we can persuade ourselves that we may have been mistaken in our call, or that the Lord may have changed His purposes for us. It is the one who has learned the lesson of constancy who usually holds fast. He has learned to keep on in spite of discouragement. The Lord can depend on him. So too can his fellow workers.

You can't enjoy real success without such perseverance. The story of missions everywhere demonstrates this. But, like faith, constancy isn't something you can work up overnight. Instead it is the result of persistent practice in dependability: in employment, in studies, in social relationships, in family obligations, etc. Have you come to the place where people can always depend on you? If not, start practicing!

Missionary work calls for leaders. Whether they want to or not, those who go out as missionaries have to take places of leadership. This is true even when their work becomes subordinated to the authority of the national church. The leadership then may be less obtrusive and more subtle. But it is leadership, just the same.

Bringing men to Christ is only the beginning of the work. The missionary needs to be able to lead new Christians in their spiritual development. He needs to lead them in the formation of a functioning church. He needs to lead in the training of national workers who will sooner or later take over the whole work. He must break the way in Christian literature and a dozen other lines of work— things that are needed for the full expression and development of the Christian life. His work is essentially that of the trailblazer. So he must have the qualities that go with leadership—especially initiative and responsibility.

BASIC—BUT HARD TO MEASURE

The ten qualifications we have mentioned are essential for good missionary service. Insofar as a missionary is weak in one or another of these items, his work is bound to suffer. They are qualifications that have marked the ministry of the really great missionaries.

But they are extremely hard to measure. How can a mission board tell what amount of each is needed before it accepts a candidate and sends him out? Can they possibly tell how much he really has? How do you measure such things as love and spirituality? Clearly this list is of most use to the candidate himself. He can use it in examining his own heart and life. He can see where his weaknesses lie and try to strengthen those parts. Getting by the board is incidental. To be true to himself and to his Lord, he wants to become a real missionary!

12

MISSIONARY QUALIFICATIONS— PHYSICAL AND EDUCATIONAL

THE SPIRITUAL QUALIFICATIONS given in the previous chapter are essential for missionary service. But in the very nature of modern missions other requirements are usually made. The requirements differ from mission to mission and from field to field, so all that we can do is explain general principles or trends. You need to find out the demands of any particular mission from the mission itself.

But remember that under some circumstances the mission may make exceptions. Of course it only makes exceptions for what it thinks are good reasons, and always at its own discretion. The mission, you see, tries to look at the candidate as an individual and not as a mere collection of qualifications. It tries to visualize how that particular person might possibly fit into its needs and program.

Note too that some boards are very strict in their requirements, while others are notoriously lax. If you want to have the happiest and most fruitful service, set your aim high. Try to make it with the best board you can find, a board with which you would be proud to be associated.

PHYSICAL QUALIFICATIONS

We begin with the physical requirements because they are the most obvious and the easiest to judge.

AGE

Naturally no one is too old or too young to witness for Christ. But when it is a matter of choosing a messenger who can go to a foreign land and make known the message of Christ among a strange people, a man who can establish and build up a church there, the question of age takes on real importance.

The *general principle* is this. The candidate needs to be young enough: (1) to learn well the language of the people to whom he goes; (2) to adapt himself physically and mentally to a new culture and new conditions of living; and (3) to look forward to enough years of ministry to warrant the necessary expense for his equipment, his passage to the field, and all the special training and apprenticeship he will have to undergo before he becomes a fully effective missionary. On the other hand, he needs to be old enough to be mature in thinking and acting, so he can take on the serious responsibilities of a missionary's life and work.

In *practice* some missions will accept young people in their very early twenties. However, most of them will contend that the middle twenties, about twenty five or twenty six, is a much better age to enter the work. It gives more time for thorough preparation and the needed maturity.

Again, many missions set thirty as the maximum age for a candidate under normal conditions. Others extend the limit to thirty five, especially where more preparation is required. Even this maximum age limit may be set aside in some cases. It is regularly done for doctors, for instance. The reason is that their period of training is quite prolonged. Also the effectiveness of their ministry is not so closely tied with their ability to use the native tongue as that of the evangelistic missionary. It may also be done for others with specialized training. That is, it will be done if the mission happens to need their special abilities badly enough to offset the disadvantage of their age. There is actually greater flexibility in this maximum limit than there used to be. Missions have been finding that certain candidates who are beyond the usual age limit work out very well when they are accepted. Their experience in Christian life and work and their greater maturity give a stability that is to be desired. Each such case is decided on its own merits.

HEALTH

The average missionary works in fields and under conditions that make serious demands on his health and strength. The situation is not nearly as bad as it used to be, however. The mortality rate among missionaries has been greatly reduced in recent years, and the conditions of life and work in most fields have been improved. Still the job does call for a sound and vigorous constitution.

Then, too, in spite of the noble work being done in so many fields by the medical missionaries, and in spite of a larger and better native medical practice, there are still many places where the missionary cannot count on competent help in illness. Sometimes the nonmedical missionary not only has to care for the health of his own family, but from his limited knowledge of medicine he has to try to help the nationals.

Of course there are wide differences between fields. Each mission sets its standards according to the need in its own field. But *in principle* the candidate needs to be sound and robust when he leaves for his field of service. He will have to be able to adjust himself readily to a new climate and environment. He must be healthy enough to carry on an active life and take up the heavy responsibilities of his mission without undue strain. He needs the physical resistance to combat any unforeseen illness that may come, with reasonable expectation of success.

To assure this *in practice,* the mission usually prescribes a rigid physical examination for each candidate. The mission itself prefers to choose the doctor who makes the examination rather than depend on the candidate's personal physician. The reason is twofold. The mission's doctor is likely to be more objective and thorough. Also he is more familiar with the mission's requirements and the demands of the work. In some areas a number of missions share the services of a single physician, who may himself have served in the mission field.

It is not at all uncommon for the examining doctor to find some weakness or dormant ailment of which the candidate was not aware. Some of these things can easily flare up into activity under the strains of missionary service. Others can be corrected without serious difficulty. However, they may cause a delay in the candidate's acceptance or departure for the field. Those that are more serious may even block the way entirely.

For this reason, if you are thinking of foreign missionary service, it is a good idea to get a thorough physical checkup if you have not already done so. Do it even before applying to the mission or finishing your course of training. That is, of course, unless you are already on the verge of applying. In only a few cases will the examination reveal some unexpected ailment that might close the door to foreign service. But there is no keener disappointment than that of the young person who has dedicated his life for foreign missions, has spent a number of years in preparation, has built up his plans and hopes about it— and then discovers through the final medical examination that he can't go.

In speaking of health the average layman is likely to overlook matters of *nervous and mental stability.* So let us add a word here. By experience the missions have learned to take these things into account. Excessive nervousness at home becomes greatly aggravated under the strains of missionary life. It may even become dangerous. And, if anything, mental health and balance are more necessary for an effective ministry than bodily soundness. The mental and spiritual strains of missionary service are really greater than the physical strains. They can scarcely be comprehended by those who have not actually served on the field and experienced them.

A further practical note. Two of the most important factors in preserving missionary health are personal cleanliness and neatness. This is largely a matter of habits. They are habits that you can build up before going to the field and adjust to meet the conditions there. Slovenliness is both irritating to those with whom you have to live and it opens the door to needless disease.

Do keep this in mind too: A condition that would keep you from the field today may not be a permanent bar. You may be able to correct it within a year or two so that it will no longer stand in the way. The very experience of overcoming a handicap is the best possible training for service on the field.

Of course there are some physical handicaps that you can't completely overcome. The loss of a leg or an arm, or the crippling effects of poliomyelitis are permanent handicaps. They sometimes close the door to missionary service. But not always. There are some places and kinds of work where the possession of two good arms or legs is not essential. Then if you have the special ability or training that is needed, you may find the mission ready to overlook your handicap. Teaching in an established station or doing literary work are just two of several types of service that a physically handicapped person can perform.

EDUCATIONAL QUALIFICATIONS

The matter of educational qualifications calls for special attention. It is perhaps more misunderstood than any other requirement.

Missionary work is first of all a spiritual service. As such there can never be any satisfactory substitute for a real personal knowledge and experience of Christ. No amount of education can cover up a lack here. If we had to choose between a candidate with little formal education but a vital relationship to Jesus Christ, and another with a very high scholastic record but a very superficial experience of the power of the gospel, the choice would be easy. The first would make by far the better missionary.

But such a theoretical case probably never occurs. What does often happen is that the mission is faced with candidates whose religious experience is more or less similar, but whose educational qualifications differ widely. Given the same amount of spiritual life and leadership, the one with the better educational background is sure to prove the more useful on the field.

Missionary work makes great demands on the intellectual ability and preparation of the missionary. Some types of work demand more than others, but they all demand an ability that is above average. The reason is the work that the missionary has to do. His ministry, you see, is primarily mental and spiritual.

Sometimes the people at home get absorbed in the physical side of missionary life. They like to hear of the missionary's adventures, his physical hardships, the problems of living in another land. But really these are only incidental. They are interesting but not fundamental. Sometimes the missionaries themselves get irritated because people are always asking what they have to eat. "As if that were all that mattered!" exclaimed one missionary in disgust. "Why don't they ask about the work?"

It is true that at times the missionary's work does include building, repairing, traveling, and a good many other such activities. But these are not the purpose of his being there. He does them because he has to do them in order to accomplish his main task. His main job has to do with the souls of men. This spiritual ministry may not take most of his time but it is the heart of his work.

He tries to sway men's thinking. He seeks to change the course and objectives of their life. The arms of his warfare are spiritual. Words are his most valuable weapons— preeminently the Word of God. He plants thoughts and nourishes them until they bear fruit. The fruits of his labors are changed hearts and minds. He stimulates the fellowship of the saints and helps guide their worship. With wise counsel he multiplies his usefulness and sees re-created in others that spiritual life and development that Christ has already brought to him. He deals in thoughts, in souls, in life.

To do this he must be prepared. And while years of school work don't always show the amount of training a man has had, we don't have any other very usable gauge. So missions will continue to use this one. They will keep on stating this requirement in terms of years of schooling, courses taken and degrees obtained.

Remember this: The missionary usually has to do his work in a language other than his own. He has to learn that language, not superficially so as to bargain in the marketplace or to give orders to a construction gang, but thoroughly. He has to be able to teach the people *in their own tongue* the sublime truths of Christianity, the most profound truths the human mind is capable of grasping. Unless the people understand his message, all his work is in vain. Among primitive people his task is, if anything, even more difficult than among the more advanced. It is always true that the greatest simplicity of expression calls for the greatest depth and breadth of knowledge.

Remember too that a missionary, no matter how humbly he may want to serve, soon finds that he has to take a place of leadership. His work demands it. And while leaders may often arise from among the self-educated, they never come from the ranks of the uneducated.

Besides all this, it is a mistake to think of missionary work only in terms of ignorant, uncultured, primitive peoples. Many of the people to whom we take the gospel are far from uncultured. They are civilized, cultured, and, in some cases, highly educated. We have a marvelous message to give them, but don't get it confused with the fictitious notion that we are superior to all other people. We aren't. We have much to learn from others, even from the so-called "primitives."

The fact is that even in many of the "underdeveloped" countries to which the missionary goes he has to deal with some very well-educated people. Most mission fields, just like our own country, are far from static. They are changing, and changing rapidly. They are upgrading their educational systems. Thousands of their young people are pursuing courses of higher education, many of them right here in our own country.

It is no wonder that some missionaries, after a time on the field, begin to feel a lack in their own educational background. Some of them on furlough are enrolled in our schools right now. Some ask for extended furloughs so they can complete more work than a normal furlough would allow. Some who did not have college training before are getting it. Others are taking additional training to improve their ministry.

In reality the educational *needs* for the foreign missionary are greater than for the worker at home. He does the same work and more. But he has to do it in another language. The circumstances are much less favorable. Also he has to get along with only a fraction of the equipment available at home. Or, what is quite common, he has to improvise, invent or manufacture his own.

The *principle* involved in the educational requirement is this: Education should be preparation for living. Therefore the missionary must have an education that will enable him to live among the people in such a way as to win their respect. But education is also preparation for service. So the missionary must have enough education, and of the right sort, to enable him to do efficiently his part of the missionary job.

This principle is very broad, I know. The reason is that missionary work itself is so broad. Different kinds of societies demand different measures of adaptability. Different kinds of work call for different kinds of training. And some ministries require longer preparation than others. Generally speaking, a broad cultural education plus Bible training lay the best foundation.

In *practice* most of the denominational missions require graduation from a four-year college course as a basis. In addition they require seminary or Bible institute training of those who are not going to engage in some specialized work, such as medicine, general education, agriculture, etc. Even for this specialized work they may require at least a year of Bible training, since all these efforts must contribute to the chief missionary aim.

The faith missions, and some small denominations, set a minimum requirement of graduation from high school plus Bible institute training. Note that this is a minimum. They may strongly recommend more. In fact, the trend is toward a raising of these requirements.

For specialized work there are of course special requirements, depending on the job to be done. Some are set by the mission and some by the country to which the missionary goes. Both of them, for example, will insist that doctors be fully qualified to practice in their home country. In addition the government may insist that they meet local requirements for certification. Educational missionaries must have the proper training to make them good teachers. This often means securing a teaching certificate from their own state or province. The requirements for any specialized ministry differ a great deal from country to country, and from time to time. The best thing to do is to get the advice of the mission's candidate secretary during the period of training.

We have stated that missionary work demands an ability that is above average. This doesn't mean that every missionary is expected to be an intellectual genius. Each one will of course show more talent in one direction than another. But the best thing is to have a well-rounded development, rather than extreme brilliance in a limited field. A high average scholarship, in spite of a few low grades, is good. For any type of service one of the most valuable traits is an aptitude for teaching others.

13

MISSIONARY QUALIFICATIONS— PERSONAL CHARACTERISTICS

PERSONALITY

BESIDES ITS PHYSICAL and educational requirements, the mission is always interested in the personality of the one who seeks appointment.

Our present-day use of the term *personality* is very hard to define. It seems to be the total effect of our manner of acting upon others. So we say a man has no personality if he fails to make any deep impression, either good or bad, on others. He has a good personality if his good qualities, as we see them, impress us more strongly than his bad ones. And a bad personality is just the reverse.

These things don't have to bear any relation to reality. The man with the good personality may be a scoundrel of deepest dye, and the one with no personality have the strongest character of the lot. We are dealing only with the outward appearance and the impression it makes on others. The Scripture recognizes this difference between the reality of an action and the impression it makes on others. It says, "Let not your good be evil spoken of." It urges us both to do good and to see that the impression is good.

A bookkeeper doesn't have to worry about the impression he makes on anybody but the boss. The main thing is to have his records neat and accurate. This is not true of the salesperson, however. The volume of his sales and the commission he earns may depend on such impressions.

A research scientist may be a very disagreeable person to meet, while at the same time he may be highly regarded for his contributions to science. But a minister of the gospel can't even get a hearing for his message if he continually rubs people the wrong way.

The missionary, of all people, needs to make the right kind of impressions. He not only has to get a hearing for his message, but that message is so closely tied in with his own life that the impression of his life and the impression of the gospel are likely to be the same thing. Then, too, his whole ministry revolves around his relationship with other people. He can't do his work in a corner.

Even such a scholarly task as the translation of the Bible requires contact with the people. The translator has to immerse himself in the life of the people until he can express the living message of the Bible in the living tongue that they use every day. He has to draw out from them the words and phrases he needs, with infinite patience and understanding. But he can't do it until he first wins their confidence.

Then add to these things the fact that the missionary must both work and live with other missionaries under conditions that are not always conducive to harmony. And remember that this relationship is not one that he can terminate on two weeks' notice.

No wonder the mission is very much interested in the personality of its candidates.

If you ask which elements in the personality are the most important, no one can say. Perhaps no two missionary leaders would ever agree on a list of them. Even when there is fairly general agreement on one trait, such as congeniality, we have to admit that there have been some outstanding exceptions. That is, there have been some who lacked that trait, or were weak in it, and still made good missionaries.

The reason is that personality is not a collection of independent traits. It is a composite in which the many traits are fused together into a whole being. We like one man and we dislike another without stopping to analyze their personalities to determine just what elements we like or dislike in them. When we weigh them in the balance of our likes and dislikes, we never estimate just how much generosity it takes to counterbalance an ounce of jealousy. We just react to the total impression they make on us.

It is to get that total impression that missions seldom depend wholly on the questionnaires they send to the candidate and his references. The questionnaire only deals with definite and specific items. The mission doesn't even depend on a few personal interviews, which can be more general and allow them to gain some personal impressions. Often they try to arrange for a longer personal contact with him in the affairs of daily life. If all other indications are favorable, they invite him to spend a time in the mission home or candidate school—maybe a week or so, maybe a longer period. There he lives, works and studies along with other candidates. The leaders see how he gets along with others. They get a general view of his personality.

There are some things about the personality and character of the candidate that the mission is particularly interested in. Sometimes they ask their questions of the references the candidate gives. Sometimes they seek the answers in other ways. Below are a few typical questions for which they want answers. They are stated in such a way that the preferred answer is obvious. Thus the prospective candidate can look them over, check his own weaknesses, and perhaps make improvements.

1. Does the candidate have real strength of character? Or does he usually run along with the crowd and let others make his decisions for him?

2. Is he self-centered, or does he take a real interest in the affairs of others?

3. Is he easily discouraged by difficulties? Does he usually finish what he begins?

4. Does he work well when not under supervision? Can he be depended on to fulfill all his obligations?

5. Is he usually tactful and reasonable, even under moderate stress? Or does he easily lose his head?

6. Does he have a good supply of common sense?

7. Does he show the initiative and willingness to take responsibility that a leader needs?

8. Is it difficult for him to cooperate with others, or to obey those in authority?

9. Does he readily adapt himself to new situations?

10. Has he learned to endure hardness *without complaint?*

11. What about his emotional stability? Is he given to fits of despondency? Does he have a good sense of humor?

12. Can he stand criticism, and even ridicule?

13. Is he willing to serve in any capacity if needed, no matter how humble?

14. Does he have a teachable spirit?

CHRISTIAN EXPERIENCE

Now a word about Christian life and work as a qualification for missionary service.

The spiritual qualifications we began with are essential. But as we said, the mission boards find it hard to evaluate them. For practical purposes they inquire into certain definite matters about the candidate's life and experience.

Of course they want to know first of all if he gives good evidence of real Christian life and character. They ask this of his references and of any others who may know him.

Then they want to know from the candidate if he has any definite convictions about the missionary call, motives and purposes. Why does he want to be a missionary?

In the matter of doctrinal beliefs there is quite a difference of procedure. Some missions merely require the candidate to sign the doctrinal statement of the mission. Some want an independent statement from the candidate himself in his own words telling what he believes. Some quiz him on certain special items that they think are significant. The whole purpose is to make sure he is in harmony with the fundamental principles of the mission.

Experience in Christian work is very important. The missionary should not go out as a novice. If he hasn't learned to serve Christ and bear an effective witness in his homeland, he isn't ready for overseas service. Sometimes a mission will even recommend that he spend a short period in the pastorate or in the home mission field before he is approved to go abroad. At the very least he should have a record of voluntary service in his home church.

One last question is frequently put to the candidate in somewhat this form: What are your devotional habits? (Note that we say *habits*, not occasional practices.) Our devotional practices are very deliberate in their beginning, and the atmosphere in which most young people live is not very conducive to keeping them up with regularity. It is only through constant repetition over a long period of time that they become habitual. Then they show the mold into which the spiritual life has been cast.

ENGAGEMENT AND MARRIAGE

It may seem strange that we put the matter of engagement and marriage under the heading of qualifications for missionary service. But they bear a clear relationship to the subject. In considering the qualifications of a candidate, the mission always wants to know whether he is married, engaged or single. It makes a difference. They don't want single missionaries for some kinds of work. For others they do. They may even consider that some candidates would be acceptable if married, and otherwise not. And of course if there are children, their number and ages would influence the decision.

The great majority of missionaries are married, either before leaving for the field or at some time afterward. This in spite of the popular misconception that single young women outnumber all other missionaries. The mission seldom insists on marriage for appointment, except in certain areas. But it does figure on it as the usual thing. Often it expresses a definite preference for married couples. This is especially true in places where custom demands that all women must have husbands and any unattached woman is not considered respectable. But marriage does present some problems that each candidate needs to understand.

There are real values in having a missionary family on most fields. So the mission as such is not opposed to marriage or families. Neither does it presume to judge whether a young man's intended is the right one for him. That is a purely personal matter. But these things do have an effect on the work. That is what concerns the mission. Let's see if we can make the problems clear.

One of the problems became especially acute shortly after World War II. That war interrupted or postponed the training of many young men for missionary service. On their return from military service after several years of absence, it was only natural that many of them should decide to get married before continuing their training. The government itself favored such an arrangement by increasing its educational allowance for those who had wives and families.

In time these young people applied for appointment to the mission field. One day the director of a large mission asked me, "What are we going to do with these young couples who apply to us with three or four children? We don't want to turn a man down simply because he has a family. But you can see the problems it raises."

Of course I could. It means a much larger expenditure for outfit and passage. It means more support on the field during the long months of learning the language, getting introduced to the many phases of the work, and becoming adjusted. It means not only increased problems of housing during language-school days, but also the problem of caring for the children so that the parents may have time for classes and study. It means all the burdens and distractions of caring for a sizable family at the time when the young couple should be getting a grasp of the work.

But, in spite of such problems, the missions do send out families, especially where they are well qualified. The most conservative will accept those with only one child. Many do not quibble at two. Most have no set rule but decide each case on its individual merits.

Aside from the problems presented by the children, the candidates ought to understand that the mission often expects both the man and his wife to be missionaries. Some will appoint a missionary, accompanied by his wife. But others prefer to appoint two missionaries, with both of them measuring up to the usual standards of acceptance. The wife's ministry will probably not be the same as if she were single. It shouldn't make her neglect her family responsibilities. But it is a real missionary ministry and it requires ability and good preparation.

What does the mission do when, for health or some other reason, one of the two is not acceptable? What can it do but reject them both? It is a hard decision to make, but an unavoidable one. It has been made many a time.

For the young couple this may seem like a tragic disappointment. But it doesn't need to be. If you have let the Lord lead you in the choice of your helpmate just as sincerely as in the other affairs of life; if you are sure that He has brought you two together and means for you to be together; then the rejection can only mean that He has another place of service for you. You should consider such a rejection in the same light as if it had been the rejection of both individuals. For in God's sight you two are in truth "one flesh."

It is customary for missions to require that couples

be married for at least a year before actually leaving for the field. The major purpose is quite simple, yet very important. Marriage itself involves many adjustments in the lives of the young couple, adjustments they don't often think about ahead of time. Little things like the time for meals, or what to do of an evening, or whether to buy a new 'rug for the living room are things that no longer can be decided by each one individually. And there are a hundred and one other adjustments to be made in the blending of two hitherto independent lives.

When we go to foreign lands as missionaries of Christ there are many other adjustments to make. There is a different climate, different conditions of living, a very different people whose ways of thinking and acting seem very strange to us. There is a new etiquette to learn and abide by, a new lack of privacy even in our own home, and a radically new diet to get used to.

To make two sets of adjustments of such a radical nature at one and the same time is too much to require of anyone. Besides, the honeymoon is not the best time for learning a new and difficult language. So the mission likes to allow a year for adjustment to married life before the adjustment to missionary life is begun.

A similar situation faces those engaged young people who go to the field single, expecting to be married after they arrive. But here it is the adjustment to missionary life that they need to make before facing the adjustment to married life. The mission usually has them wait for one or two years after arrival. That is, they wait until they have adjusted to the field and the work and have gained an acceptable knowledge of the language.

There is a further complication for engaged couples. The mission has found that it is wise to put them in separate stations until marriage, sometimes at a considerable distance. This means that they don't have the frequent opportunities to see one another that they enjoyed in the homeland. It also means that one of the stations is going to lose a worker just at the time when he is becoming really useful. Or maybe after marriage they will both be sent to an entirely different station. But this problem is unavoidable.

If you inquire whether it is better to get married before going to the field or wait until after arriving, you will get all sorts of answers. No one answer will fit all cases. The idea of getting married first seems more attractive to the young people at first thought. But the mission will point out several dangers. There is the danger that you may get sidetracked into some other line of service while waiting. Or the arrival of children may postpone your leaving for the field or even preclude it altogether. Each candidate has to make his own decision in the light of all the facts and looking to the Lord for guidance.

14

MISSIONARY PREPARATION—
THE INDISPENSABLES

CONTROLLING FACTORS

HOW DOES A YOUNG PERSON go about getting prepared for
missionary service? The answer to this question is not easy.
It depends to some extent on the point in his life at which
he makes his decision to volunteer. Maybe he is already
near the age limit. Then he doesn't have much time for
special training, though he may already have some training that will be useful. But if he makes his decision in his
teens he has plenty of time to carry through with a complete,
well-planned course of preparation.

Still, there are other things to consider. He wants
to be a missionary. But what kind of missionary? Maybe
he has only a vague idea of what a missionary is and does.
Is he to be an evangelistic missionary? An educational
missionary? A medical missionary? A technical missionary? Each of these requires special aptitudes and preparation.

The personal characteristics and abilities of the young
person enter into the problem too. Just because you think
it would be nice to be a missionary doctor doesn't mean
that you can be one. Do you have the aptitudes for it? Are
you willing to spend the long years of preparation? And
don't think you are fitted for "pioneer work" simply because
you would like to go where no one else has been before.
It takes a special kind of person to make good in this sort
of work.

As for formal schooling, there are many missionary

training schools. Some are good, some not so good. They range all the way from a few months in a so-called "boot camp" to the specialized studies in some graduate schools of missions. But none of them does the whole job. They all build on a basis of previous training. A few don't specify the amount of previous education. But they still take it for granted that you have completed the usual public school program. Others insist on a background of graduation from high school. Still others accept only students with degrees from colleges or universities. What each is able to do depends both on its own program and on what its students have learned before.

How do you choose a school for missionary training? There are many factors that enter into it that only the prospective missionary can evaluate. For instance there is the question of the denominational school versus the independent school; the school that offers degrees versus the one that doesn't; the large school or the small one; the theological position of the school, etc. Besides these things it is well to find out: (1) whether the graduates of the school are readily accepted by the mission boards; (2) whether the missionary subjects are taught by teachers who are fully qualified by experience as well as study; (3) whether facilities for instruction, such as the library, are adequate, especially in the missionary area.

But really much of the training for a missionary doesn't come from schools or books. It is gained in other ways. Success in missionary work depends fully as much on this extracurricular preparation as it does on the school work. For a missionary is a witness to Christ and to the Christian life. So he must know that life by living it.

THE INDISPENSABLES

There are several things in missionary preparation that we might call indispensables. That is, they are not only important, they are so valuable that to miss them would inevitably cause our ministry to suffer. They are things so fundamental that without them there can't be a real missionary ministry at all. They are things we can't do without. Let's take a little time to talk about them. Then I think you will see what we mean.

I may seem strange to say that there is any particular kind of preparation that *all* missionaries ought to have for *all* fields. Even more strange to say that there is any type of preparation that is really indispensable for them all. After all, there is a great deal of specialization in missions today. There has to be. And surely the technical specialist doesn't need the same kind of preparation as the evangelistic missionary.

In a sense he doesn't. His training as a technician is quite different from that of the evangelist. But remember that he is a *missionary*. If the word *missionary* is to have any meaning at all, it must mean that those who bear that name have certain things in common. It is those things that make them missionaries. It is like those who call themselves Christians. By occupation they may be almost anything. But in that name they are united in a common faith, a common Saviour, a common standard of right and wrong, etc.

The true indispensables in missionary preparation are all spiritual. Classroom work plays a part, but it is not effective by itself. It is too easy to learn lessons for an examination without having them affect the course of our lives. We can take the finest course of preparation offered in any school and still be unprepared for missionary service. Some have done it. We need something more, something in addition to the school work.

In general there are four indispensables in the preparation of the missionary. *First,* and fundamental to all the rest, there is the training of our inner life—what we might call spiritual training. *Second,* there is the training to show forth that life in our relation to others, a matter of vital importance in all missionary service. Some would call it our "testimony," the actual living of the Christian life. *Third,* of course, is our training in the message we are called to deliver, the gospel itself. The missionary is God's messenger, so he must have his message well in hand. *Fourth* is the matter of experience in presenting the message to others, the training that comes from practice. With this experience also comes maturity, that seasoning that we can only get by actually coming to grips with real life and with living persons.

SPIRITUAL PREPARATION

In the vitally important line of spiritual training the least systematic work has been done. The mission boards look for certain spiritual qualifications in those who apply, but the schools don't offer courses in the subject. It may be that they count on the churches' doing the job. If so, they are making a big mistake. The training given by most churches is quite haphazard. Even when several young people offer themselves for missions from the same church, the amount of spiritual training they have had is never the same.

One candidate, for instance, was born in a devout Christian family. At an early age he accepted the Saviour. Shortly afterward he offered his life for service on the foreign mission field. This allows for years of development before he actually sails. The Bible becomes a familiar book; family devotions and private prayers make their mark on his life; Sunday school lessons, sermons, conferences, Bible camps, young people's societies, all help to foster and strengthen the growth of his spiritual life.

Another, however, did not know of Christ's salvation until some time during his college days. He comes from a nonchristian background and has already delved deeply into the sinful ways of the world. But then he allows Christ to enter his life and it is transformed. In the enthusiasm of his new found faith he too volunteers for missionary service. He hasn't the background of the first candidate, but he is not a whit behind him in sincerity of purpose.

He may even excel him in warmhearted zeal. He joins the church and takes an active part in its affairs. He associates with other Christian young people. He takes counsel with his pastor and drinks in avidly the messages he hears.

Now it is possible that the second young man may one day outstrip the first in his spiritual development. Then again, maybe he won't. It is something that is hard to prophesy. In any case he is not likely to find that any course has been planned for his spiritual development. Certainly not in college. Even in seminary the chief aim is to give him an intellectual mastery of certain truths and to help him develop certain skills. His spiritual profiting will depend mostly on his own initiative and his associations outside the classroom.

Of all preparatory schools the Bible institutes seem to have made the most definite provision for the training of the spirit as well as the mind. What they do is not enough. They themselves would be the first to admit it. But it is a part of their program and an important one. Student life there is more closely regulated than in other schools. There is an emphasis, often repeated, on the devotional life and practical Christianity. Every student is assigned to do some practical Christian service, which makes him exercise the spiritual life he already has and helps him grow. But even so it is not enough.

What kind of spiritual training does the missionary need? Let me mention briefly a few items with which not many will disagree. Devotional habits are very important— habits of communing with God in prayer and drawing help and instruction and inspiration from His Word. These are almost the breath of life to the missionary. Now it takes constant and regular repetition to turn an occasional practice into a habit. This is a part of missionary preparation.

With these habits should go the constant application of Christian principles to everyday living. A course in Christian ethics at school is not of much value as long as it is kept in the abstract. The principles don't begin to have real meaning and value until they are applied to definite situations. For instance, it is easy to repeat that all lying is wrong. But it is not so easy to tell the truth when a lie would apparently save you from an embarrassing situation. How do you know the principle is true if you don't apply it? A missionary must be sure!

Also, what good is it to know the theological definition of faith, or to be able to expound Paul's teaching on faith in Galatians, if you don't know how to exercise faith in the affairs of life? There are many times, even in student life, when faith is called for. And do take notice that to the heathen, religion is as much experience as it is theory, if not more so. He won't be interested in any new theory or doctrine that isn't borne out by experience.

SOCIAL PREPARATION

Training for your own spirit also comes through learning to deal with others about their soul's needs. Here our first indispensable merges with the others, especially with the second one, the one that deals with our relationship to other people. Personal evangelism is the very cornerstone of missionary work everywhere, and the same preparation of heart that you need for it here at home is what you need in foreign lands. Personal counseling, too, is one of the missionary's most common jobs, and one of the most demanding. Its principles are pretty much the same wherever you go. One of those principles is that the counselor must show a real interest in the one who seeks his help. In fact, the missionary needs to be, of all people, one who is unselfishly interested in others, one who is willing to make their burden his own.

In a missionary's life, too, relationship to others involves the matter of leadership. Whether he wants it or not, people do look to him for leadership. Now some seem to think that leadership is a purely natural gift, that some people are born leaders while others will always be followers. It is perfectly true that some do have an exceptional talent for leadership. But it is not true that all of our leaders come from those talented few. Instead, it is perfectly possible for those who don't have such a gift to develop real ability as leaders. Often all they need is the opportunity and the encouragement to step out and lead.

We said that missionaries are expected to be leaders. Whether they get proper training for it or not, the circumstances of their life make them take on the responsibilities of leadership. If they have had good training and experience, they can do a creditable job. If not, they will probably become petty dictators. And this will bring harm to the work.

What does leadership training involve? We can give only a limited amount in class instruction. That is, we can explain some of the basic principles and how to apply them. The student can learn much more by observing those who lead and by following their example. But more important than either of these is experience in leading. The one who wants to be a leader needs to take every possible chance to exercise leadership.

Several things are fundamental. The leader needs to have a definite *objective;* he must know where he is going. He has to be ready to make *decisions,* not merely follow along with what others decide. And he must be prepared to accept the *responsibility* for those decisions, not blame someone else if they don't work out well.

The one who finds it hard to make up his mind, who always hesitates to commit himself for fear he might make a mistake, had better practice making decisions on every possible occasion. He will make mistakes, of course. Who doesn't? But his mistakes will be just so many valuable lessons that will help him to make better decisions the next time. And the one who doesn't want to take responsibility just isn't material for a missionary.

Another thing, the one who is to be a Christian leader needs to learn the lesson that Peter taught, that we are to take the oversight of God's flock, not "as being lords over God's heritage, but being ensamples to the flock." We show real leadership when we can get others to do what we have in mind, while all the time they are convinced that they are doing what they want to do.

PREPARATION IN THE MESSAGE

Our third indispensable has to do with the mastery of the message we bear to others. All too often one who has some special technical training or skill asks the question, "Is there a place on the mission field where I can be used?" What such a person usually presumes is that a missionary work we need laboratory technicians, printers, builders, teachers, nurses, etc. But that is all wrong. We need *missionaries!* We need young men and women with a message! They may be educational missionaries, industrial missionaries, medical missionaries; but first and foremost they must be missionaries. As a doctor in the Congo once wrote, "If I thought my job out here was just to heal men's bodies, I would stay at home!"

All of the various types of work in which missionaries engage are proper and useful only insofar as they contribute to the one great aim of missions. They must be related to the task of bringing Christ to the people, of winning them to Him, and building them up in Him.

Every missionary must be a man with a message, and he must know that message well. The mission field is no place for one who has serious doubts about his faith. Neither is it the place for one who is not quite sure just what his message is. He doesn't have to be a finished theologian. He doesn't need to be a profound student of the prophetic Word. But he does need to know the essential elements of his faith and be fully persuaded of their truth. He does have to show to the people that he has a working knowledge of the Scriptures. And he must be able to show them how that message touches their lives.

Please understand that the people to whom the missionary goes are not ignorant. They may be illiterate, but that is quite another thing. Among illiterate people there are often some of the keenest minds to be found anywhere. They are remarkably acute in their evaluation of the missionary. They may overlook his halting speech, his apparent faulty logic in some of the things he says, and even his ignorance of many things that don't bear directly on his work. But two faults they will not excuse: a failure to know his message, and an insincerity in professing what he doesn't fully believe or practice.

Bible training, then, is indispensable to all missionaries, no matter what their type of service.

PREPARATION THROUGH EXPERIENCE

Our final indispensable is experience in presenting the message. We have already said something about maturity in the spiritual life, which comes through experience. We have also spoken of experience in such a matter as leadership of others. The Bible, too, becomes a living message to others largely to the extent that we who preach it have experienced its power in our own lives. It is remarkable how these indispensable elements in missionary preparation are intertwined with one another. It is only in our thinking that we try to separate them. In life they merge into one another.

Christian service. The matter of experience in presenting the message is very important. Mr. Moody knew its value and stressed it in founding the Moody Bible Institute. He made practical Christian work an integral part of the course of training. It still has that place of importance at Moody as well as in other Bible institutes.

Yet in spite of such experience during their school days, I have had students come to me as they neared graduation, saying, "I don't believe I am ready to go out as a missionary. If I am to be a leader on the mission field I feel that I need more experience in dealing with souls, more experience in meeting the spiritual problems of real life." So some of these young people have gone into home mission work for a short time to get that experience before going abroad.

Such young people have shown a real perception of what it means to be a missionary. On the mission field you are not reciting lessons. People don't quiz you on the subjects you had in school and allow you to show why you got top honors in theology or church history or some other subject. In fact, what may disturb the missionary most is their complete indifference to what he has to say, even when they are polite enough to listen while he talks.

You are a missionary. So what? That doesn't mean anything to them except that you are an object of curiosity. Can you engage them in conversation and so direct the conversation that it will turn to matters of the spirit? It is not difficult in many fields. Other peoples often show more interest in religious matters than do the folks at home. But once you have begun the discussion, can you keep it in the main channel where you can present the Lord Jesus Christ in all His desirability? Can you disregard the minor matters and get to the heart of the question so as to reach the heart of the man? It takes practice.

Oral expression. Again, missionary leaders are insisting, "We need missionaries who know how to express themselves!" Well, that is just where experience comes in. You don't learn to express yourself by reading a book or answering a set of true-false questions. You need practice. They say you "learn how to write by writing." You also learn how to express yourself orally by repeated efforts to tell others what is on your mind.

The aim of missions is not simply to proclaim the gospel. It is to proclaim it in such a way that men will listen to it, understand it, and be moved to obey it. Differences of language don't mean too much in this matter. If you can express yourself in English you can learn to express yourself in another tongue. But if your thoughts are hazy and disordered, and your expression is anything but clear in English, there is no magic in learning another language that will straighten you out. You need this preparation before going to the field. You need this experience in oral communication.

Counseling. One last thing. We have mentioned the missionary's need to give counsel on the field, counsel of all sorts. More than anything else this calls for experience. You need to know people through much association with them. The missionary cannot be a hermit. You need to know something of the forces that move men, the problems that most of them face. It takes experience as well as tact to draw them out and to avoid the pitfalls that go with snap judgments. "Advice is cheap," we often say, for there is so much cheap advice on the market. It is given without any background of experience to make it valuable. Yet when a troubled new believer, or a national pastor, comes to the missionary with a vital problem, he doesn't want cheap advice. He has come to God's messenger and he looks for God's message. How humble it should make the missionary feel, and how dependent on God!

CONCLUSION

These things, then, are indispensable in the preparation of the missionary candidate. Other training is useful, but this is fundamental. Some of it can be provided in the school curriculum. Perhaps we can do even more along this line. Some can be given in the church, if the church is alert to its opportunities.

But much of it, in fact the very heart of the whole matter, depends on the individual. The candidate must not depend on others to prepare him for the mission field. They will do what they can, but it is limited. On the candidate himself rests the responsibility of such a close walk with God, and such a full determination to serve Him well, that the Holy Spirit, the master Teacher, can accomplish that indispensable work of preparation that is His own special ministry.

15

MISSIONARY PREPARATION — SPECIAL SUBJECTS

THERE IS NO ONE COURSE of preparation for all missionary service. There can't be. The things that missionaries do are too varied. Their fields and the requirements of their work are too different.

For example, two missionaries to Central America took identical courses of missionary preparation. The course included some elementary medical and dental instruction. It might seem that if either of them needed that training, they both would. But it didn't turn out that way.

Here is what they told me. One had worked in and around the capital of his country. At the end of his second term of service he remarked, "I have never had to use a single day of that medical instruction I took." The other had his field among the lowland Indians of the Caribbean coast. After an even shorter period of service he said, "With just that little bit of dental instruction I have already pulled a thousand teeth!"

This seems quite confusing. How are you going to know what training to get? How can you tell which course of preparation to follow? Is there any answer that will cover most situations?

There is indeed. It is a threefold answer. *First,* there is some preparation that is indispensable. We have already talked about this. *Second,* there is some training that is so generally needed that nearly everybody ought to get it. We'll talk about this in a moment. *Finally,* there is some training that depends on the needs of a particular field or mission, or else it depends on your own talents and interests. This last is the most difficult to talk about because of the many variables. Every case is different. Not only will each prospective missionary face different circumstances wherever he goes, but it is questionable whether he really knows his own abilities and limitations.

STUDIES GENERALLY NEEDED

Now let us give attention to some of the more generally needed types of training.

LANGUAGE STUDY

The matter of language study is a critical one for missions. We have already said that ability to express yourself in English is indispensable. To learn how to do it in another language is almost as important. There are not many fields where you can use English effectively in missionary work — not even in such places as Nigeria, where English is taught in the schools. It is true that educated people there have learned to read, write and speak English to some degree. But a message delivered in English doesn't mean nearly as much to them as a message in their native tongue. As an educated Filipino once remarked to me about his own people, "English speaks to our heads; but our own language speaks to our hearts!"

"That's all right," someone will object; "I know you ought to do a good job studying the language on the field. But what can one do about it here in the homeland? Our schools don't teach many of the languages we need for missions. Besides, how can a candidate fit language study into an already full course of preparation?

Usefulness of any language. The objector does have a point. There aren't many cases where a missionary can study in the homeland the language he will have to use on the field. But that should be no excuse for omitting language study completely from the course of preparation. In fact, you may find that some missions will insist that you take language study of some sort before they send you to the field. One thing they want to find out is whether you are likely to have much difficulty in learning another language. Also they know that the study of any other language than your own is likely to help, whether it is the one you are going to use or not. It helps you to see that *differences of language are not just differences of words.* They represent different ways of thinking and of expressing thought. Once you have learned any other language than your own, you find it easier to adjust your thinking so as to learn still others.

Actually it isn't hard to fit a foreign language into your course of preparation. Nearly all our high schools offer instruction in one or more foreign languages. In some cases it is a prerequisite for entering college. Many colleges, too, require at least two years of a foreign language for graduation. And if somehow you missed it before, the Bible institutes and Bible colleges offer such instruction.

For missionaries it is usually best to choose the modern languages. That is because they are actually spoken today. They are also usually taught in a different way from the so-called "dead" languages. But there are cases in which the dead languages may be more useful. For example, if your work is likely to involve translation of the Bible, then by all means take up Greek and Hebrew if they are available. You will do a better job.

Specific languages. Sometimes you can study at home a language that you will use on your field. Then do it. You can get Spanish, for example, in nearly all our high schools and colleges. Spanish is what you will use in most of Latin America. French is also taught in most of our colleges and in many high schools. You will need French in large parts of Africa that were once under French or Belgian rule. Portuguese is not so commonly taught, but it is given in a number of schools. It is necessary for Brazil and for the large Portuguese possessions in Africa. In fact, no matter where you learn it, you will probably have to know

Portuguese before you are admitted to Angola or Mozambique. This is not the case in French-speaking Africa, but it is still advisable to know French before arriving and having to learn one of the tribal or trade languages as well. This is why many of the missions make it a practice to send their missionaries first to France or Switzerland for language study before they proceed to French-speaking Africa. Of course if you need another language that is not so commonly taught, such as Japanese, Chinese or Arabic, it will be a little more difficult to get it in the home country. There are schools that teach these and other languages, but they may not readily fit into your program.

Why study at home? There was a time when many missionaries advised against studying in the homeland the languages that would be used on the field. Some of them still do. They usually mention two reasons. One is that you may not learn the language correctly, especially when it comes to pronunciation. You need to live among the people to get it right. The other reason is that you may start talking to the people before you understand their ways and know what is wise to say.

There is a good deal of truth in both these reasons. The trouble is that their importance has been exaggerated. We admit that, in spite of our improved methods of language teaching and learning, and in spite of a growing number of competent language teachers, there are still some who don't speak well the language they are teaching. They learned it in school themselves and have never had to use it in everyday life. But actually most of their mistakes are those of pronunciation and idiom. They usually are able to give a good foundation in grammar.

Of course poor pronunciation is a definite handicap. It is possible to develop fixed habits in this line that are exceedingly difficult to correct later. But most of our school courses are neither long enough nor intensive enough to do this. Rather, those who have studied the language in the homeland usually find that they can make the corrections in a fairly short time. In addition they are able to enter fully into the work much sooner than others.

As for the second reason, it is true that a new missionary might possibly say some very unwise things. It is possible, but it doesn't often happen. The fact is that most new missionaries are afraid to say much, if anything, for fear of making mistakes. They have to be encouraged to talk. Often they are hesitant even to go out on the street for fear someone will talk to *them,* and they may not understand.

Missionaries often do make slips of the tongue. But not just the new missionaries. Some of the most serious blunders have been made by those who have been on the field for a number of years. Neither is it noticeable that those who learned some of the language at home make any more awkward mistakes than those who didn't.

We have said that some people exaggerate the disadvantages of studying a language in the homeland. We don't want to go to the other extreme and exaggerate the advantages. There are some advantages. They are very real advantages. They warrant your taking classes in the language while you are preparing for the field. If the course is a concentrated one, it may even warrant your delaying your departure for a while to take it. But don't spend a year or more after you are otherwise ready for the field just in taking one of our ordinary language courses. You can do much better on the field.

There are at least three advantages in beginning the study at home:

First, it gives you a grasp of the grammatical foundations of the language. As a result it isn't entirely strange and confusing to you when you first reach the field. Those first days are confusing enough, with all the new things you have to learn and get used to.

Second, such study takes you through the first period of discouragement. There always comes a time when you think you will never get the language, a time when you wonder how anyone could ever learn to talk such stuff. Better to undergo that first discouragement here than out there.

Third, that study may shorten your stay in the language school if there is one. This means that you will be able to take part in the work sooner. It will save time and money for you and your supporters.

An added dividend is the attitude of the people to whom you go. You will find that they deeply appreciate those who can speak to them in their own tongue from the beginning, even though imperfectly.

General linguistic studies. Still there are many languages missionaries use that can't be studied in the homeland. Some of them are not taught in our schools. Others have not yet been reduced to written form. Those who plan to go to places where these languages are used have another alternative. They can take classes in linguistics that will help them to learn any language.

A class in general phonetics, for example, particularly if it has a missionary slant, is valuable for all missionaries. Phonetics deals with the sounds of human speech. It treats not only the limited number that are found in our own language but others that may be found elsewhere, such as the clicks of South Africa. In such a class you learn about the various vocal organs that produce and modify the sounds of speech. You practice making many of the more common speech sounds and learn how to identify them when you hear them. You are taught a system for describing and classifying any sound that is used.

If you are dealing with a well-known language, phonetics helps you to learn its sounds more quickly and to produce them more accurately. If you come in contact with an unwritten language, it enables you to distinguish the sounds it uses and to reproduce them. It also gives you an accurate way of writing down words and phrases so you can repeat them later and teach them to others.

There are various schools that offer classes in phonetics, sometimes in connection with a course of missionary preparation. Classes that teach methods for learning the language from the people are much rarer. A special one-month course that includes both phonetics and language learning is offered each summer at the Toronto Institute of Linguistics, to which a number of missions send their candidates.*

Most missionaries do not really need more than this. However, those who are going to give their primary attention to linguistic work on the field, especially those who reduce a language to writing and translate the Bible into it, need much more. Without doubt the most useful training of this sort for missionary candidates is that provided by the Summer Institute of Linguistics (Camp Wycliffe) on several university campuses.† You can take the foundational course in one summer session of a little less than three months of intensive work. An advanced second-year course is also offered.

MEDICAL STUDIES

A second type of training quite generally needed is in the line of medicine. That is, it is medical instruction for the average missionary, the one who does not intend to be a doctor or a nurse.

Every missionary ought to know the elementary things about anatomy and physiology, hygiene, first aid, and care of the sick. There are still many fields where competent medical help is all too little and too widely scattered to take care of all the needs. The missionary ought to know at least how to care for himself and his family in ordinary circumstances. He also ought to know how to care for an emergency until he can get a doctor.

Another thing. In some places where the law does not

*Suite 200, 1835 Yonge Street, Toronto 7, Ontario, Canada. The classes are given at Victoria University.
†Box 1960, Santa Ana, California 92702. The universities in the United States are North Dakota, Oklahoma and Washington.

forbid it, a nonmedical missionary has an opportunity to treat illnesses among the people as far as his knowledge and ability go. Of course he is not a doctor and needs to recognize his limitations. But when no doctor can be had, he does what he can. The opportunities for this medical work by nonmedical missionaries are getting less and less. There are many more fully trained doctors than there used to be, both missionary and national. Many countries, too, are trying to restrict the activities of unauthorized practitioners. But there are still places where the missionary may be free to carry on such a ministry for some years to come.

Just how much medical training should the general missionary have? There is no general agreement. Too much depends on the particular field, the government restrictions, and even the personality of the missionary. The amount of training that might prove very useful to one missionary might even be dangerous for another with less discretion. However, we can say that everyone ought to get instruction in the basic subjects mentioned above: anatomy and physiology, hygiene, first aid, and care of the sick. For tropical lands one should know something about the more common tropical diseases, such as malaria, and how to treat them.

TEACHER TRAINING

A third type of training, which is even more generally needed than medicine, is training in teaching. We are not talking here about those who are going to give their full time to a teaching ministry. Every missionary is a teacher. No matter what his special ministry may be, he is called on to teach others. He may teach printing, or nursing, or carpentry; or he may teach Bible and theology. But whatever his ministry, teaching is a part of it. He is never just a workman doing a specific job. He is also one who inspires and teaches others to do what he does.

So each missionary ought to take some training in the

principles of teaching. That training doesn't have to be as complete as that of the professional teacher. Nevertheless it should be enough to give him a good grasp of the funamentals. In addition he ought to get some experience in teaching. If he can get it under the direction of a skilled teacher, so much the better. But, if not, by all means he ought to have the experience of teaching others somewhere.

BUSINESS TRAINING

For a fourth type of needed general preparation we must mention bookkeeping and business management. It may amaze some that such subjects are listed as needed by most missionaries. Yet mission leaders have been urging the matter for many years. They are not thinking about the general accounts and the business affairs of the whole mission. For such things they can usually get someone with special training and experience.

But every mission station has accounts to keep and business affairs to handle. Building, repairing, hiring laborers of all sorts require good business judgment and the keeping of accurate accounts. Schools, Bible institutes, even "bush" schools, make the same demands. So do such things as hospitals, printing plants, colportage work and even Bible conferences. Many a mission treasurer has groaned over the seeming inability of some missionaries to keep simple accounts and render intelligible financial reports.

What the individual missionary needs is not a complete business course, though that certainly would increase his usefulness. But he does need to know the principles of bookkeeping, which he can take in high school and even some Bible institutes or colleges. And he also should have some business experience. Actual classes in business management of the simple sort the missionary needs are not as available as bookkeeping. But if he can't get a regular course in the subject, at least he will find that business experience is a great asset.

SPECIALIZATION

Specialization is the order of the day in our American civilization. Men concentrate their studies not just on one field of knowledge but on a fragment of one portion of that field. Such intensive work has produced marvelous results in the realm of the physical sciences. Many people don't see why it wouldn't do just as well in missionary work.

Doubtless it would. That is, it would if the missions had enough money to employ the large staff of specialists they would need in each field. Also, it would if there were enough trained specialists volunteering for the work. And, it would if the people we work with didn't insist on being treated as individuals instead of a collection of parts on an assembly line, and at the gospel as a whole gospel for a whole man. But these conditions don't exist.

Complete specialization in missions is out of the question. There are always some specialists, some who give their whole time to just one phase of the work. Their number is increasing. But the majority of missionaries have to be ready to take on various kinds of work. They are not really jacks-of-all-trades, but neither can they limit themselves to just one. There are so many things to be done and so few to do them that actually the missionaries sometimes pray, "Lord, deliver us from the specialist, the fellow who isn't ready to do whatever needs to be done!"

Yet because specialization is valuable, there has always been some of it in missions. Every missionary has some things that he does better than others, some interests that attract him more than others. No matter what job he is assigned, he will always find the time and place to stress his special interest. Beyond this there will always be certain types of work that, more than others, demand the full-time services of specially trained workers. Under present conditions those needs are increasing for specialization.

THINGS TO BEAR IN MIND

So if you want to be a missionary, keep these things in mind. *First,* most missionaries have to do more things than the one thing they like to do most. Doctors, for example, often have to do building and repair work. *Second,* if you have real talent and training in a line that is useful to the work, sooner or later you will have the chance to make use of your specialty. People like musicians often make a special niche for themselves in the work. *Third,* in some specialized fields your chances to be used full time are quite broad, while in others they may be very limited.

SPECIALTIES IN DEMAND

Medical work more and more calls for the fully trained, full-time doctor or nurse. There are still a few places where the nonmedical missionary can give some medical help, as we said before, but the number is rapidly decreasing. On the other hand, the demand for well-trained missionary doctors always exceeds the supply. Nurses, too, are generally needed. But not in all fields. There are some fields where foreign doctors are not allowed to practice. There are others where the local doctors can meet most of the need. So the medical missionary candidate has to expect some limitation in his choice of field. He may not get to go to the place of his first choice.

Teaching is another specialized field that often calls for the full-time services of trained men and women. There are many kinds of teaching, and not all are carried on in any one field or mission. The teaching and directing of primary schools is of course the most common, if we don't count the Bible schools. However, nationals are rapidly taking over this work. Teaching on the high school and college levels offers fewer opportunities to begin with, but the need is likely to continue for a longer time. The supply is usually short of the demand.

Printing is done by many separate missions, as well as by several missions working together. It usually calls for a full-time printer who can also train and supervise national help. Trained men are very important in this work and are usually in demand. But since there is a trend toward using commercial printing shops where they are available, a printer may have less choice of field than a doctor or a teacher.

As we get into other technical fields, we may find the opportunities even more limited. Full-time *builders* are needed, but only by the larger missions. The same is true of *business managers. Laboratory technicians* can be used only where there are hospitals. *Airplane pilots* usually need to double as *mechanics.* They are being used in a limited number of fields where commercial aviation cannot meet the needs.

Radio technicians are needed where missionary radio stations are in operation. They are also needed where a mission has set up a short wave communications system between its stations. *Agricultural experts* are very useful in some fields, as well as *teachers of the crafts.* There are other useful specialties too numerous to mention. You can see, though, that full-time service in any one of these specialties may be limited to certain fields and missions.

EXPERIENCE NEEDED

There is another type of specialization that we ought to deal with. It is the type that we can best illustrate by speaking of literary work. Very seldom does a mission send out a new missionary specifically designated to do literary work in another language. Instead, when they set aside someone for this ministry it is usually a veteran missionary who has demonstrated interest and ability.

The reason is simple. Training in writing or journalism at home is designed to reach people of our own language and culture. It is good as far as it goes and does give basic principles. But it usually takes some years for a man to learn another language well enough to produce literature in it, or even to edit it. Besides, the missionary has to learn something more than the language. He also has to learn to know the people. He has to learn what needs to be written and how. He needs to learn how the people think, what the background is for their beliefs and actions. He needs to learn how to write, insofar as a foreigner can, from their point of view. This calls for experience in the land and with the people.

There are other specialties like this, such as teaching in a Bible institute or seminary. The basic principles can be learned at home, but their development and application require field experience.

GETTING THE BEST TRAINING

Most of our courses of missionary preparation suffer from one serious weakness. They are not specific enough. Many of the students have no other purpose than just "to be a missionary." If you ask them, "What kind of missionary?" they find it hard to give a clear answer. They have only a vague idea of what missionary work involves.

To get well prepared, a missionary candidate should find out as soon as possible in what kind of ministry the Lord can best use him. He may have major and minor interests, but he does need to have objectives. He needs to realize that evangelism is itself a specialty and takes special preparation. How can he say that he expects to be an evangelistic missionary if he hasn't learned to do personal evangelism? Or hasn't learned to preach in his own tongue? Or isn't on familiar terms with the gospel message? Or shrinks from contact with new people?

As for other specialized ministries, if the prospective missionary wants to be really effective he should get the best possible preparation.

Medical missionaries need to be fully qualified to practice in their own country first. Teachers in recognized schools also need to be certified at home. Both of them, in addition, may have to fulfill other requirements in the country to which they go. A certificate allowing them to practice their profession at home does not necessarily qualify them to do so in another country. They may have to take additional courses.

For each of the technical specialties, too, the missionary should get the best of training. Those who handle airplanes need more than a private pilot's license. A sound aviation program calls for a pilot with at least a commercial license, and usually a license in aircraft and power-frame maintenance.

We can't go farther into the matter of specialized preparation. But we do need to remind ourselves again that training in these specialties does not exempt a candidate from the basic preparation required of all missionaries. Specialists are expected to be missionaries too. They must be motivated by the same spirit as the evangelistic missionaries. Otherwise the work will suffer. Experience has shown us that each new worker added, if he is not a real missionary, dilutes the spiritual effectiveness of the work. We do need specialists—but *missionary* specialists!

16

WHY MISSION BOARDS?

MOST PEOPLE TODAY accept the existence of mission boards without any question. They are quite the normal thing in missions. They have certain rather definite functions to perform, and they have clearly been used in the expansion of the missionary enterprise.

However, there are a number of sincere and devout Christians, including some missionaries, who are opposed to mission boards. Some base their opposition on doctrinal grounds, claiming that such organizations are not scriptural. Others are governed more by their personal situation and interests. In addition there are some today who believe that mission boards are outdated, that we need to find new forms of missionary ministry.

We can state the opposition on scriptural grounds quite simply. Generally those who hold this position are opposed to most forms of organization in the church. They take it for granted that the New Testament gives us a complete and detailed pattern of all that a Christian church ought to be and do. This includes the methods by which we are to carry on missionary work. We should have no other organization than what we find in the pages of the New Testament. And of course we find no mission boards there.

We respect the sincere faith and earnest zeal of those who hold this view. Some of them have done very good missionary work. Yet they represent the view of only a small minority of all earnest Christians. And most of us don't find in the Scriptures any claim to such finality in matters of organization and methods. In doctrine, yes. The New Testament does present Jesus Christ as God's final and complete revelation. It pronounces an anathema against all who would preach any other gospel than what it presents. But we think it is a mistake to extend these claims of finality in doctrine to matters of organization.

In fact, the New Testament itself does not give a unified picture of organization and procedure. What it does give us is a picture of development under the guidance of the Holy Spirit, a development in organization to meet the needs as they arise.

Christ left only the nucleus of an organization in the eleven apostles. After His ascension they chose another to complete the original number of twelve. The church in Jerusalem grew so fast that they soon had to create the office of deacon to take proper care of needy members.

We don't know when the elders in Jerusalem were first chosen, nor why. But we can see the similarity to the Jewish synagogue with which the believers were familiar. We can also see the need for such officers when the apostles themselves began to die off or leave for other fields. When Barnabas and Paul started the first churches in Asia Minor, they reversed the procedure. They appointed elders first, since the apostles didn't stay with the churches. The deacons seem to have come later as they were needed.

Mission boards in their modern sense don't appear in the New Testament. In fact, we have had them for less than two hundred years. But the basic principle on which they are organized is not inconsistent with New Testament teaching.

As we stated before, Christ laid the responsibility for carrying out His Great Commission on the church as a whole as well as on individuals. Clearly the New Testament church recognized to some degree that responsibility, even though it didn't see just how far it was to go.

So when Philip started the work in Samaria, the church at Jerusalem sent an official delegation to confirm it. When Peter preached to Cornelius, his conduct was officially reviewed by the church. The decision in that case was to be the deciding factor years later in their approval of the work of Barnabas and Paul. When the church began in Antioch, the Jerusalem church sent Barnabas to confirm the believers in their faith. And when Barnabas and Saul started on their first missionary tour, it was the church at Antioch that sent them forth, by the direction of the Holy Spirit. They also reported to the church when they returned.

The church did not take on financial responsibility for any of its missionaries. That is a very modern development. Neither did it presume to tell them where they were to go nor how they were to carry on their work. These men were pioneers, and there was no one qualified to instruct them. However, later on Paul himself did give some very definite instructions to the younger missionaries, Timothy and Titus. Also, though the church at Antioch didn't provide the financial needs of its missionaries, other churches did send help to them on various occasions. And of course, as sometimes happens today, the people to whom they ministered often saw to it that they had food and shelter.

Those who contend that mission boards are outdated also have some grounds for their opposition. It is true that missions has become in a sense "big business." Our societies tend to follow the pattern of Western commercial organizations. Sometimes one gets the feeling that there is little room left for the leading of the Spirit. Increased efficiency doesn't always result in spiritual effectiveness.

Yet the burden is on the objectors to provide us with new and more effective instruments. The tremendous advances of Christianity in the past century and a half were made possible through the mission societies. Any new proposal must either aim at different goals or prove itself to be more effective in the present day.

Values of the Boards

THE CHURCH AT WORK IN MISSIONS

The modern mission board is intended to represent the church in the carrying out of its missionary task. It is formed within the church and is the servant of the church. Its constitution and practices reflect the church it represents. Since there'are a number of different denominations, the boards do have different practices. The funds that any mission board has to use are the gifts of the members of the churches. So the board is responsible to the churches for its handling of them.

Of course there are a number of boards that are not denominational. But they are still representative. They represent a large and growing number of independent churches, plus many groups and individuals within the various denominations. These are people who for one reason or another decide to support their work. Such boards may not seem to be so immediately responsible to the churches. But the fact is that their very continuance depends on keeping the interest and support of the churches. Since this support is likely to be more spontaneous and less regular than that of the denominations, these boards are apt to be even more sensitive to the attitudes of the supporting churches.

EFFICIENCY IN THE WORK

We need mission boards for the effective, systematic spread of the gospel, just as the Jerusalem church needed deacons for the fair, systematic distribution of material help to needy believers. It can't be done on an every-man-for-himself basis. It is the church's business, and that means cooperation. But cooperation on a large scale always calls for some sort of organization.

Take for example the handling of the church's contributions to finance missionary work abroad. In a large mission operating in several fields this is a big job. It isn't just a matter of receiving funds and forwarding to each missionary a stated salary. That would be simple, even if you had to vary the salary with the size of the family. But there are other things to consider. Living costs are different in every field and they often change rapidly when inflation hits. Money exchange rates are constantly fluctuating. The American dollar that is worth five dollars of the local currency in one country may be worth only sixty cents in another. Or it may drop in value next month. The board takes all this into account.

Then there are expenses for building, for running schools and hospitals, for printing, for travel, for a multitude of other things that are involved in carrying on a mission. Besides, the churches don't always give with regularity. Giving reaches its peak just before the end of the year, partly because of Christmas but even more because of the income-tax deadline. On the other hand, the summer months are very slim. Business is slack, church attendance is off, and many are spending their money on vacations instead of missions. Yet the missionary has the same needs for support in the summer as in the winter. The board plans the handling of funds to take care of these matters.

And what about planning? There is much talk about mission strategy. But strategy necessarily involves planning. It involves coordination of efforts. This can never be done on an individual basis. Some kind of organization is called for. The modern response has been the mission society or board. It is the board that establishes the basic principles of the work, that sets up priorities in the distribution of personnel and funds. While it does make mistakes, in general it has been a very efficient instrument in the carrying out of the church's missionary task.

It is true that the creation of separate mission societies seems to imply that the work of "missions" is somehow distinct from the other ministries of the church. It puts "missions" in a class by itself, while many believe that it should be just a part of the total ministry or "mission" of the church. But in any case the church would still find it necessary to set up a board or commission to supervise the "overseas ministries of the church."

LIAISON WITH THE HOME CHURCH

We need the mission boards also to represent the work to the church at home. If missions is the church's job, if the churches are to support the work spiritually and financially, they must have regular reports on how it is going. Interest has to be fed by information.

Now it is entirely possible for the individual missionaries to keep up a certain amount of interest through their personal letters and by means of visits to the churches while on furlough. This is good, but it is far from enough. Most churches don't keep in touch with more than one or two missionaries, if at all. Then, too, most missionaries themselves are not well acquainted with the work outside their own stations. Their letters from the field and their talks on furlough deal mostly with their own personal experiences.

The mission board, on the other hand, is in a position to view the whole field. It can present a balanced picture of progress and needs. It usually tries to do this through the mission publication or through visits to the churches by secretaries and others. Sometimes it sponsors the taking of motion pictures, or filmstrips with narration, which it makes available to the churches to represent the work. Or it helps promote missionary education in the churches, providing the needed plans and literature. Or it plans and conducts missionary conferences or schools of missions.

Of considerable concern to many individual donors, the mission is also a legal channel through which tax-deductible contributions can be made for missionary work. The American income-tax law does not allow deductions for gifts to individuals.

It seems rather obvious that mission boards are needed to secure, examine and counsel missionary candidates. The local church is not in a position to do this. It may know the candidate and his spiritual fitness for the work. But what it doesn't know is the field and its particular needs. Neither can it provide the accepted candidate with the orientation he ought to have before departure.

When the newly appointed missionary is preparing to leave for the field, he also needs counsel and help in such matters as purchasing equipment, shipping, getting the necessary papers and transportation, etc. In this and many other ways the mission board proves its practical value.

Specific Criticisms

We have stated that mission boards are usually taken for granted. Yet there are many who criticize them without good reason. Some think they are too expensive for the work they do.

Some years ago a certain writer published the claim that one denomination was spending 87 percent of its missionary income on overhead expenses. He justified this claim on the ground that each missionary at that time was getting a salary of $1,000 per year. When he multiplied that amount by the number of missionaries, it only accounted for 13 percent of the total expenditures. All the rest, he concluded, was overhead.

This was far from true. The salary of the individual missionary was indeed $1,000. But that didn't include rent, medical allowances, group insurance, pension payments, and extra allowances in certain fields where inflation was rampant. It didn't even include allowances for the children. The actual average support for each missionary that year came to more than $2,000.

But that was not all. Missionaries had to be transported

to and from the field at mission expense. They had to travel on the field in carrying out their work. They had to be equipped for their job. They had to have literature provided. Equipment and supplies for hospitals and dispensaries were expensive. Seminaries, Bible schools, and schools of other types took money. As a matter of fact, the board's report for that year showed less than 9 percent of its income spent at home, while more than 91 cents out of every dollar contributed was spent on the field.

It may be that some boards are not as economical as they should be. But there is probably no business concern doing business abroad that is getting by with as low a percentage of overhead as even the most extravagant mission board.

Another criticism that is better founded argues that mission boards tend to "go by the book" and not make allowances for individual differences among their missionaries. Some young people get the idea that mission boards discourage innovation. They don't welcome new ideas, new approaches to the task.

It is true in any organization that the "organization man," the one who follows precedent and doesn't disturb the status quo, is most likely to get along with his superiors. No supervisor likes the "odd ball," the fellow who doesn't fit into the pattern. This applies to missions as well as to other organizations. But it would probably amaze many people to know how much experimentation actually does go on in missions. Some missions encourage it more than others. As a result they are making valuable contributions to the work. But none of them allows a new missionary simply to follow his own inclinations. This is too much like a little boy playing with his new chemistry set. He needs some guidance.

17

TYPES OF MISSION BOARDS

DENOMINATIONAL

MOST MISSION BOARDS may be divided into two general types: denominational and independent. We shall talk about the denominational boards first. They were among the first to be set up and they still carry on a large proportion of the Protestant overseas work. In recent years some of them have been changing their structure and they have steadily been losing ground in the percentage of overseas workers. Yet numbers of workers is not the only, nor even the chief, measure of the significance of a work.

In one sense many of the boards, especially those in Europe, were independent in their origin. That is, they began among the churches of a particular denomination. They got their missionaries from that denomination. But they were separately organized through the vision and initiative of a small group of missionary-minded individuals within the denomination. In some cases, especially in Europe, there are several missions supported by members of a single denomination.

In the United States, however, most of these boards have now come under the overall control of the denomination. They have come to be that branch of the denominational structure through which the overseas ministries are carried out. In short, they are the denomination at work abroad. This means that it is usual for each denomination to have only one such board. It is under the control of the governing body of the denomination and makes regular reports to it.

Denominational missions of course depend on the churches of their denomination to provide both the funds and the manpower for their missionary work. Candidates are expected to belong to churches of that denomination. Only occasionally do they make any exception.

The larger denominational boards have work in a number of different fields. Although they may set up a field organization in each of these fields, the board at home has the overall supervision and retains final authority. In earlier days the missionaries often had reason to criticize the boards because they didn't understand the field situation. Today this is not nearly so true. It has become the custom for boards to appoint experienced missionaries as secretaries. Then they have them visit the fields periodically to keep in touch with what is going on.

Though each church in the denomination may be given a quota for its missionary giving, the offerings are still voluntary. The board may make an appeal for money, but that is as far as it can go. Its income depends on the generosity of the members of the churches. It draws up its annual budget and makes its plans on the basis of what it estimates will be the probable giving during the year.

Nevertheless, when the board appoints a missionary it puts him on a regular salary. This salary is almost always small, and it has no relation to the value of his work. Missionary salaries are not competitive, as are salaries at home. Perhaps we ought rather to call them living allowances. The amount varies from field to field according to the cost of living there. It is proportionately more for those who have children, since it is based on needs instead of merit. And because it is intended only to cover the needs of the missionary and his family, the mission does not usually care to appoint missionaries who have dependent relatives or unpaid debts. They wouldn't be able to meet these extra obligations.

One problem in mission financing has always been hard to solve. People just don't like to give to mission boards. Whatever the reason, many of them prefer to give to individual missionaries or to special projects. This has forced missions to adopt various plans of "personalized giving."

Generally the idea is that one or more churches may take on the support of a missionary and consider him their missionary. The missionary then keeps in touch with his supporting church. If it is not his own home church he is expected to visit it when he is home on furlough. The church has little to say about the amount of his allowance. That is set by the board. But the responsibility to provide it is assumed by the church.

INDEPENDENT MISSIONS

There is an increasing number of missions that are not under the control of a church or denomination. These we call independent missions. In most cases they have a self-perpetuating board of directors. That is, if one member of the board resigns or dies, the others elect a man to take his place. In many cases the missionaries themselves are not considered employees of the mission but members of it, having a voice in all its affairs. Sometimes churches and individuals who contribute to the mission more than a stated amount per year are considered members with a right to vote in the annual meeting.

A large part of the independent missions, though not all, are called "faith" missions. They got this name, not because they claimed to have more faith than others but primarily because of certain financial principles. In general they have made it a rule not to solicit funds directly from men but to depend on God for the supply of their needs. In most cases this does not preclude giving information about needs. Some have adopted a sort of watchword: "Full information; no solicitation." They believe that God will move upon the hearts of Christians to give for any work that is truly of Him. Of course under these circumstances they cannot assure their missionaries of any stated salary. They expect each one to look to the Lord to send in what is needed. The plan sounds utterly visionary. But it works. In fact it has proved successful in many missions.

The independent missions get their support from the growing number of independent churches as well as from many individuals and even churches within the denominations. Some simply prefer the independent missions to their own denominational missions. Some are interested in the special ministries that the independent missions represent. Others have enough interest in missions to make these contributions above and beyond what their quota is in the denomination. Denominational stalwarts don't like the idea. They do their best to pressure church members into making all their missionary contributions through the denomination. But they usually find many who resist and even resent such pressures.

Some of the independent missions, especially among the Baptists, are really denominational in character. They are not under the control of the denomination, and sometimes they adopt the faith principle of financing, but in other ways they are denominational. If they are Baptist, all the members of the mission have to be Baptist. Candidates are advised that they must be Baptist "by principle, not for convenience" in order to be appointed. And the churches they establish on the field are Baptist both in name and practice.

But perhaps the largest part of the independent missions are interdenominational faith missions. That is, their membership and support come from different evangelical denominations as well as from the independent churches. They are all conservative in theology. They hold to a brief statement of doctrine that covers the fundamentals of the faith but usually omits some of the controversial points that have separated the denominations. On this basis they welcome Presbyterians, Methodists, Baptists, Congregationalists and many others into their fellowship.

The first of these interdenominational missions, and one that has served as a pattern for many others, was the China Inland Mission, now known as the Overseas Missionary Fellowship. It was founded in England in 1865 by Dr. J. Hudson Taylor. Taylor had spent several years in China as a missionary and then returned home, broken in health. But he had a continuing passion for the conversion of the Chinese people.

Without going into details, these are the facts that led to the starting of the mission. Taylor was burdened for the vast interior of China. But it was not really open at the time. Besides, the missions already in China did not believe they could take on any more responsibilities than what they already had. To reach the interior a new mission would be needed. But it wouldn't have any denomination to sponsor it.

Now Taylor in his experience had come to several personal conclusions. One was that "God's work done in God's way will not lack God's supply." If this was true, then it would be wrong to go into debt. Why should we try to borrow from men what God has seen fit to withhold? Taylor was also sure that evangelism was the great need of inland China. For that purpose it was not necessary to insist on missionaries who had all the educational preparation usually required. He believed the mission boards were passing over many who might prove to be very useful missionaries.

But while Taylor had learned to trust God for his own needs without making appeals to men, it would be different to form a mission on that basis. What if he should get young people out to China, and then the funds should fail? Could he carry such a responsibility? His reluctance was not overcome until he came to realize that if God was moving him to start the mission, the responsibility was God's not his. In that confidence he went ahead.

In the missions that have followed the example of the

China Inland Mission the following principles are generally observed:

1. No solicitation of funds or missionaries is permitted.
2. No debts are allowed.
3. No salary is guaranteed.
4. Missionary candidates from any evangelical denomination are acceptable.
5. Evangelistic work is to have first place.

PLANS OF FINANCING

Even though they hold to the faith principle of
financing, the faith missions do not all understand it in the
same way. So it should not surprise us to find them following different policies in financial matters. They themselves are inclined to stress most their interdenominational
character rather than their financial setup.

Looking realistically at these missions today, we notice
that basically their constituency, both for funds and personnel, has changed since the days of Hudson Taylor. No
longer is it composed largely of isolated individuals who
may feel a special burden to assist a work outside their
own church. There are still many of these, of course. But
there has also grown up a substantial body of churches
and other Christian groups who customarily channel their
missionary interests through the faith missions. There
are even some small denominations who have adopted
one or another of the faith missions as their own mission,
rather than establish a separate denominational society.

Many of these churches want to be informed about
specific financial needs. They are also willing to put a
mission or a missionary on their annual budget for a specified amount of support. It is still their own choice and
may be revoked at any time. Yet the regular contributions
from these groups have come to form a major part of the
income of the faith missions.

The missions have been adjusting their own plans to
the situation. For instance, many are now insisting that a

missionary's support be underwritten by churches or individuals before he departs for the field. This, they contend, does not denote a lack of faith, for there is no firm guarantee that the promises of support will be fulfilled. Yet it is a departure from earlier procedures.

Just how are the missionaries supported? Here we must describe two basic plans, though they are subject to innumerable modifications.

Pooling plan. First is the pooling plan. Under this plan the mission puts all contributions for missionary support into one common fund or pool. When the regular distribution is made, usually once a month, each missionary gets his share, up to what is considered to be a full allowance. Single missionaries in the same field all get the same amount. Married missionaries get larger amounts, depending on the number of children they have. There are numerous other details, but the principle is that of share and share alike.

The missions usually set up some definite amount for each field as a full allowance, an amount that they think will cover the missionaries' needs. The difference between this and a stated salary is that there is no guarantee that the full amount will be paid unless the funds come in. The larger missions can usually foretell their probable receipts with reasonable accuracy, so they draw up a budget on that basis.

The pooling plan has several *advantages.* It avoids inequalities among the missionaries, since all share alike. The missionary with a thrilling story to tell gets no more than the one whose service is more humdrum but perhaps just as valuable. Even if people at home try to bypass the pool and send their contributions directly to the missionary, it makes no difference. He usually has to report these receipts and they are counted in the common pool and deducted from his next remittance from the mission.

Most missions do, however, allow bona fide gifts for such things as birthdays, Christmas, a new baby, etc., with-

out their entering into the pool. In fact, the mission itself
will gladly transmit such gifts for the donor. They can
usually do it with greater safety than he can. They will
issue him a special receipt for the amount. At the same
time the donor needs to be aware that such personal gifts
may be disallowed as income-tax deductions.

The plan also impresses upon the missionary the need
of praying for the needs of the whole mission and not just
his own. When one profits, all profit; when one gets a
short remittance, they are all short. No one is ever left completely without support, even if his supporting church
drops him. This tends to greater unity in the mission
and emphasizes the mission rather than the individual
missionary.

But the plan also has some *weaknesses.* Much depends
on the confidence in those who administer the funds. It
has happened that a mission under this plan has unwisely
sent to the field more missionaries than it could properly support. Then all the missionaries suffered hardship.
(Though it should be said to the credit of the missionaries
that they didn't complain.) But the greatest weakness is
the attitude of the donors. Many of them insist that they
want their contributions to go exclusively to the individual
missionary they are supporting. They don't want them
pooled. No amount of explanation will satisfy these donors.
If their missionary doesn't get for his work just what they
send, then they won't send.

Individual-support-plan. That is one thing that has
given rise to the second plan, the individual-support plan.
Under this plan the individual missionary gets exactly whatever his friends and supporters contribute for him and his
work. It may be much or little. But it must be specified for
him. The mission will provide donors with information
about the amount he should have, but it doesn't take the
responsibility to see that he gets it.

However, it does make this provision: All unspecified
contributions go into a general fund. This fund is meant

to cover expenses of the work that are not included in the missionary's personal support. If the missionary does not get enough personal support for his needs, the mission may make up the difference from the general fund, providing there is enough money to do so.

The individual-support plan also has some *advantages.* It capitalizes on the desire of so many donors to contribute toward the work of individual missionaries. It creates a close bond between the donors and the missionary they support. It also spurs the missionary to keep in touch with those who support him. He can't count on being carried along by what others do.

But it also has its *weaknesses.* Contributions to the general fund are usually inadequate. Too many people prefer to contribute for the work of an individual they know rather than for the overall work of the mission. Some missionaries also enjoy better support than others whose work is equally valuable. Either they have more friends or they may be better at inspiring interest through their talks and letters. And because the worker stands out more than the work, the sense of unity in the mission is weakened.

The picture we have given of these two plans is far from complete. We have oversimplified it. Most missions today use some modification of one or another of the basic plans. This is particularly true of those that use the individual-support plan. Tax rulings have made it necessary for them to have effective control of the funds contributed. At the same time they are allowed to accept contributions toward the salaries of individual missionaries or the work under their charge. So their official receipts usually indicate that they are "for the work under the charge of" a certain missionary.

It has become quite common for the faith missions to expect their missionaries to get both personal and service support. That is, of the amount that each missionary is expected to receive, a certain part is designated as service support. This money is to cover services rendered by the mission on behalf of the missionary but which he does not personally pay. It may include such things as the cost of sending his money to him, his rent or other provision for housing, the costs of administration, and his share in any number of other expenditures that benefit his work. This relieves some of the pressure on the usually depleted general fund.

Each mission is willing to explain its particular plan of financing to any donor or candidate on request.

18

HOW TO CHOOSE A MISSION

THE PROBLEM

TO MANY PEOPLE the choice of a mission is no problem at all. They are members of one of our Protestant denominations. They are either responding to a general call, or they believe they are called to a specific field or work in which their denomination is working. Moreover, they see no reason why they should not be accepted and work in harmony with their denominational board.

There are advantages in working with the mission of your own denomination. As a missionary it makes you feel that you represent not just the local church to which you belong but the whole denomination. Other churches besides your own presumably have a concern in your work.

In addition, you work on the field with other missionaries who come from churches like your own. Their doctrinal views are largely the same. The churches they have started use an organization you are familiar with, and in many other ways you are made to feel at home. Sometimes too, you will find in the mission an organizational and financial stability that is not always present in the independent missions.

But, for some, even in the denominations, the matter is not all that simple. There are reasons why some hesitate to ask for appointment under their denominational board. Boards, and even pastors, don't always appreciate those reasons, but to the missionary volunteer they are very real.

One of the main reasons is theological liberalism. Not in the official statements of belief; probably none of the denominations have officially adopted creeds that are clearly liberal, even though there are trends in this direction. It is the prevalent interpretations of these statements of faith that are disturbing, or the more or less obvious omissions. So a great deal depends on the local leadership. Even in the more liberal denominations there are individual churches that do not follow the liberal trend. It is also true that there are many members of liberal churches who are not in agreement with their liberalism but have not yet come to the point of leaving them.

Conditions are not the same in all denominations. Neither are they the same in all mission fields of the same denomination. Generally the churches in mission lands have tended to be more conservative than the churches at home. Yet it is not at all uncommon to have a young person say, "I would prefer not to serve under my denominational board; it is too liberal."

We have mentioned that the board doesn't always appreciate this viewpoint. Sometimes it insists that it has no objection to the candidate's holding to his own more conservative beliefs if he wants to. It can't understand why he won't be just as tolerant of the beliefs of others.

But it is more than a matter of personal viewpoints. It is a matter of basic principles. We can be tolerant of others' beliefs if the differences are not important to us. We can't be so tolerant if we believe they are basic issues.

In such a case it seems to us that the candidate's hesitation is perfectly proper. If the missionaries are not agreed on their message, how can their mission be successful? And if a missionary cannot have spiritual fellowship with the other members of his own mission, how can he stand the strain of missionary life and render good service? Some have tried it and have given up.

There are others who do not want to work with their denominational boards because they believe they have been called to another field or type of ministry than the ones in which their board is engaged. Sometimes this happens when the board's ministry is almost wholly institutional and not evangelistic. For it is true that in some of the major denominational missions, evangelism holds a very minor place.

Then there are some who might like to work with their denomination but can't meet the requirements, especially in the matter of education. Also there are actually quite a few young people who have come to dislike the narrow denominationalism of their churches and would like to serve in a broader fellowship.

Add to these the members of the many independent churches, and members of denominations too small to support an extensive missionary work of their own, and you have a large group of young people who need to know how to choose a mission board. Their choice is made doubly hard because many of the independent missions work in only one field. Thus the choice of a mission is also the choice of a field.

How to Proceed

In those cases where the volunteer is *sure of his field,* the following suggestions may prove helpful:

1. Find out what boards are in that field.

2. Get all the information you can about the missions there and the work they are doing.

3. Write to those with whom you might be interested in serving. Tell them of your interest and ask for more information about the mission, its organization, principles, requirements, etc. At the same time don't fail to tell them something about yourself, your age, preparation, present situation, and motives for seeking appointment. They need to know whether to encourage you to pursue the matter with their society.

4. If possible, have personal interviews with mission representatives and individual missionaries.

5. Above all, and through it all, be sure to wait on the Lord for His guidance.

You may possibly experience a special divine call to a certain work. But whether you do or not, you should come to a wholehearted conviction that the mission you finally choose is the one with which the Lord wants you to serve.

If the prospective missionary is *not sure of his field,* he may do one of two things. He may wait until the Lord shows him the field. Or he may choose a mission after prayerful consideration because he believes it is the sort of mission in which he can work with greatest harmony and effectiveness.

This latter course of action is usually the better. We have already seen that a missionary call is not necessarily associated with any particular field of service. It is quite the common thing for zealous young missionary volunteers to be uncertain about the precise field in which they are to serve. If they waited to be sure of the field before approaching a mission, many would never reach any field.

The relative unimportance of knowing the exact field is to be seen in the fact that many a missionary today is serving, and serving successfully, in another area than the one he originally had in mind. In fact, hundreds of missionaries have been transferred from one field to another without losing any of their effectiveness. As an example, see what happened to many of the China missionaries after that field was closed.

Much more important is the mission board. A real missionary is seldom disappointed in his field after he gets there. But there are all too many occasions when he becomes disappointed in the mission with which he is working. It is amazing how little attention many seem to pay to this matter. As if the people you work with in the Lord's service were always easy to get along with! Or Christian leaders were always wise and considerate!

Evaluating a Mission

There are a number of specific things about a mission that every candidate ought to find out if he can. We shall list them here in the form of questions. They are not necessarily in the order of importance.

DOCTRINAL STANDARDS

What is the theological position of the mission and its missionaries? It is easy to get an answer to this question. The mission usually has an official doctrinal statement that it publishes from time to time in its magazine. If not, the mission will gladly send it to you. Do you agree with it fully? If you have any hesitation, move slowly. Of course, if you are not in full sympathy with what it stands for, the mission probably wouldn't accept your application anyway.

FINANCES

Are the mission accounts regularly audited? Is the audit published so that anyone may examine it? For most people it makes dull reading, but you can well be suspicious of any mission that does not publish such a statement.

What plan of missionary support does it use? Is it pooling, individual support, or some modification? You may not have any preference, but you ought to know which is actually used.

Are the missionaries well cared for? This is not always easy to find out. It might influence your decision though, especially where the funds are pooled.

ORIGIN AND AIMS

How and why did the mission start? If it is a split-off from another group, then why? If the reason was good and sound, the mission itself will not hesitate to tell about it. If it does hesitate, be careful.

Is the mission meeting a real need? That is, is it performing a service that is badly needed and that no other group is doing or could do? Or is it in the same area with other good missions and competing with them? There is more of this than the people at home realize. It may be best to get this information from sources outside the mission itself.

ORGANIZATION AND METHODS

Young people are not always the best judges in the matter of organization and methods. They haven't had enough experience. Yet they should not be so willfully blind as the pastor who wrote us for information about a certain mission. He said, "Please tell me about its doctrinal position and its financial honesty. I am not interested in its methods."

Is the control in the hands of one or two individuals? In some very small missions this may not be significant. However, a personal or family dictatorship never works out well. Incorporation doesn't mean a thing in this regard. It has mostly to do with financial responsibility.

On the other hand, it is just as dangerous for the individual missionary to have too much independence. There needs to be authority that is recognized and obeyed.

Who is on the governing board of the mission? Who sponsors its work? Don't be misled by the so-called "councils of reference." These are just lists of men who have consented to having their names used to recommend the mission. They may know something about its affairs, but just as often they know little more than that they have a good impression of its leadership or its work. They are window dressing. They are not the actual leaders. They have no authority in the mission itself.

FELLOWSHIP

Relations with other missionaries on the field are so close that it is important to have a good basis for real fellowship. A fellowship that might be very enjoyable to one person might not suit another at all. For this reason it is good to have an opportunity to get acquainted with some of the missionaries before actually applying to the mission.

Often a young person, after meeting the leaders of the work, can well ask himself this question: Are these the kind of leaders I would be glad to follow? Are they people who can inspire me to do my best in the Lord's service?

Another practical question: Are the other missionaries of your nationality and culture? It is not easy to be a foreigner in a foreign land and at the same time feel that you are a foreigner in your own mission. Some of us can work very congenially with those of another national or cultural background. But we may as well face it that the adjustment is more than many can make very readily. As fellow Christian workers we ought to be able to do it, but all too often we don't.

REPUTATION

Does the mission have a good name among other missions? Remember, other missions in the field are in a better position to judge the value of a work than are the people in the homeland. In most cases they are inclined to be charitable in their judgments. One or two might possibly give a bad report of another mission through jealousy. However, if several agree in such a report, you do well to be wary.

You can judge the interdenominational missions on this point by seeing whether they are members of the Interdenominational Foreign Mission Association of North America (IFMA).* Only missions that have a good reputation among others are accepted into this association. In addition to being interdenominational, they must also be evangelical in their theology, follow the faith principle

*54 Bergen Avenue, Ridgefield Park, New Jersey 07660.

of missionary operation, and publish an annual audit of their accounts. Missions in the association have a total missionary force of well over eight thousand missionaries.

MISSIONARY TURNOVER

Do the missionaries generally stay with the mission? Allow for some who have to leave the work because of illness or some other good reason. But does the number of those who leave the mission within a limited time seem unreasonably high? Do they go back for a second, third and other terms of service? An unusually high turnover always means there is something wrong, regardless of the reasons the missionaries may officially give for their leaving.

Although the suggestions we have just made are useful, they will not settle the question for you. The decision is yours. You are the one who will have to live with it. Besides, there are some factors in the decision that are known only to you and to God. Be utterly frank with Him and trust Him to lead you to the best choice.

19

INDEPENDENT MISSIONARIES

WHO THEY ARE

ON THE FRINGE of the missionary movement are a great many independent missionaries. They are called independent missionaries because they are not connected with any organized missionary society. Each one carries on his work independent of anyone else on the field, and usually independent of any authority in the homeland.

There are a number of reasons for these independent missionaries. Many of them originally went to the field under some organized society. Then, for one reason or another, they withdrew from the society but decided to keep on working in the same general area. Some of them are individuals who find it hard to work in harmony with others, or to submit to authority. In other cases their mission itself may have been at least partly at fault. In any case they are missionaries who don't join another society but go on working alone.

There are others who go to the field independently because they haven't found a mission that would accept them. It may be a matter of health or age or some other lack in their qualifications. At any rate, the regular missions have turned them down for one reason or another. Yet somehow they find a way of getting enough financial support to go out on their own.

A third group are those who believe they have a call to a specific field but can't find a satisfactory mission in that field. There may be some extremists among them who are very hard to please, or even some who really don't want to be limited by authority over them. But often their argument is perfectly valid. There just isn't any suitable mission for them in that particular field.

A last group, and one that we want to deal with separately, is what are commonly called "nonprofessional" missionaries. Some of them are Christians whom circumstances, such as employment, have taken to other lands, where they do what they can in a missionary way. Others are earnest believers who have deliberately chosen to go to foreign countries to practice their trade or profession in order that they might do some missionary work. They support themselves by their earnings, try to live a consistent Christian life, and devote their spare time to witnessing for Christ.

QUESTIONS TO CONSIDER

The two groups to which we are going to give most of our attention are the second and third. These are the ones who deliberately choose to go to the field independent of any mission society and give their full time to missionary work. They are continually approaching missionary counselors, explaining what they want to do, and then asking, "Would you advise me to go out independently?"

I have never yet heard of an experienced missionary who answered *yes* to such a question. He will usually mention a number of reasons why such a course would be very unwise. But he is often too polite to raise *two basic questions* that the inquirer ought honestly to face.

The first is this: "If the regular mission boards have turned you down, are you really fit for missionary service?" The missions do sometimes make mistakes. Sometimes they turn down a candidate who would make a good missionary. More often they accept one who should not be accepted. But they are much less liable to mistakes than is the individual. Before going ahead, make doubly sure that it is really the mission that is making the mistake and not you. Remember that if you were judged unlikely to succeed in the mission, with all the assistance it offers, you will stand even less chance independently.

The second question is for those who can't find a satisfactory mission in their chosen field. "Just why are you so sure that you should go to that field and not to any other?" Sometimes the candidate speaks quite confidently of having had a call. And of course if it is God's calling, none of us would want to stand in the way. But there are so many imitations of the call of God. There are so many young people who feel attracted to certain fields without knowing a thing about the real situation there and what the needs are. It is the field that attracts them, sometimes little more than a name on a map, and not needy human beings. So be sure that it is God's call you hear and not simply the echo of your own desires.

THEIR HANDICAPS

Now there may be an overpowering reason or a distinct call that will lead a missionary into independent work. But before he decides to undertake it, and before any local church or individual decides to sponsor it, they should both know some of the handicaps that he will confront.

ENTRANCE INTO THE COUNTRY

First of all, there are some countries today into which no missionary can gain an entrance unless he comes as the representative of a recognized society. This is not because the government discriminates against one form of Christianity or another. It is simply that it has found it much better to deal with responsible organizations than with every Tom, Dick, and Harry.

CHOICE OF LOCATION

Second, just where are you going and what is the need there? When a well-organized board decides to open a new field, it doesn't blindly plunge into it. First of all it makes a careful survey to find out what the needs are. It

consults with other missions in the field so as not to dupli-
cate what they are doing. In the light of these studies it
plans its occupation of the area.

The independent missionary almost never does this.
His choice of location is largely a hit-or-miss proposition.
More often than not he hits on a well-known place where
he comes into competition with other missions. Of course
he seldom mentions this in his letters home.

It is true that there are great needs in nearly all fields.
So if the independent missionary will work in cooperation
with others, letting his work supplement theirs, he can
often find a niche where he can make a real contribution.
He may even, after a time, be welcomed into the ranks
of one of the established missions. It has happened. But
most independent missionaries are not of this nature. They
are intent on starting a work all of their own, be it ever
so tiny and lacking in stability.

EXPERIENCED COUNSEL

Third, a serious practical difficulty faces the independent missionary from the beginning. It is his lack of
experienced counsel. He doesn't know what kind nor how
much of an outfit to take with him. In normal times he
experiences little difficulty in arranging transportation
to the principal ports or airports of a country. But when
the newcomer without help tries to proceed inland, away
from the well-traveled routes, he soon finds himself at
the mercy of any glib swindler with a smattering of English.
Of course he doesn't yet know the language of the country,
and he is not familiar with its currency nor the legitimate
prices. Not knowing where to find lodging, he usually takes
advantage of the hospitality of some other missionary. (I
have often admired the long-suffering generosity of missionaries in the major cities. How often they are imposed
on!) At every step in his inexperience he makes unnecessary blunders from which the counsel of others could have
saved him.

SIZE OF THE WORK

And what work is he going to do? Supposing he has somehow learned the language, and found or built a suitable house, and learned how to get along in the land. What will his ministry be? At home he would be called to the pastorate of a church already established. That would be a big enough job for one man. Here he can't possibly do all that needs to be done.

There is the literature, for example. Even supposing the Bible has already been translated by someone else into the language of his people, where is he going to get the other Christian literature—the Sunday school lessons, the devotional books, the Christian magazines—that are so helpful to the pastor at home? He must depend on others. And who will teach his teachers? Who will train his young people for Christian service? He can't do all of this by himself. Missionary work is just too big for any one person. It calls for cooperation.

Even as the work is too big for the independent missionary working alone, so the independent church resulting from his ministry is too small for satisfactory Christian fellowship and service. We often see this in what happens to the young people. When the time comes to marry, they are told that they should marry in the church. Yet their own church fellowship is so limited that they have little choice. The result is that many marry outside the church and are lost to it. And who has ever attended a conference of churches on the mission field and has not been thrilled to witness the joy of the believers as they gathered? How much it means to them to realize that their small congregation is only a part of a much larger fellowship!

DEPARTURE FROM THE FIELD

But the final and often the greatest test of the work of the independent missionary comes when he must leave that work. It may be for furlough; it may be permanently. Furlough is always a problem. It is a problem even when another missionary can fill in for the one on furlough. But in the organized mission the problem is minimized. Usually the mission can assign someone to fill in temporarily for the absent missionary. Or, if not, it will make some other provision to take care of the work. It is not likely to abandon it.

The independent missionary, however, has little choice. In most cases he must either give up the idea of a furlough, or he must abandon the work for the time his furlough lasts. In the first instance he may be jeopardizing his health or sacrificing important contacts with his supporters at home. In the second he is risking a breakdown in the work during his absence. Whichever he does, the work is likely to suffer.

Sometimes young people have objected, "But he ought to have a national worker prepared to take over by the time he goes on furlough." Such a statement shows lack of experience and understanding of missionary work. Unless he is building on a foundation that someone else has laid, the missionary will rarely have a worker prepared to take full responsibility for the work in just one term. If he could do so, what would be his justification for going back after furlough? But it just doesn't happen that way.

Of course there inevitably comes a time when the independent missionary dies or has to leave the field permanently. Then the situation is likely to be even more critical. The best thing would be for some mission to take over and continue the work. Sometimes this occurs. But perhaps more often the work is simply abandoned.

NONPROFESSIONAL MISSIONARIES

We have already explained what nonprofessional missionaries are. In one sense they are independent, for they are not definitely connected with a mission society. In another sense they are not, for they seldom attempt to carry on a complete missionary ministry apart from what others are doing. We might rather call them auxiliary missionaries.

VALUES

There are some very real values in the service of these part-time missionaries. One is the same as the value of the testimony of the Christian businessman in the United States. It helps people to realize that Christianity is not just for the preachers; it is a vital faith in everyday life. Rightly or wrongly, some people get the idea that Christianity for the preacher is a livelihood; for the businessman it is a conviction.

Besides this, the businessman can sometimes reach individuals and even groups that are closed to the missionary. In his contacts with other businessmen and in his relations with government officials he can often speak a word in season about his Saviour. He may even get into a lengthy discussion of the Christian faith with them. People don't think this is inappropriate in other lands. Often they are much more ready to bring religion into an ordinary conversation than are our own people.

A third value of the nonprofessional missionary is that he may at times gain an entrance into lands that are closed to the regular missionary. That is, he can go in not as a missionary but as a businessman, an engineer, a professor, or something else. If he is wise and tactful in his approach he may possibly be the opening wedge for a full proclamation of the gospel at a later date. At any rate he has the opportunity of demonstrating Christianity by his own sincere profession of faith and his Christian manner of living and dealing.

HANDICAPS

But don't think there are no handicaps! There are a number of them and one should understand them clearly. If you do understand them it will take away the false impression that this is an easier and more effective way of doing missionary work. It is surprising how many get this false idea. We insist that it is a valuable service, and one in which we wish many more Christians would engage. But it is not easy, and its effectiveness is not to be compared with that of the full-time missionaries. Here are three of the reasons:

Full-time job. First, the one who is hired to do any secular job is expected to give full-time service on that job. He is not paid to be a missionary but to be a geologist, an engineer, a doctor, or whatever his profession or vocation is. It is only his spare time that he can devote to missionary work. That is, aside from casual conversations in the course of his employment. Besides, after a full day of hard work, it takes real consecration to take on other responsibilities of a missionary sort. Of course, too, his missionary service is necessarily limited to the vicinity of his place of employment. He is not free to itinerate, as a missionary does, except on vacation.

Foreign employee. He usually encounters a second handicap in the very nature of his employment. Most such men are in the employ of foreign companies. So quite naturally the people think of them primarily as employees of the company. Presumably their interests are the same as the company's interests. If the people think, as they often do, that the company is exploiting them for its own advantage, then its foreign employees must be simply a part of the plan. If any of them preach the gospel, it must be so the people will become more pliable tools of the company. Even full-time missionaries are often accused of being paid agents of their own government. How much more the employee of a large foreign corporation.

Company relations. In the third place, the one who plans to be a nonprofessional missionary is likely to find himself seriously hampered by the ones he works for and with. The company itself will not be much interested in his missionary purpose. In fact, it may be strongly opposed. Not that it opposes Christianity as such. Rather, it just doesn't want its employees engaged in any activities that might put the company in a bad light or jeopardize its earnings. In some countries this is not much of a problem. In others, as in strongly Muslim lands, it may be a serious one. In such places some companies oblige their employees to sign an agreement that they will in no way interfere with the religion of the people.

Aside from this, the employee needs to realize that he will probably be working in a nonchristian land with other foreigners who are not Christian in their manner of living. That is, many of those who go overseas for business reasons may be members of Christian churches at home. But all too often they appear to leave their Christian principles, with their membership, at home. Dan Crawford once wrote about Central Africa, "In this climate European meat goes bad, European dogs go bad, and European morals go bad."

The employee may be fortunate enough to find some good Christian fellowship in his work. There are indeed a number of fine Christian businessmen in other lands. But in most cases the situation will be just the opposite. The Christian must be prepared to stand alone, if need be, and to resist the constant pull that would bring him down to the level of the others. His very loneliness will make the temptations, when they come, all the stronger.

No, it is not an easy service, and the visible results are often disappointing. But it is a valuable service, *principally for those who could not qualify for full-time missionary service.*

This one thing must be borne in mind: It is a challenging opportunity for those who have not been called to a full-time ministry but are willing to carry on their trade or profession in a foreign land, where their witness for Christ may help bring men to Him. If supposedly Christian businessmen abroad were as zealous for their faith as are the Muslim traders in Africa, what a tremendous effect their witness could have!

20

WHAT A MISSIONARY DOES—
PRELIMINARY TASKS

THE TITLE OF THIS SECTION is presumptuous—almost ridiculous. Who could possibly compress into two or three chapters all the multitude of activities in which missionaries engage? And who could describe the activities of a missionary in Latin America and presume that the same ones would be carried on in New Guinea?

Yet it seems wise to attempt some sort of description of a missionary's ministry. If for no other reason, the people at home have conjured up such a fictitious idea of a missionary's life that they need a corrective. Besides, the young people who are volunteering for missionary service ought to have some idea of what that service involves.

Actually, in spite of the great variety of missionary activities, there are some that are common to all lands and to most missionaries. There are also some principles that are valid everywhere, though the way we apply them will differ in different circumstances. We are not going to try to give a complete picture. We are going to concentrate on just a few features, trusting that this rough sketch will be reasonably accurate and suggestive of the many details we shall have to omit.

Judging from the questions they ask, most people seem to think of the missionary as a sort of combination itinerant evangelist and handyman. They are usually inclined to think that he has a rather hard life. Some, on the contrary, would insist that the picture has been overdrawn and that missionaries have it easy. They must live a sort of "life of Riley" among the poverty-stricken natives. All will agree that there must be something of glamour and adventure in missionary life. All faraway lands and strange people are glamorous from a distance.

As for the missionary's work, they think it consists almost entirely of preaching sermons and getting people to join his church. Of course they realize that his work involves travels and dangers—look at David Livingstone! And the missionary may have to turn builder or medicine man on occasion. But most of all he preaches to ignorant, uncultured natives.

It is not enough for us to say that this is a very distorted picture. Nor even that it is insulting to the people to whom the missionary goes. It is not enough to remind people that the world is changing and that we are not living in the days of Livingstone. We need to present a more realistic picture. We need to give some idea of the complexities of the situation the missionary faces.

LANGUAGE STUDY

The *first task* of the new missionary is to go to school. Does this sound strange? You might think that after all his years of preparation in the homeland he should now be ready to begin his ministry. But not so. In most cases he still has the task of learning the language of the people to whom he is to minister. And this is not easy.

In fact, because it is such a job, there are always some who try to shortcut language study or to bypass it altogether. Many have attempted to carry on a ministry through interpreters. Shortly after World War II a number of American evangelists went to Japan and preached by interpretation. They sent home marvelous reports of the success of their efforts. When some questioned whether the results were not more apparent than real, they became indignant. One young student, a member of a youth team, vehemently insisted that they had had wonderful results—he had seen them himself! How he could know what was going on in the minds and hearts of the people when he couldn't understand a thing they said is a mystery.

Interpretation does have its values. It is useful when the people are so interested in the speaker himself that they are anxious to get any sort of message from him. This often happens when a strange foreigner appears. Curiosity draws a crowd. It isn't the message so much as the speaker who interests them. They want to hear him even if they don't understand what he is talking about.

It is also useful when the speaker has a message whose importance the people recognize and which they couldn't get in any other way. They know they won't get it perfectly, but at least they will get some of the main ideas. This is true in important conferences where persons of various nationalities attend. Addresses given in one language have to be interpreted for those who speak others.

Yet speaking by interpretation is always a poor substitute for speaking directly in the language of the people. I remember with amusement the introduction a Central American pastor once gave me to his congregation. It was a congregation that had had to listen to a number of interpreted messages by foreign visitors during the preceding months. In concluding his introduction he remarked, "You will be able to understand him. He speaks our language!"

To realize the ineffectiveness of the interpreted message, just put yourself in the place of the other person. Suppose a Buddhist missionary came to your community to try to win converts for his faith, but he could not speak English. Since he has come from an Oriental country, you might be curious to see and hear him for a time or two. Of course you would have to sit twice as long as usual to get his message, since he first says a few things in his own tongue and then the interpreter tries to tell what he means in English.

If the interpreter seems to be very fluent in his interpretation, you naturally wonder just how much of his own ideas he has put in. Or if the interpreter is himself a convinced Buddhist, and so is interpreting with great fluency, you wonder why he doesn't do the preaching himself. Except, of course, that a foreigner does attract the curious. And if the interpreter is obviously being very careful to interpret accurately, and so speaks rather awkwardly, what becomes of the oratory, the fine reasoning, the warm passion of the original speaker? These are things that can't be interpreted on the spur of the moment.

Of course if interpretation is not very effective in evangelizing, it is much less so in teaching, in building up and guiding a newly founded church, etc. Yet these are some of the most important activities in sound missionary work. Really there is no substitute for the accurate learning of the national language. Shortcuts are just blind alleys.

There are various ways in which new missionaries learn the language. The best way is usually the language school. Sometimes a large mission like the Overseas Missionary Fellowship conducts its own language school. At other times, as in India, the language school is a sort of joint enterprise and missionaries from all missions attend. The language school has several advantages. It usually has a carefully planned course, experienced teachers who give full time to the job, and no other obligations to distract the new missionary from his main job of learning the language. In some cases, as in two or three of the Spanish language schools in Latin America, many of the students are not even in the country where they are to serve. It is after about a year in the language school that they move on to their assigned posts.

For French- and Portuguese-speaking territories in Africa the missionaries have to learn at least two languages. They must know the language of the government as well as that of the tribe in which they work. This often means language study in Europe for perhaps a year before going on to Africa.

Still there are many other cases where the missionaries have to be taught right on their stations. It may be that only one or two new missionaries arrive in any one year to begin work in this particular language area. To conduct a language school just for them is out of the question. So either a senior missionary has to take on the task or a national must be hired to do the teaching. Then unless the national is adept in both languages, it often works out best for the missionary to teach the grammar, while the national teaches pronunciation, conversation, reading and writing.

Of course some missionaries face languages that have not yet been reduced to writing and for which there are no grammars prepared. Here the missionary has real need for the special linguistic training available today in the homeland. Also he must expect that it will take him much longer to learn the language than others who have the advantage of grammars, dictionaries, trained teachers, etc.

The length of time for language study varies. Some languages are more difficult for one who speaks English than others. Also the concentrated course in a language school is bound to take less time than the one class a day that a senior missionary can possibly give. A full year in the language school is not at all unreasonable. At the end of that time the student is still far from having a complete mastery of the language, but he will probably be able to enter fully into the work. His mission may then require that he do further study and reading after he reaches his station.

Sometimes people who have never learned another language wonder why it takes so long. They think there must be some easier way. They point to the fact that little children seem to "pick up" a language in short time. Why can't older people do the same thing?

There are several reasons. It is true that little children often get a fluency and an accurate pronunciation that puts their parents to shame. But we must realize that their habits of pronunciation in English are not yet so firmly fixed that they can't adjust readily to new sounds. Then too they are not so afraid of being embarrassed. They mimic the words and expressions they hear, repeat them over and over to themselves, and blurt them out at every opportunity, even when they don't fit. So what if they do make a mistake? What if people do laugh? The children can laugh right along with them, and they learn from the mistake.

Besides this, little children are very limited in their conversation. If the missionary were willing to confine himself to childish prattle he wouldn't need to study so long. But a proper use of the language in conveying the profound truths of the gospel calls for much more than this. After all, how many years do we have to study English in our schools in order to become acceptable ministers of God's Word? And this in spite of the fact that we started to speak it before we were three years old.

What most of us fail to realize is that learning a new language is more than just learning a new set of words to take the place of our English words. Language is a means of expressing thought. And the thoughts of other people are not always the same as our thoughts. Neither do they use the same way of expressing similar thoughts.

For instance, we have a common word "to lack." But Holman Bentley tells us that in a certain tribe in the Congo there is no one word that bears that meaning. If you mean "to lack something you never had," you use one word. But if you mean "to lack what you once possessed," it is a different word. Americans studying Spanish are always confused by the fact that a Spanish-speaking person never "likes" anything. Instead it "is pleasing to him," thus reversing subject and object.

So the new missionary confronts this problem. He must not only memorize a complete new set of words, with an entirely different sort of pronunciation. He must also learn new patterns of thinking and new ways of expressing thought. It is through the language that he begins his job of getting into the life of the people. He must understand them, and they must understand him, or else his ministry will be in vain.

We have dealt rather extensively with this first task of the new missionary. This is because it is so little understood or appreciated at home. Yet it is so very vital to the work. If we were to pick out one of the most glaring weaknesses in the missionary enterprise as a whole, it would certainly be the failure of so many missionaries to get a really good command of the native tongue.

KNOWING THE PEOPLE

The new missionary also has another important and related job. It is to learn to know the people. At the same time that he is studying the language he is learning something about the people. But he needs to know more. Sometimes a veteran of many years will say, "I suppose we never do get to think just the way the people do. Maybe that is why we are not more effective."

But whether the missionary ever does get to think just exactly as the people do, he tries to understand them as best he can. This is a vital part of his ministry. In this he tries to follow Christ, the master Missionary, identifying himself as much as possible with the people to whom he is sent. If he doesn't entirely succeed, we still know that he has probably gotten closer to the heart of the people than any other outsider.

It is no wonder that missionaries on furlough sometimes speak of the people as "my people" or "my tribe." Perhaps less often the people themselves speak of the missionary as one of themselves. Yet one Presbyterian missionary in Shantung actually had the experience of being adopted into a Chinese family as a daughter. And in Japan another missionary won popular acclaim by attending classes in school along with Japanese children so as to learn their language better.

The missionary doesn't think of his learning to know

the people as a job. It isn't a subject that he can very well study in the classroom. Yet it is something that does take a good deal of his time and attention.

He soon finds that you can only learn to know people as you come into personal contact with them. He must visit much with them in their homes. He must eat with them, often dipping his fingers into the same bowl of food. He must enter into their sports, where they don't conflict with Christian principles. He must also enter into their sorrows. You can often learn more about people at a wake than at a church service. He must welcome them into his own home and perhaps spend long hours conversing with them — about nothing in particular.

It all takes time, time that impatient missionaries often think could be better spent at more productive tasks. But it is really the very fountain of productiveness. You must win the confidence of the people if you want them to trust your message. And confidence is not something that you can win overnight, especially if you are a foreigner.

JUST LIVING

One thing the missionary doesn't like to tell the folks at home about, for fear they won't understand. This is the amount of time he has to spend for just living. In fact, he often finds it irritating to himself and wishes he could do more about it. Yet in spite of himself he finds that he must keep on spending a considerable amount of his time and energy with the details of just carrying on his daily life.

What we mean is this: We scarcely realize in the homeland how convenient life has been made for us with a multitude of aids for living. We don't mean such modern helps as electric dishwashers, garbage-disposal units and air conditioners. Rather we mean the many other ordinary conveniences that most people take for granted.

Not many of our young people today know what it means to clean and trim a kerosene lamp. They flip a switch and have light. When they want a drink, they go to the faucet or water cooler, with never a thought as to the purity of the water. They can buy all of their food in one store, most of it in sanitary packages, cans or jars. If they do any baking or canning, it is either to save money or because they like it, not because they have to. They buy their bread already sliced and can even get many foods precooked.

These are just some of the common things. In fact, they are so common that we can hardly conceive of life without them. Every day new conveniences are being introduced to make life easier. The only thing that keeps us from getting most of them is the cost. Even in remote areas they are readily available from the mail-order house.

What of the missionary? Can he enjoy these same helps? In some places he can. Other countries are introducing these things as fast as they can. But often they are not available. The only way to have electricity in many mission stations is to put in your own plant. This sounds easy. But have you ever tried to keep an electric light plant in regular operation over a long period of time, with no repairman within a day's journey? Even if you are a competent mechanic yourself, it is going to absorb quite a bit of your time.

And drinking water. Boiling the water for drinking is just routine for many a missionary family. Sometimes it has to be both filtered and boiled. That takes time. And don't think this concerns only the out-of-the-way places. Some of the world's principal cities do not have safe drinking water.

Even cooking may be a problem. Electric stoves are usually out. Gas stoves using bottled gas are a possibility in some places. Kerosene and gasoline stoves are perhaps more often used, but they do need quite a bit of attention. There is sometimes a clogged generator to clean or a troublesome wick to attend to. And many missionaries must depend on wood, charcoal or sawdust for their heating or cooking.

Then the food. Many a missionary remembers with longing the supermarket or even the corner grocery at home. Of course if there is a daily public market nearby, he can send there to get whatever is available, though this means that the wife can never be entirely sure just what to count on in planning the meals. Also, there won't be many prepared foods. The preparing will have to be done at home. As for the marketing itself, it saves time to hire somebody to do it, since often a great deal of bargaining is involved. But it doesn't save money.

In most of the mission fields the automobile has proved to be very helpful in the work as roads have been built. But again, automobiles mean repairs, and repairs take time. But for all that, even in the old days, when most missionaries counted themselves fortunate to have a good horse or a mule for traveling, it took a lot of time to feed and care for these animals.

What we have tried to do in this section is simply to give some impression of the multitude of "chores" that occupy so much of a missionary's time. We have only touched the fringe, and of course we know that the situation is different in every field. But if you ask any missionary, he will probably admit to you that he has to spend a lot more time than he wants to, just on the details of living in a foreign land.

21

WHAT A MISSIONARY DOES—
MAJOR ACTIVITIES (I)

LEAVING ASIDE some of the other details that fill up a missionary's life—letters, reports, dealing with government officials and the like—let's turn to a brief view of five major missionary activities: evangelism, counseling, church establishment, leadership training, and Christian literature.

EVANGELISM

When we talk about evangelism, everybody thinks immediately of *preaching*. Of course missionaries do preach, even where a national church already exists. They preach whenever and wherever they can. It may be in a church building; it may be in the open air. It may be in a city street chapel, where people are continually coming and going. It may be in the village council house, where they gather specially to hear the message. It may be in a large convention or in a neighborhood meeting in somebody's house.

Missionaries are likely to preach more frequently than ministers in the homeland. I remember the amusement of a mission director when he told me about one applicant to his mission. The young man apparently thought he would impress the mission with his abilities and experience. "I think I would be able to do the work all right," he wrote. "I am used to preaching. I preach at least twice every Sunday and once in the middle of the week, besides occasional sermons at other times. The director laughed and said, "I told him we didn't have a missionary on our field who preached that little!"

197

Oh, it isn't always the best of preaching in a homiletic sense. It often has to be much less formal. How can you develop a theme with first, second and third points when you are preaching in a market where most of the people just stop for a few minutes and then move on? It is like open-air preaching in the homeland.

And many times you can't get by with a ten- or fifteen-minute sermonette. The people are there to hear God's message and it may be a long time before they will get another chance. They want "the whole counsel of God"— or at least as much of it as they can get. Some of them came many miles on foot just to hear that message. So keep on, preacher, give them good measure!

Late one Saturday a dusty traveler reached our home. He was a Christian from a town where there were no other believers. He had trudged two or three days on foot to reach our city. He stayed with us over Sunday. Then early Monday morning he started back, another two or three days' journey. Why did he come? "Every once in a while," he told us, "I get so hungry for Christian fellowship that I just have to come down here for a Sunday and hear a sermon or two. Now I am going back well fed."

The *invitation* is a standard part of an evangelistic meeting in the United States. At the close of the sermon, usually while the congregation sings a hymn, people are urged to accept Christ as their Saviour and to indicate that decision by raising their hand.

In most mission fields this just doesn't work. As a missionary to Africa once wrote us, "If we did such a thing here, every hand in the place would go up! But it wouldn't mean a thing." Others have insisted, "If people are really converted, they ought to be able to stand up and say so!"

And they do. On a visit to Puerto La Cruz, Venezuela, where I had been invited to speak to the church, my sermon was interrupted right in the middle. A woman stood up in the congregation and said in a loud voice, "I want to accept Christ as my only and sufficient Saviour!" Then she sat down. Nobody was shocked. Nobody thought it was unusual. After a brief pause the sermon went on.

Of course *personal evangelism* is the foundation of all evangelistic work. After the beginning, the people themselves do most of it. With a little instruction they can do a better job at it than the missionary. But the real missionary never ceases to be a personal evangelist. Some give a great deal of their time to this ministry. Even in many of his talks with groups, the missionary often just "gossips the gospel" as if in a private conversation.

Some missionaries spend a great deal of time *traveling* for evangelistic purposes. They have to if they are to do a good job. You see, the missionary is not supposed to be the settled pastor of a single congregation. His work is far broader than that. His objective is to get the fires burning over as wide an area as possible.

Now travel always sounds attractive to those who like to read books of travels. Sometimes they get just enough of it themselves during the summer vacation to wish they could do a lot more. But they are thinking in terms of their own country, where nearly everybody travels and traveling is made easy.

Often it is not so on the mission field. True, there have been many improvements in travel in recent years. For instance, the word *safari* in Africa no longer means a long line of porters trudging down a narrow trail bearing the missionary's equipment and sometimes even the missionary himself. Now the missionary can pack everything into a station wagon or truck and take along just a helper or two when he travels. In some places, even in such primitive areas as the jungles of eastern Ecuador, he has the airplane at his call. But that doesn't mean that travel is easy. Or that it no longer takes much time.

Take the missionary in India, for example. Suppose he wants to go on a tour of the villages of his district. There are airplanes in India, but they won't do him much good for such local travel. There are railroads too. But the railroads aren't much help in reaching many of these villages. So the missionary takes a truck and makes use of the highways as much as he can.

He has to plan his trip carefully, however, and take a great deal more equipment than we might imagine necessary. In the first place he is not likely to find a conveniently located hotel or rooming house. So he takes a tent. Then that means taking along all the necessary equipment for sleeping, washing and eating. For of course he can't just drop in at a restaurant, come mealtime. Even if there is a market where foods are prepared in the open air, he finds it wiser to have his meals cooked under his own supervision.

Then there are the implements of his work. He may need to have a portable organ along, or some other musical instrument. He needs tracts, Scriptures and other books for those who read. Charts, flannelgraphs and other such aids help reach both the children and the older people. It may be that he can even take along a projector and show films or slides, using his truck to provide the electricity.

But the missionary to India has an easy time traveling compared to some of the missionaries among the lowland Indians of South America. At times these missionaries do have the advantage of airplane transportation to and from their stations. This is a tremendous help. But it does involve work that we do not always remember. An airplane must have a place to land—a large, level, cleared space, free of trees, stumps and underbrush. It is a real job to make such a clearing, even with plenty of cheap labor available. It is also a job to keep it clear, for, in the moist tropics, vegetation seems to spring up overnight.

Then, too, the missionary must have some way of contacting the plane when he needs it. This means shortwave-radio communication, which is all very lovely until the set goes out of order. And of course no one can tell when nor how often that may happen.

For the ordinary evangelistic tours, however, the plane

does not have the same value. It is useful only for the big hops, not for a succession of very short trips. For the shorter distances on the ground the missionary can often use a car, truck or jeep. This is even feasible where the government has spent little or no money on road-building. One group of missionaries in Bolivia built their own road so that trucks could get to their station. It had to be a rough job, since they couldn't afford better. But it was usable, especially if the truck had a power winch to pull itself out of an occasional mudhole. In other areas during the dry season a dry stream bed does duty as a road.

But beyond the roadhead there is still need for traveling. Then it may have to be on foot, muleback, or canoe. Travel by foot is much less common than it used to be. But the inland waterways are still an extremely important highway system in some areas. So there are times, sooner or later, when the traveler has to take to the "flowing road."

We moderns are losing the fine art of *visitation*. That is, we are rapidly losing out on the pleasant and sometimes stimulating conversations that used to be the very heart of the visit. Now when a visitor appears, he often gets the uncomfortable feeling that his host wishes he would hurry up and leave. Maybe it is just because his presence is keeping the host from looking at his favorite TV program. Or just as often it may be that they don't find subjects of common interest and importance to talk about. We are so much in a hurry to get things done that we consider leisurely conversation a useless waste of time.

Even pastoral visitation is becoming a rarity. Pastors seem too busy with a score of other activities that they feel are more pressing. (Though sometimes one may wonder whether they are not just avoiding a task that can be very demanding spiritually.) In some cases the church employs a "church visitor," usually a woman, to do the visitation. It helps fill the gap, but few consider it a real substitute for a pastoral call. In most cases, however, the visiting just isn't done.

Visitation on most mission fields, though, still holds much of its former position of importance. The visitor is usually welcomed. He is welcomed even when his host radically disagrees with his point of view. After all, how are you going to understand the other fellow's point of view if you don't talk with him? If you want an opening to do personal evangelism, here it is.

Some years ago I made a sort of survey trip out along the Gulf of Paria in Venezuela. In the small port of Cristobal Colon I was held up for about a week, waiting for a way to proceed homeward. While there I spent considerable time visiting among the people, but without positive results as far as I could see.

Two or three years later, after our return from furlough, the missionary then in charge of that district was visiting in our home. "You will be interested," he said, "in a report I just got from up the coast. Do you remember a woman in Cristobal Colon who was very much interested in the gospel when you were out that way?"

I told him I couldn't remember any such person. But then, I had done a good deal of visiting in the town.

"Well, anyway," he continued, "this woman says you spent a lot of time one day explaining the gospel to her and several others. She wasn't quite ready to accept it then, but she did later. And now word has come saying that she has died trusting in the Saviour, thanks to your visit."

And still, the most that I ever could remember was that one day a storekeeper had courteously offered me a chair outside his little store. His wife and a number of others gathered around, as in a leisurely fashion we carried on our conversation. An hour? Two hours? I really don't know how long we talked. But that woman may have been one of the group.

COUNSELING

Visiting is often closely associated with the work of counseling. Whether in the homeland or on the mission field, those who need our counsel do not always seek us out. Many a time we must go and find them.

Now counseling is a most demanding sort of work. Young people who have never occupied places of leadership don't understand just how demanding it can be. They are likely to think of it simply as the giving of advice.

"Advice is cheap," some say. But that proverb about the cheapness of advice probably got started because there is so much cheap advice in circulation. It is cheap, not only because it is given without charge but because it didn't cost the giver anything—not even so much as a few minutes of serious thought.

Opinions and superficial advice are easy to express. But what if a life depended on your judgment? What if following your advice might possibly bring anguish and remorse? And what if it meant the eternal destiny of a soul?

Every missionary is called on for counsel. Not just for the common spiritual problems that confront the pastor or Christian worker here in the homeland. The variety of subjects on which the counsel of the missionary is sought is astounding. Somehow he is expected to be an authority on almost every subject under the sun. Yet he knows that he is not.

What is he going to do? To some of the people he has become a spiritual father. And fatherhood means care. Are the children to blame if they don't understand just what kind of subjects their father can best counsel them about? Isn't he supposed to know? How can they tell the difference between a spiritual problem, a social problem, and an economic problem? Just what is the difference?

Counseling takes a lot of time. Probably there is no other job the missionary has that is more time-consuming. Even when a man does come to you for counsel, he may beat around the bush for a long time before he comes to the point. Even then it may take a bit of prying to find out what really is the heart of the matter. Ask any dean of students.

No job calls for more understanding. This is one of the reasons why missions want young people as candidates who are mature in thinking and acting. Maturity that is born of experience shows itself more in counseling than perhaps anywhere else. In counseling, as in medicine, the first problem is to diagnose the case. It calls for patience to lead a person to reveal just what is the trouble— patience, and obvious sympathy that inspires confidence. It takes discernment to see just what is the issue involved, and then to restate the case in such a way that the person himself will see it. It takes tact and self-control to avoid saying, "This is what you'll have to do," and to say instead, "This is what your decision will mean; but the decision is up to you."

It is in this field of counseling that the missionary can best show his spiritual leadership. It is important from the beginning and it continues to grow in importance. There will come a time when national pastors and evangelists will do the preaching, when national teachers will displace the missionary teacher and even take over the work of supervision. But there will still be a need for the counselor, for the one to whom people turn in confidence to help them solve the many problems they constantly face.

THE CHURCH

We have already said that a part of the aim of missions is to establish the church. This should be the natural outcome of evangelism. In fact, a working fellowship of believers must result if evangelism is to have any permanent effect. So one of the missionary's most vital tasks is to help the church get started and to guide it in its early years. It also takes plenty of tact and spiritual leadership.

The faith missions, which have always strongly emphasized evangelism, tended to give comparatively little attention to the church in the early years. Their emphasis on evangelism was of course needed at the beginning. But sometimes they found that after the first ingathering of believers the work did not progress as it should. Instead of becoming stronger and more vigorous every year, it often showed signs of weakness. It continued to depend too much on the presence of the foreign missionary. They then came to realize, at least in part, that without reducing their zeal for evangelism they needed to place more emphasis on the building up of the church.

Looking back now, it is easy to say that they should have known better. Didn't Paul lay great emphasis on the church in all his missionary work? Wasn't that part of the secret of his success? Nevertheless, there are still many, both in the faith missions and in the denominational missions, who have not learned that lesson. They are not convinced that the principles used in the first century can be applied today. They feel that the circumstances are different.

But, on the whole, missions today are laying greater stress on the church than ever before. Especially since World War II and the closing of China we have come to see the importance of developing a strong national church that is not dependent on the missionaries. To this matter the missionary has to give a great deal of attention.

We are used to churches in the Western world. Even though our churches differ from one another to some extent in organization and procedures, there is still a great deal of similarity between them. Fundamentally they are all voluntary associations in which the members have a great deal to say about what is done. Whether the pastor is appointed by a bishop or chosen by vote of the congregation, his authority is limited by the will of the people. Democratic procedures are the general rule, procedures with which we became acquainted as early as our grade-school days. And there is so much similarity between the usual orders of service that a visitor might find it difficult to tell the denomination of the church he is in, if he didn't already know it. Most of us are familiar with these things from childhood.

This is not true in many mission fields. The people's previous manner of life has been entirely different. Society is organized on a different basis. Many haven't the foggiest notion of what a democracy is, or how democracy functions. A large part of them are used to chiefs, to dictators of one sort or another. They think it only natural that this pattern should be carried into their church life.

For example, a young Bible-school graduate in one South American country went to be the pastor of a church. His country was one of those that have usually been run by strong-armed dictators. He had been taught parliamentary rules and church government in his Bible-school days. But a few years of formal teaching can hardly overrule a lifetime of experience.

Within a short time he got into trouble with his church officers and some of the older members. The whole problem was a difference of political viewpoint. He became so wrought up that, without bothering to follow parliamentary procedure, he promptly excommunicated all of those who disagreed with him. "Long live the Dictator!" Fortunately for the church he didn't last long.

Church life is something entirely new to many people. Their religious life has been on an entirely different basis heretofore. Religion is more a part of daily life than it is among us, but regular weekly services are often lacking. Of course witch doctors don't preach sermons. Besides, religion is often for them a community affair—the whole town or tribe has a single religion, with no dissenters allowed. So it is quite a new thing to come into a church— an *ekklesia* or "called-out group." How does one act in a church? And how does a church act in society?

We can't go into the details of this problem. But we trust we have said enough to show that it is something to which the missionary has to give long, careful and prayerful attention. How to lead the people to understand the scriptural ideal of the church? How much of our Western church organization to introduce? (We Americans love to organize to the limit—or even beyond it!) How much of the native pattern of life to adapt to church purposes? When to stay in the background and allow them to run things—letting them make their own mistakes instead of making them all himself? How to encourage the development of a national leadership? And so on, without end.

One thing is certain. The church will usually take on much greater importance in the life of the people than it has at present in our American life. We have turned over so much to the state and to secular organizations— education, charity, relief, social affairs—that the church often does little more than minister to what we call the "strictly spiritual." Even in a funeral service the mortician rather than the minister is in charge of affairs. Some individual churches have indeed tried to assume a more activist role in politico-social affairs. But in so doing they have often alienated much of their constituency.

In mission lands the situation is different. In fact, because it is so different, many of our American missionaries find it difficult to understand and they are slow to adjust to it. You see, in coming out of a nonchristian society into the church, the people have had to break many of their former connections. It is not just a matter of attending a different type of religious service. They have to build a different life pattern.

Sometimes they have to find a different way of earning a living. A maker of idols cannot continue in that craft. He may need help to get something else. Usually their social life is changed. Sometimes this means only a change of companions. The activity itself may be good, as with some games or other social affairs. At other times it involves a disengagement from previous social activities, such as drinking parties, gambling, and lewd dances. Then something else that is wholesome, if not specifically Christian, needs to be substituted. Man is, after all, a social being.

It is in the church that people have found spiritual life. In the church they find a new and delightful fellowship. So it is only natural that they look to the church to satisfy other needs of their new life.

Just before the war in Korea the Yung Nak Presbyterian Church started in Seoul. It was a refugee church, one among many. The pastor had managed to escape from the terror in North Korea and in the capital he had found many other North Korean refugees who were Christians. They met for worship in increasing numbers. Soon there was no auditorium large enough for their services.

But they did other things also. They all knew what it was to abandon all their possessions and escape to a strange part of the country. Here they had no jobs, no homes, no friends but their fellow Christians. They would have to help one another. So through the church those who had arrived first began to assist later arrivals. As they were able, they provided them with food. For some they provided clothing. They set up a sort of employment bureau and helped many to get jobs. Then as each one got on his own feet he began to take a part in helping others.

They didn't question whether this was the church's job. From where else should they get help if not from their brethren in Christ?

22

WHAT A MISSIONARY DOES—
MAJOR ACTIVITIES (II)

LEADERSHIP TRAINING

YOU CAN'T HAVE CHURCHES without leaders. The leaders may not be given titles, but they are leaders just the same. The question is, what type of leaders will the church have and how well will they be prepared for their task?

Of course it is entirely possible in some places for the missionary himself to assume the place of leadership. To him it may seem to be the easiest way. Then he has no training problems. Also there is no question about whether the work will continue in the way he has planned it. But the poor missionary soon finds himself burdened down with responsibilities without number. And in spite of all his efforts, for some reason the church doesn't seem to progress. If he were to have to leave the field, as has happened, the work would fall to pieces.

Another alternative for the missionary is to note those new believers who seem to have the gift of leadership and to turn over to them at least a part of the responsibilities. It might work. That is, it might work if the one appointed has more than the usual amount of humility, tact, patience, perception of spiritual principles, understanding of the Scriptures, and a few other gifts. But the odds are against it. Paul knew what he was talking about when he wrote against giving leadership to a novice. He knew the danger of pride, the danger that such a man would fall into the enemy's trap. It has happened time and again. More than natural ability is needed for leaders of the church.

The only satisfactory plan is to train leaders. But this is not as simple as it sounds. You just can't pick out a promising young man, send him away to a school for a few years, and then have him come back all ready to do the leading.

CHOICE OF LEADERS

In the first place, the missionary's choice of leaders is not always the best choice. This is not to depreciate the missionary's judgment. But many a time a missionary has selected and sponsored the schooling of a young man, only to find out later that he is not accepted as a leader by his own people. Sometimes the very fact that the missionary has chosen him is a handicap. He is the missionary's stooge, the people feel, not a leader who has arisen from among themselves. He may be made to feel the resentment that we all express toward a "teacher's pet."

It is not always easy to find the Lord's choice for leadership. He may be, like David, the one considered least likely. As Samuel remarked, "Man looketh on the outward appearance, but God looketh on the heart." So the missionary has to be careful not to rush ahead and anoint the first promising candidate. He may have to try them out for a long time first. Then he may be able to commend some to the church as Paul commended Timothy when he sent him to Philippi: "I have no man likeminded, who will naturally care for your state. For all seek their own, not the things which are Jesus Christ's. But ye know the proof of him . . . ."

MORE THAN SCHOOLING

Second, training for leadership is not just a matter of sending young people away to school for a few years. In fact, there are not many schools that are good training grounds for leadership. Sometimes the best students in school are those who conform most readily to the pattern. They faithfully and intelligently do what they are told, but they often lack the initiative, the imagination, the aggressiveness that a leader must have. The leader may sometimes be a headache to deans and teachers. He goes off into paths that the teacher hadn't thought of, and raises questions that are not covered by his set lectures. He thinks things out for himself.

Obviously the first place for leadership training is right at home, in the home congregation. Here much depends on the vision and initiative of the pastor, if there is one. Otherwise it may depend on the missionary. Someone has to encourage the believers to take an active part in the work. Someone has to counsel them in the doing. Someone has to introduce them to the treasures of the Scriptures and show them how to apply them to daily living. Someone has to set before them the challenge of a loving service for Christ in a spiritual ministry to others.

BIBLE STUDY

You can't have *Christian* leadership without Bible study. But Bible study must be for more than just the leaders. The wise pastor or missionary realizes this and plans regular Bible teaching for all the people. The Bible teaching in the Korean churches has been a model in this regard. What good is it to have the leaders instructed if the people are kept in ignorance? It will not be long before the leaders too are dragged down. We need to raise the whole level of the church in biblical understanding. This is a tremendous task, but a blessed one.

Neither can you have leadership unless the leader is ahead of the people. This does mean special training for some. It was strongly impressed on me one day when a woman from the Women's Bible Class came to see me. She explained, "Mr. Cook, we love our teacher. We admire her Christian life and her sweet spirit. But can't you do something to help her? She doesn't know any more than we do!" It is one of the problems of missionary life that those who are the most willing to serve are not always the most able. And those who intellectually seem to be the most capable often lack the devotion, the self-sacrificing zeal of the more mediocre.

How can you inspire a gifted young person to give his life in the Lord's service when the world offers so many more material advantages? How can the missionaries in Africa, for example, turn their talented young people to the ministry when they see the pastors living in need, but government service offers a comfortable living? How can you take the humble young people of one talent, but with lots of devotion, and help them to polish that one talent and use it with such effect that they become true leaders of the church of Christ? How? The missionary would like to know. In his work he needs to know. It is a part of his job.

PROBLEMS OF SCHOOLS AND SEMINARIES

Just a word about our Bible schools and seminaries. We have them on nearly every field. They are doing a most important job. But they have a great many problems the folks at home don't know about. It sounds great to talk about training national preachers. Just think how much better they will be able to do the job than the missionary! How much more the missionary's own work will count if he gives his time to this teaching ministry!

This is true. The trouble is that not every missionary is qualified for such a job. In reality it is one of the hardest of all jobs to do well. Besides, it isn't as romantic as it may sound.

For one thing, it isn't a job for the newcomer. Sometimes a young missionary candidate in the homeland tells the mission board that he has been called to teach in the Bible school. He has never had any experience in that sort of work, but he thinks the job would be most interesting and important.

The director of one Bible institute told me of such a young man. He reached the field, studied the language, and then was actually assigned to the Bible institute. He spent just about a year there. Then he went to the director and said, "I was mistaken. I don't think this is the work for me. I'd like to be assigned to regular station work." So he was.

The problem is not just that some people are teachers and others are not. Nor is it the fact that one really needs to be thoroughly familiar with the language before he can do a good job of teaching. This is a job that calls for experienced workers because they are the ones who know the people, know something of their background and what can be expected of them. Through their work in the field they also know something of the situation the graduates will face when they leave the school. They can plan their courses accordingly. You see, a good teacher has to know much more than just the subject he is to teach.

Then there are problems that we don't usually have to worry much about in the United States. For instance, many of those who go to the Bible schools overseas have had very little previous education. How can you expect much study from people who have never learned to study? An hour or two of preparation for each class? Many of them have never studied a full hour at one time in their lives. As a result they may have to spend more time in class and less in study.

Also, how can you teach effectively without textbooks? By the lecture system? Our American students flounder badly enough under such a system. And those who have difficulty writing at all are at a complete loss in a lecture class. Yet textbooks are scarce in a large part of our fields. They are scarce because there has been no one to prepare them in the language of the people. Or because there wouldn't be a large enough circulation to warrant the cost of printing them. Or because there just isn't enough money available for the purpose.

Then if you have a Bible school or seminary without many churches, what will happen to your graduates? After they have spent several years in getting this special training, will they then be willing to go back to their old homes, take up their former jobs and give voluntary part-time service to the church? Are there churches enough, and are they financially able to support all those who graduate? Will the young people feel that since you have trained them for Christian service you are responsible to see that they find suitable employment in that service? These problems are not hypothetical. They are problems that missionaries are actually facing in many fields.

CHRISTIAN LITERATURE

We have spoken about the lack of textbooks for our Bible and theological training schools, a situation that adds to the missionary's work. But this is only one phase of our great need for Christian literature in the mission fields. Actually the *two greatest challenges for missionary service today are in the field of leadership training and in that of Christian literature.* Mission leaders are all aware of these needs, but we haven't met them yet. One of the major reasons is that, just as in leadership training, the requirements for doing a good job in literature are very high.

Literature also is not a job for the newcomer, no matter how well trained he may have been at home. There is much that he has to learn right on the field. But if he has any talent at all, he can be practicing while he is learning and getting ready for this most important ministry.

LEARN THE LANGUAGE

First of all, of course, he has to learn the language. But he needs to master it much more thoroughly than the missionary who will use only the spoken language. When you are speaking you can use facial expressions and gestures to help put across your meaning. You can watch the people and see if they seem to be getting what you are saying. If not you can say it in another way, until finally their faces light up with comprehension. You can even get your word order wrong and still have them understand, if you get the emphasis in the right places. But not so in writing. Every bit of meaning, including the emphasis, must be conveyed by those little black marks on white paper. Any mistakes you make, any lack of clarity, is permanently fixed in print.

KNOW THE PEOPLE

Then he has to get to know the people. This is for several reasons. He needs to know what should be published for them—what will be of the most value. But even more he needs to know how it should be written. Blunt, straight-from-the-shoulder writing such as we often use in English would be offensive to many people. And when it comes to illustrations, a high proportion of those we use at home would have no meaning in other places.

I recall one missionary who in his sermon started to use the example of a railroad engineer. After he got started, he suddenly realized that no one in his audience had ever seen a railroad train. He tried to explain a train, so he could explain the engineer, but ended by confusing them worse than ever. The missionary needs to know the life of the people so he can write in terms that are meaningful to them.

All of this means that he must have experience on the field before he is ready for a ministry of writing or editing. But the writer needs still something more. Not every experienced missionary can write. He needs to have at least some talent for writing, an urge to do so, plus some instruction, together with plenty of practice. It doesn't matter too much that his writing instruction may have been in English. If he has learned to write clearly and forcibly in English, he will usually learn to do a good job in the other language.

Those who engage in a literary ministry need to have a real dedication to their task. It is not very stimulating to sit down to a typewriter to put your thoughts on paper. It is much more inspiring to speak them to a living and responsive audience. Yet the audience of the writer is many times that of the speaker. And the words he writes can be read and read again until they are all assimilated, whereas the speaker knows that his words are extremely perishable. They must be grasped at the moment they are spoken, if ever.

TRANSLATION WORK

We have been speaking primarily of original writing. Some may think that the answer to our need for Christian literature lies in the translation of what we already have in English. "We have so much good material in English," they say, "why can't you just translate it into the other languages and save all that work of writing something original?" Missionaries, too, sometimes get this idea. One of the first literary tasks a new missionary attempts is a bit of translation. It seems it should be so easy.

But translation is far from easy. At least to do a good accurate job is anything but easy. To make a smooth translation into another language that is reasonably true to the sense of the original is hard at best. Sometimes it is practically impossible. You see, many do not realize that another language is not just another set of words. It represents another set of ideas expressed in a quite different way. Some of the ideas are partly like ours, and others are quite different. The pattern of expression is sure to be different. The one who tries to translate word for word is bound to make serious mistakes, sometimes ridiculous ones. A missionary, for example, tried to translate into Spanish the expression "spring of truth." He looked in his dictionary, found that the word *resorte* meant "spring," and used it. What he apparently didn't realize was that *resorte* is a spring like an automobile spring.

What makes translation particularly hard is that it always involves interpretation. You can't translate without interpreting. That is, you can't translate without having in your own mind a clear idea of what the author is trying to say. The reason is that you have to try to convey that same idea to an audience with a different background and through words and phrases quite different from those the author used.

Holman Bentley, in translating the Bible into a language of the Congo, found that the people had no word for "brothers" in the general sense. They had separate words for brothers on the father's side, brothers on the mother's side, or full brothers born of both parents. In the passages that speak of the brothers of Christ he faced a problem. They could not be full brothers, since that would make Joseph Christ's father. He had two other choices. He could call them brothers on the mother's side, which would mean that they were later children of Mary and Joseph. Or he could call them brothers on the father's side, which would make them children of Joseph by a previous marriage. Rightly or wrongly, he chose the latter. He had to interpret in order to translate.

Albert Schweitzer, who knew both German and French from childhood, refused to translate one of his books from French to German. He contended that the languages were so different that it couldn't be done properly—even by the author himself. So he rewrote the whole work in German.

PUTTING A LANGUAGE INTO WRITING

The literature problem is different on every field. Some missionaries go to fields where the language has not yet been reduced to writing. There the missionary has to begin from scratch. First he must patiently try to dig the spoken language out of the people, carefully recording all he learns. He must use some system of phonetics in transcribing the sounds he hears. After he has gathered a certain amount of material, he uses those data to try to work out an alphabet for the language—a letter for each meaningful sound, and not more than one letter per sound.

As soon as he can understand a little, he begins to figure out the patterns of speech the people use—the construction of their words, and the ways they combine them into sentences—the grammar. As soon as he can, he tries writing a few little things in their language. Of course they can't read them yet, but he reads them aloud to see if they comprehend. All of this takes time—a tremendous amount of time. Even with the modern improved methods of linguistic study it calls for years of devoted, patient application.

LITERACY CAMPAIGNS

Writing the language is only the beginning. If it is to be useful the people have to learn how to read it. So the missionary embarks on a literacy campaign, teaching the people to read and write their own language. Then they will be able to read for themselves the Word of God that he is trying to translate for them.

Literacy campaigns, however, are not just for those in the first stages of getting a written language. Illiteracy faces the missionary in many fields. Many not only have written languages but a great deal of literature in those languages. The missionary rightly feels it is disgraceful when the people have the Bible in their own tongue but most of the Christians are not able to read it. How can a church grow spiritually in such circumstances?

WHAT TO PRINT

But literacy is only the opening of the door. Those who have learned to read can pass through. To what? What are they going to read? Obviously the most important single book is the Bible. But putting the whole Bible into the language of the people is a tremendous task. It is seldom accomplished by a single missionary. Many have engaged in the work over many years and there are now parts of the Bible in over thirteen hundred different languages. Yet the great majority still do not have the whole Bible.

We don't wait for the whole Bible, however, before providing other reading material. Almost from the beginning the people need hymns, for Christianity is a singing religion. Very few missionaries are poets and musicians, so they have to reverse the usual hymn-writing technique. They take a Western hymn tune and then set words to it. The result may not be good poetry, but usually it carries a message and is singable.

Another publication that is soon started, even among those who are just beginning to be literate, is the periodical. It may be just a four-page leaflet, or it may become a sixteen-page paper with illustrations. But it is issued at regular intervals and is much more important in the work than a similar paper would be here at home. However, periodical publications do call for a steady flow of writing. Also they usually have to be printed on the field. The task is a big one.

Tracts are read far more often in mission lands than they are at home. Sunday school literature is usually scarce and so is greatly prized. Correspondence courses have proved their value wherever there is any sort of postal service, however poor. And always there is a call for Christian books: Bible-study books, devotional books, books on Christian doctrines, the home and family, on Christian history and biography, books for children, reference books. No one who has seen the pitifully small library of the non-English-speaking pastor in a foreign field can fail to be impressed by this ever present need for more books.

DISTRIBUTION

The writing, editing and printing of literature for the

people is important. But equally important is the distribution of what is already available. The Bible colporteur is a familiar figure in the mission field. In many places, notably in Latin America, he has been the pioneer to open the way for a more settled ministry. We can hardly overstress the importance of his work of seed-sowing. Colportage is one of the best ways of distributing not only the Bible but other Christian literature as well.

There are also other ways. A full-scale gospel bookstore is usually too big a job for the average missionary, unless he is set apart for that ministry by the mission. But there are multitudes of missionaries who on their own initiative carry small stocks of books to sell to the people as they have opportunity. It is just one of the many odd jobs a missionary does. Its profits are usually more spiritual than material.

Many a missionary, too, maintains his own private circulating library. To those who can't afford to buy a book he will lend one for a short time. Of course there is so much work in trying to keep track of the books loaned that the library is in constant need of replenishing. But again it is time and money well spent. Books are meant to be read. And if good books are read there is bound to be some result.

CONCLUSION

What does a missionary do? He may not do everything we have mentioned here. He most probably does many other things we haven't mentioned. There is no typical missionary, and there is no typical missionary work. Missionaries have become "all things to all men, that they might be all means save some." What they do depends on the field and the circumstances in which they are placed, on their own abilities and resources, and on the Lord's leading.

This we can say: There are some parts of the missionary's work that appeal to the people at home. These he learns to tell about in his missionary talks. But there are other parts that are hard to make sound appealing. They may sound just like what they are—plain, tiring, even monotonous work. The second are just as much a part of the missionary's life as the first. Perhaps even more so. They probably consume more of his time and more of his energies. In many cases they are what really produce results.

23

A CHURCH MISSIONARY PROGRAM— HOW TO CREATE INTEREST (I)

WE HAVE ALREADY SAID something about the church's responsibility to missions. Now we want to come to some practical suggestions for carrying out that responsibility. It is the local church that we have in view, not the denomination. In fact, we want to think primarily of the church of average size, not the big city church. These are the ones who would appreciate help. They are also the ones from whom a great part of the help for missions comes.

THE PASTOR'S PLACE

The life of any missionary program in a local church depends largely on the leadership. Someone has to have the interest, the vision, the initiative to inaugurate a program, plus the persistence to carry it through. Normally the pastor should be that leader. People usually look to him for leadership, and in this matter they expect him to be much better informed than the members. Besides, he must cooperate if missions is to be a church concern and not just a fringe activity of a small group within the church.

Now this doesn't always happen. The pastor isn't always willing or capable of taking the lead. Then it is up to someone else in the congregation, though he will have a much harder time. In any case it is important to win the support of the pastor. For purposes of our discussion here, we are going to assume that the pastor is the leader.

It is important that the pastor be sold on missions. That is, he needs to be really enthusiastic on the subject.

The enthusiasms of the pastor tend to spread to the people. Not to everyone, but to many. If the pastor is thoroughly convinced, the program is bound to follow. We may make suggestions here that are helpful, but apart from the hearty endorsement of the pastor they are of no value. If he is only mildly interested, you may be sure that the program— even the most excellent program—will languish.

Three things the pastor needs to see if he is to be enthusiastic about missions. *One* is a matter that we have already treated—that the Scriptures present missions as essential to the church and not as just an extra. A *second* is that the church itself will get a great blessing from taking an active part in the work. This has been so amply proved by the experience of so many churches that sometimes we fear that a few pastors are taking up missions for the wrong motives. They use missions for its publicity value. A *third* thing, which is not always so readily recognized by the pastor of a small church, is that he and his church have a really important part to play in the work. A great many of our best missionary candidates come from small churches. In addition, proportionately some of the small churches are far more generous in their giving than the large ones.

SEVEN OBJECTIVES

When the pastor is really in earnest about a complete missionary program for his church, he will want to have before him several objectives. They may be stated as follows:

1. To create interest and enthusiasm for missions on the part of as many members as possible. He may not be able to interest everybody, but he should try. The more who are interested, the greater the blessing.

2. To support that interest and enthusiasm with accurate and up-to-date information. Information is the food that interest grows on. But misinformation or out-of-date information can soon dull the appetite. The information

can't be as up-to-date as the daily paper. In some countries things don't change very rapidly. But when you quote as present facts statements that were published more than thirty years ago (as we have heard on several occasions) you are on shaky ground.

3. To secure as much prayer support for missions as possible. The missionaries on the field need this more than we realize. Their success depends on God's working through them, not on their own unaided efforts to do the job.

4. To contribute material support for missions in as large a measure as possible. This is one of the objectives, but don't think of it as the only one. It is not even necessarily the chief one.

5. To provide personnel for the missionary enterprise. That is, to provide missionaries. It is surprising to see how many people are willing to give their dollars but not themselves—not even their sons and daughters.

6. To train prospective missionaries as far as the local church can do that job. Sounds strange, doesn't it? How can a local church train a missionary? Well, just look back at the indispensables in missionary preparation and see how much can be done at home and through the home church.

7. To assist in such other ways as its particular circumstances may enable it, such as the promotion of joint missionary conferences, etc. The church's objectives don't have to be limited to its own membership. Neither do its objectives have to be limited to the six above. Sometimes it can do more. And if it can, it should.

Now don't think that these objectives are separate and distinct from the other objectives of the church. They are closely related to them and sometimes actually blended with them. For instance, you can't busy yourself in the training of young people who may become missionaries without training some who will never be missionaries but will be better Christians. Actually you can hardly promote the missionary objectives of the church without benefiting the whole work of the church. The task abroad and the task at home are just two different phases of the same task. The church exists both for fellowship and evangelism. And evangelism in its full sense embraces the whole world.

Carrying out the Objectives

Now for some practical suggestions in connection with these seven missionary objectives. These will carry us through most of the remainder of the book. For greater simplicity they are put in outline form.

I. Creating interest and enthusiasm for missions

A. The pastor's own ministry

Many a young pastor is called to a church that has little or no interest in missions. When he himself is vitally interested, he often asks, "How can I get my people interested, when they can't see it?"

1. Don't try to force it on them.

There is no surer way of turning disinterest into opposition. Missions must come from the heart. Your first job is to find out just where the people stand. Then, beginning at that point, try to lead them out step by step. If they already have some sort of missionary program, don't try to throw it out. Use it as a starting point for something better.

2. Get down to the fundamentals.

Missions is not the major issue. The real issue is a vitality of faith that constrains us to witness for Christ. When the church begins to feel its obligation to witness to others, missions will soon follow.

3. Use missionary illustrations in your sermons.

The story of missions is full of apt illustrations for most of the truths you present in your regular preaching. You don't have to drag them in; they just fit. If you are preaching on faith, the experience of Hudson Taylor can give you an outstanding example. If your subject is persistence, you can find it illustrated in the life of William Carey,

who claimed this as his only talent. It will be surprising
if the people don't want to know more about these men
after they have had a taste or two. Of course up-to-date
illustrations may be even more helpful. Who would not
thrill to the tale of that Korean pastor who interceded
for the Communist murderers of his two sons and actually
took them into his own family?

4. When the occasion offers, preach on missions.

This is one of the advantages of expository preaching. It
would be hard to give a series of messages on any extended
passage in the New Testament without dealing with missions
in normal course. You don't have to look for a reason to
deal with it. It comes in naturally. Of course the Acts is
preeminently a missionary book. Or if you follow the church
calendar, Pentecost Sunday gives you an excellent occasion
to speak on missions, remembering how people of so
many different tongues heard the gospel on that day. Or
Christmas Sunday, when we celebrate the coming of the
greatest of all missionaries.

5. Take a trip to the field.

When the church wants to do something special for
its pastor as a token of love and esteem, suggest a trip
to a mission field. Some such trips today are well within
the capacity of even the smallest churches. It is more than
just a vacation trip for the pastor. It is an investment
from which the church will draw dividends. When the
pastor has actually seen the field and witnessed the missionaries in action, he comes back with a new understanding and a new zeal for the work. He cannot help communi-
cating some of his enthusiasm to the church.

Planning the trip and making all the arrangements
on an individual basis can be quite a chore. However,
some missions are prepared to take care of most of the
details for you if you will go with a small party. Periodically they plan specially conducted tours for pastors and
other interested church members. The mission provides
guides and interpreters. It arranges for transportation,

housing and meals. It plans the itinerary to cover the most interesting features within a reasonable time. And it usually does so more cheaply than a professional tourist agency.

B. Using missionary speakers

Without doubt, good missionary speakers can do more to stir up missionary interest than almost anyone else. But many pastors and leaders don't know how to use them effectively.

1. Whom to invite.

a. Missionaries on furlough.

These are usually the most popular speakers, because they can speak of their own experiences in the work. A recent survey shows they are more than twice as influential as anyone else. Many churches try to get missionaires "fresh from the field." This may be all right at times. But usually the missionary just arrived from the field needs to get a rest and to become readjusted to home conditions and to a free use of the English language, before he does much speaking. He is then able to do a better job than at the beginning. He can see things in better perspective and know how best to present them.

1) Those recommended by your denomination.

It is easy to get in touch with the deputation representative of your denomination's mission board. He can usually tell what missionaries may be available in your area, and when. But don't fail to ask for his recommendations. Some missionaries do best in a small gathering. Some have a special attraction for young people. Some, who are not gifted speakers, may possibly be used for a brief testimony. Be sure to ask for a speaker long ahead of time when you will need him. On short notice you may find that no one is available in your area.

2) Those from well-known interdenominational missions.

Independent churches as well as many denominational churches enjoy the inspiration that some of these missionaries bring. Unless you have a particular missionary in

228 AN INTRODUCTION TO CHRISTIAN MISSIONS

mind and know that he is making his own appointments, just write to mission headquarters for information. Write well ahead of time if possible. Again, don't hesitate to ask about the capabilities of those who may be available. Not every good missionary is a good public speaker.

3) Others whom you may know or who may be recommended to you.

Go slowly here. You are safest in inviting those who are from the well-known missions. (Membership in such organizations as the IFMA or EFMA is a good recommendation.) Some very able speakers represent works that are highly questionable. If you are not sure, investigate. Don't invite the speaker until you are satisfied. (One pastor wrote us asking about a certain mission after he had already completed arrangements for it to hold a conference in his church.) It is easier to keep an undesirable speaker out to begin with than to explain to your people later that you made a mistake.

b. Mission secretaries, deputation representatives, etc.

There are times when these are to be preferred to the missionary on furlough. In fact, many of them are experienced missionaries whom the mission has kept home for this special ministry. They are usually effective speakers. These are the ones to invite if you want a broad picture of the whole work of the mission. The missionary on furlough speaks principally of his own station or work and his own personal experiences. This lends vividness to his talk. But he doesn't always see how his work fits into the overall program of the mission.

c. Accepted candidates.

Many churches pay scant attention to accepted missionary candidates unless they are personally acquainted with them. The candidates haven't been on the field yet. They only know the work at secondhand. So what kind of message can they bring? The answer is simply this: they can bring the inspiration of their example. If they are wise enough to make much of their personal testimony of the Lord's dealing with them, you will find that they can bring real inspiration to the church. They may lead some of the young people to wonder if perhaps they too might not be usable on the mission field. They will also move older people to a deeper devotion by their example of youthful consecration. It is not necessary to give them a whole church service. But you can very profitably give them a few minutes for a personal word.

2. For what services?

This is largely a matter for the discretion of the pastor or leader. However, to get the greatest profit you will definitely want to have a good missionary speaker at a time when most people will be able to hear him. Don't use him as bait to try to increase attendance at an otherwise poorly attended service. His presence may possibly increase the attendance somewhat, but the blessings of his ministry will be lost to those who didn't get there. They are often the ones who need it most. Also don't overlook the possibility of having him minister in the Sunday school and the young people's society. But by all means let him know ahead of time just what services he is to have. Even veteran missionaries need to prepare their messages ahead of time in order to do their best.

3. When to invite.

Invite your missionary speaker as much in advance as possible. Even when they live in your city, you will find that the better speakers have their schedules filled months ahead. If he comes from a distance you will want to reduce transportation costs by inviting him at a time when he is already planning to be somewhere in your neighborhood. That means your invitation should reach him while he is planning his itinerary. When a missionary responds that he will be able to be with you on a certain date, and that date is acceptable, be sure to confirm it in writing. That way there won't be any slipup.

4. Financial arrangements.

These are sometimes hard to make because the missionary hesitates to put a price on his services as if he were a professional man. Yet money is important to him. The following suggestions should help:

    a. Give him at least as much as you would give to a regular pulpit supply, if the missionary takes a church service.

    b. If he comes from any distance, see that his transportation is cared for.

    c. If he has to stay overnight, at least take care of his lodging.

    d. Faith missionaries will not ask for remuneration and may even request that no collection be taken.

However, this does not prevent your doing what we have mentioned above. Neither does it keep you from putting an offering plate near the door, into which people may drop an offering if they wish. The only thing is that they do not want people pressured to give.

    e. In some other cases churches like to take a free-will offering for the missionary in addition to, or in place of, the regular church offering.

5. Instructions to the speaker.

Even the experienced missionary speaker needs to be told precisely what you expect of him.

    a. Be sure to tell him the exact time of the meeting, the lenght of time for his message, and the type of service it is to be.

If your people don't like the service to run overtime, let him know. Some missionaries need this reminder.

    b. Tell him how to reach the church; and if you are arranging accommodations for him, let him know it.

    c. If you want him to use pictures of any sort, find out if he will have his own equipment and let him know what equipment you can provide.

> d. If you don't want a sermon, tell him so.

Don't blame the missionary for not giving a missionary talk in a Sunday morning service if you didn't tell him what you wanted. Make it clear just what kind of message is desired.

6. Conduct of the service.

> a. Make sure the missionary's time is not cut short by lengthy announcements and other needless preliminaries.

This is a common failing. If you want his message, give him his full time to deliver it.

> b. Lengthy introductions are unnecessary.

Say just enough to let the people know who he is and to whet their appetites to hear him. Then sit down. The longer you talk the less time he has for his message.

> c. If the pastor can't be there, make sure that someone capable is in charge.

The speaker finds it very awkward to have to take charge of the whole service in a strange church as well as give the message.

7. Hospitality.

There are two ways of providing lodging and board for the missionary speaker when it is needed. One is for the pastor or some other member of the church to entertain him in his own home. The other is for the church to secure him a room in a nearby hotel or motel and arrange for his meals either in a private home or at a restaurant.

If the missionary has been traveling and speaking a great deal, the idea of a hotel room has special attraction. It offers him the opportunity of relaxing in private and perhaps even catching up on his correspondence. However, he also knows the value of fellowship with a Christian family and the opportunity it offers him of a unique ministry there.

This personal and familiar contact with the missionary is of great benefit to both parties. Many a family has testified of the blessing the missionary has been in the home. Often his visit deeply affects the children. At the same time the missionary finds that the family's interest in his work is now put on a deeper, more personal basis than before.

Just this word for those who entertain missionaries: The ideal host takes care of his guest, but he does it in such a manner that the guest isn't made to feel burdensome or unduly obligated. The guest on his part should not impose and should fit into the regular family schedule.

C. Use of audiovisual aids

There was a time when the curios he brought back were the missionary's only visual aids in telling his story. Later he could show photographs, and later still, the old black-and-white or hand-colored glass slides. It was left for the present generation to multiply and improve such visual aids, plus motion pictures, and add to them the dimension of sound.

It is seldom that a church is prepared to care properly for a missionary museum or permanent exhibit. Missionaries have found to their distress that curios left with the home church tend to disappear. Or else they gather dust in some neglected corner. It takes the missionary himself to use them and make them live.

However, there are many other aids that you can use effectively even in the absence of the missionary. Most important are slides, filmstrips and motion pictures, either with or without sound.

To find out what ones are available, and on what conditions, get in touch with the missionary or the mission board. Sometimes they charge a small rental fee. At other times they stipulate that an offering is to be taken at the time of the showing and remitted to the mission. Slides and filmstrips sometimes come with a printed lecture that you can read as you show the pictures. At other times there is a recording that goes along with the pictures. These are very helpful. Of course keep in mind that the better and more recent pictures usually have to be booked a good while in advance—especially the motion pictures. Motion pictures also call for an experienced projectionist, since they are expensive to replace.

These aids do require that the church own or rent equipment if it is going to use them when the missionary is not around. However, most churches today are using such equipment more or less regularly in other phases of their work.

There are a good many slide and filmstrip projectors on the market today. Many families have their own. Missionaries, too, usually carry their own along with them. But when a church is buying a projector it should keep three or four things in mind. *First,* while a 300-watt projector is often strong enough, it may be advantageous to get a stronger light for use in the larger rooms. *Second,* if the projector must be set up at a considerable distance from the screen, a "zoom" lens is advisable—one that has an adjustable focal length. *Third,* the church would do well to get a projector that can be used for both slides and filmstrips. Missionaries do not produce filmstrips, but mission societies do, and their productions are often to be preferred. *Finally,* there is the matter of the various kinds of slide-holders or magazines. They save wear and tear on the slides, but no one projector can handle them all. The best solution is to allow enough time before any showing to transfer the slides, if necessary, to the type of magazine that fits your projector.

Motion pictures call for more expensive equipment than slides or filmstrips. Of course you can use the same screen, but you need a good 16-millimeter sound projector. If the picture is not a sound picture you can still show it on the sound projector. But you cannot show a sound film on a silent projector. Don't try it.

A further word about the effective use of these aids. A common mistake in the use of pictures is to expect them to do the whole job alone. It doesn't work. You may make the pictures the heart of the program, but the whole program needs to be planned carefully to give them their full effect. First know what is in the pictures. Then plan your opening remarks to prepare the audience to view them with understanding. These remarks can be just as long as you think necessary for the purpose. But your remarks *after* the pictures should be as brief and to the point as you can make them. Perhaps they should simply point the way to what action the people should take in view of what they have just seen. *But no preaching!*

There are several other audiovisual aids that we ought to mention briefly. You can get flannelgraph stories from the mission fields from several missions. You can also buy them in Christian bookstores. Then, an increasing number of missionaries are taking tape recorders to the field and are sending home recordings. These are principally in the nature of personal reports. The quality is often not of the best. However, people appreciate them a great deal when they are well acquainted with the missionary.

D. The missionary library

The church that gives serious attention to a church library never has reason to complain of the results. No other investment pays such valuable dividends for so small an amount invested. If it doesn't work out well, the cause is usually one of three things: the lack of a dependable librarian, a poor selection of books, or an unwillingness to spend money for new books and to keep the library up.

The librarian is the biggest problem, unless the church has a full-time secretary who can also handle this work. It needs someone who is interested and will be faithful to the task, someone who will keep accurate records and be available at regular times for the borrowing and returning of books.

The biggest mistake in the choice of books is to get the ones you think the people ought to read rather than those they really want to read. It is all right to have a certain number of reference works, but most of the books should be of the sort that nearly everybody is interested in reading. When one person likes a book he is sure to recommend it to someone else. But remember that tastes differ. You will have to make allowance for this.

Of course no library will continue to be used if it doesn't continually add to its list. Some books can be gifts from interested friends. These are often the older books. But you should be purchasing new ones constantly. To know what books to buy, unless you read them yourself, consult the reviews in some dependable Christian magazine. Publicize these books, too, so that people will know they are available and want to read them. If you have a bulletin board, you can put the jacket of a new book on the board, together with a review of it.

What *missionary* books should go into the library? If your library is small you will want only a few reference works and serious study books. The larger the library, the more of these you may include. A large part of the books should be in the nature of missionary stories, mostly true stories, and biography. Books of this nature are constantly coming from the presses, both for children, young people and adults. They are books also that are rarely available in the local public library. Some of them go through only one or two printings and are quickly out of print. Others are available for many years and maintain a constant reader interest.

If you are just going to start a missionary library, you will want to get counsel. Your own reading and that of friends will lead you to some books. Missionaries can recommend others. However, remember that the missionary is a specialist in this field. What interests him may not have the same interest for the average church member. Even more helpful may be the advice of your nearby Christian bookstore manager. He knows what books have been selling well and so have popular appeal.

Of course not all best sellers are books that you would

want in your library. So pay attention to the publisher. Some will publish almost any book that is well written and promises to have a good market. On occasion they may publish a very good missionary book, or even a number of them, though this is not their major thrust. With these you need to be quite selective.

Christian publishers, of course, publish only those books that they think are consistent with the Christian message. This still leaves room for considerable variation. Some are decidedly liberal in their theological position. Others are very conservative. Get catalogs from those with whom you are most likely to agree and see what missionary books they have in print. Some, such as Moody Press, give major attention to missionary books. Others have very little to offer in this field.

Some of the larger mission societies also publish missionary books, especially about their own work or workers. They usually advertise them in the pages of their mission magazine. If your people have an interest in the work of that society, by all means get its books for your library. They will help maintain and even increase that interest.

Keeping up a library takes constant attention, though not full time. It is good to maintain a "want list" of books you would like to get when the funds are available. Perhaps you can even interest individuals or groups in donating books from this list. Remember too that books do wear out and you must make provision for replacement. This is specially true of the children's books. You may need two or more copies of a very popular book.

Just a further word about encouraging use of the library. This applies particularly to children and young people. Offer a prize for the ones who read a certain number of books within a given time. In some cases a contest will arouse great interest. Then you can give a special prize to those who read the most. Everyone who reads the specified amount, however, should get something. One church offered a trip to a mission field in Mexico as the top prize. Not many are in a position to do this. There are many less costly incentives, however. The money and effort expanded will show how valuable the church thinks it is for its young people to be alert and instructed in missionary matters.

24

A CHURCH MISSIONARY PROGRAM—
HOW TO CREATE INTEREST (II)

E. The missionary conference

One of the most popular means for stirring up missionary interest in a church is the missionary conference.* Here in a period of a few days the church centers its whole attention on missions. Such a concentrated effort is usually productive, whether in the raising of the church's missionary budget or in getting young people to volunteer for missionary service. But much of the value of the conference depends on the understanding and care with which you make the plans, and on your choice of speakers.

Where only one mission is involved, as in many of the denominational churches, the church's part in the planning is fairly simple. Since the mission has had experience in such things, you may simply agree on the dates and then allow the mission to take charge. Of course there will have to be consultation about the details. But the mission will recommend the overall plan and provide the speakers. The church's responsibility is then to carry out the plan.

But where several missions are to be represented, the whole responsibility rests on the church. And it is such conferences that are the most common. They are held even in many denominational churches. We shall give

* A 1967-68 survey of 253 new missionaries in three Spanish language schools in Latin America showed that about 40 percent were decisively influenced by their church's missionary conference to dedicate their lives to missions. No other such gathering was even a third as effective.

rather extended treatment to this type because its problems will include those of the other type.

1. Timing.

In planning a missionary conference, the first thing to do is to settle on a time for it. There is no particular time of the year that is always better than any other time. Most churches do avoid the summer months. But spring, fall and even winter months are commonly used. Churches avoid the Christmas season because of so many other activities at that time. But Easter time is popular. Often the church plans to have the conference near the beginning or end of its fiscal year, with an eye on the budget.

How long should the conference be? There is no easy answer. Local conditions have much to do with the decision. The choice usually runs from three days to a week. Very few churches find it profitable to run over a week of continuous meetings. Sometimes the conference begins with a Sunday and runs through the midweek prayer meeting. Perhaps even more often it begins with the midweek prayer meeting and ends with the Sunday meetings. Some churches have adopted another variation, where it has been difficult to get people out on week nights. They set aside a "missionary month," with missionary speakers at each Sunday and midweek service during the month. This plan does not have the concentrated impact of the other. However, it may reach more people and it does sustain the emphasis over a longer period.

2. Program.

Local conditions will determine how many and what services you can best use. The plan that works very well in one place may not be at all suitable for another. Pay attention to the following:

   a. Most people will attend the regular services of
      the church.

This means that you will have your largest congregations at the regular Sunday meeting times, with perhaps the second largest at the midweek prayer-meeting hour. People are used to going to church at these times. Even an exceptionally good speaker may not draw them out at any other time.

    b. The evening services, except on Sunday, will be better attended than afternoon or morning meetings.

This doesn't mean that you can't hold profitable daytime meetings in some places. There are people who can and do arrange their work so as to be free to attend such meetings. Of course they are likely to be the ones most deeply interested in missions, so plan the meeting accordingly. In any case the attendance will be smaller than at night.

    c. Sunday afternoon meetings are often poorly attended in the cities, where there are many other attractions.

This is something that is very unpredictable. Occasionally Sunday afternoon meetings, where there is a program of unusual interest, are well attended and profitable.

    d. A word of warning about meetings held at times that are not in the regular church schedule.

Don't make them long! Some people don't mind, but many others do. They won't come out night after night if they think the meetings are too prolonged. Better to have them wish they were longer than to feel they are too long. They won't tell you about it. They just won't come back. An hour is usually long enough for a weekday meeting.

    e. Include the Sunday school, young people's society, women's society and any other church organizations in your plans.

The women's society may have to move its regular meeting up a week, but it is usually glad to do so. The Sunday school may want a few words from a missionary at its opening exercises. Or it may plan to have missionaries speak to individual classes or departments.

    f. Usable types of meetings.

1) The Sunday morning service usually follows the regular form, except that a missionary speaker is in the pulpit.

Most people will expect a missionary message, so don't disappoint them. The music also should be missionary in nature. The Sunday evening meeting may vary.

2) Sometimes more than one missionary is available at a single meeting.

Then, if time allows, you may want one of them to take part of the time for pictures, while the other follows with an address. Or vice versa. But be sure not to extend the meeting beyond the time limit. One of the greatest mistakes is to try to crowd too much into a single meeting.

3) Sometimes it is good to follow a talk with a question period, when the audience is invited to ask the speaker questions.

This usually works out best in the smaller, more informal meetings. You may find that it is hard to get the people started asking questions. So let them know ahead of time that there will be such a period, so that they can get set for it. Also the one who presides should be prepared to get the ball rolling by asking one or more questions himself.

4) Round table or panel discussions can be very valuable if several missionaries are present.

It takes a capable and well-informed leader to handle them properly though. In the round-table discussion the missionaries discuss one or more problems among themselves with the audience listening in. To keep their interest, the audience should be allowed to interject questions also. This type of discussion works best with subjects that are somewhat controversial. It also calls for a willingness to expose differences of opinion—something that many are inclined to avoid.

In the panel discussion the questions come from the audience and are referred to one or another of the missionaries on the panel for an answer. If the leader or one of the others on the panel is not satisfied with a particular answer, he may give another point of view or add to the answer. Don't expect everyone on the panel to answer each question, however. Keep the discussion moving.

Sometimes leaders "plant" questions in the audience to be asked at the proper time. While this is not necessarily objectionable, most people dislike its artificiality. The "planted" questions are usually so stereotyped that it is obvious they didn't originate with the person asking them.

Young people keenly interested in missions usually like these discussion periods, provided the questions are spontaneous and the answers are straightforward. Otherwise, they don't.

> 5) You ought to plan for special services for the children, and sometimes for the young people.

Costumes, curios, stories, and songs interest the children. Pictures are good, but only if they are adapted to the children's interests. For the young people you may want to plan a special meeting in connection with a picnic or a banquet. Or if there is a Saturday night youth rally, you can make it a missionary rally.

> 6) Don't overlook the possibility that the local school or some civic group might be interested in hearing one or more of the missionary speakers.

Of course this calls for a speaker with tact and good judgment, in view of the present status of religion in our public institutions. In this way, however, you are spreading the blessing beyond your own church to those who might not otherwise be reached. Besides, it is good publicity for the meetings in your church.

g. Exhibits.

There are two ways of planning exhibits for the conference. One is to leave it entirely to the missionaries. In that case you should notify them well in advance that you want them to provide such an exhibit. Tell them how much space they will have, and be sure to have tables and other equipment available. Electrical outlets need to be accessible for those who may want special lighting or use other electrical devices. Missionaries usually have literature with them that can be placed on the same tables with the other displays.

Another way is to involve the church people themselves in the preparation of the exhibits. You can do this by assigning a different exhibit to each of several organizations in the church or departments in the Sunday school. A prize for the most attractive display usually excites interest.

h. Finances.

The same suggestions for contacting speakers apply to the missionary conference as for any other meetings, except that even more advance notice may be needed. The financial arrangements, however, may be quite different. They are complicated by the fact that the church sometimes uses the missionary conference to help raise its annual budget for missions. In such a case it is often best to plan a stated amount for each speaker. Then all offerings above that amount can go into the church's missionary treasury. However, many churches use another plan. They first pay the expenses of conducting the conference from the offerings. Then they divide the remainder proportionately among the missionaries taking part, or the missions they represent.

25

A CHURCH MISSIONARY PROGRAM—
KEEPING INFORMED

II. Accurate and up-to-date information

Many of the things we mentioned for stirring up interest serve just as well to keep up that interest. But they need to be supplemented by several other things.

A. Bulletin board

In many active missionary churches you will find a special missionary bulletin board. It has a variety of uses. Pictures and letters from the field often appear on it. Sometimes it carries special announcements of missionary meetings or a copy of the church missionary budget. It is a good place to advertise a new missionary book. Its usefulness depends to a large degree on the alertness of the one in charge. This of course should be a regularly designated individual. Otherwise the board is neglected. We don't need to add that if it isn't kept up it loses its value.

If the church has missionaries of its own it needs to keep them before its people. "Out of sight, out of mind" certainly applies here. The missionary is usually gone for three to five years at a stretch. Meantime the church membership is changing. Perhaps a new pastor comes. Even those who do remember the missionary find their recollections becoming rather vague. Whether on the bulletin board or in some other prominent spot, each missionary's picture should find a permanent place. With it should be his name and postal address.

B. Map

Some people find maps very dull. But that is either because they haven't learned to read them or because they haven't much interest in what the map shows. Maps are like pictures. They try to help us visualize what an area looks like if we could see it all at once. Primitive people often have trouble trying to "see" a picture. In the same way, those who are not used to maps have to learn to read them and "see" what they picture.

But most Americans can read a map if it is not too detailed. In fact, if we are at all interested in a place, we like to go to a map to get a general idea of where it is. That is why newspapers so often print small outline maps to accompany news items from abroad. It helps locate the places. And of course we all use road maps when we travel.

Just so, the church should help its people to locate their missionaries or mission fields. It doesn't call for a detailed map. The simpler the better for most people. But a real help is a general map on which the place you are interested in stands out. Put the map where the people can see it. Some churches like to put the pictures of their missionaries around the border of the map. Various devices, including tiny electric lights, can be used to indicate where the missionaries are stationed.

C. Missionary letters

The most up-to-date news from the mission fields comes through missionary letters. It usually comes in small bits, and it isn't always important. This is because most missionaries write about their own experiences, or their own particular station and work. They seldom give the broad view of the whole field. They leave that to others. But we do need the personal touch their letters give. It is from these bits of news that we can put the whole picture together.

If the church is helping support a missionary on the field, it will usually hear from him with fair regularity.

He usually acknowledges its gifts. If he doesn't he should
be reminded to do so. Here is where churches often make
a mistake. The letter sometimes gets no farther than the
pastor or the treasurer to whom it is addressed. No one
else sees it unless the women's missionary society makes
a special inquiry for any late news. No one thinks of answering the letter. Money was sent; a letter comes acknowledging receipt; and that is that.

But that shouldn't be all. The money was from the
church. So the church should see the letter — at least those
parts that interest it. Here is where the missionary bulletin
board comes in handy. Post the letters where anyone who
wants may read them.

Then go a step farther. Answer the letters. There
are pastors who have never taken the time to write a
letter to their missionary. They hear from him. In fact they
would think him very remiss if he didn't write. But they
are "just too busy" to answer. We are not going to scold
the pastor. He probably *is* busy. (So is the missionary.)
But he is missing an opportunity to minister. The missionary often is in need of a word of spiritual counsel as
well as an expression of personal interest. Not having
received any letter himself, the missionary finds it hard
to write as freely as he would like. A one-sided conversation is likely to become very stilted.

The pastor is not the only one involved. Letters come
to the treasurer and others that are never answered. Let
someone be responsible for answering them. It doesn't
have to be the same one every time. But it should be a
clear-cut responsibility. A general request in the church
bulletin for the members to write to their missionary is
too vague. Hardly anyone will write. Put the duty on a
specific person. Even give him an air-letter form for the
purpose. He will be more likely to do it, and he will get a
blessing from it.

We mentioned the weekly church bulletin. Here is
a good place to publish extracts from missionary letters.

Most church bulletins are too monotonous anyway. Spruce them up with some interesting tidbits from the mission field. The people will read them. They will read them even more readily than they will read the letters tacked on the bulletin board.

So far we have only talked about the personal letters from the missionary. We haven't mentioned form letters. Whether you think the missionaries are overdoing this form-letter bit or not, it is a fixed part of modern missions. The missionary would like to write to so many people, and there are so many people who want to hear from him, that the form letter seems to be the only answer.

Every pastor is likely to receive a number of these form letters from different missionaries. You don't have to answer them unless you want to. But they do give news that you may be able to use. In fact, some missions are so convinced of their value that they do the mimeographing and mailing for their missionaries. They also run off extra copies that they can send in packets to churches or other interested groups. These letters are more informal than magazine articles.

The missionary usually has his form letters sent to all who ask for them, or to anyone who has shown an interest in him and his work. But with his home church he faces a problem. Should he try to send a letter to every member? It means a lot of work and expense. Here the church sometimes steps in. It says to the missionary, "Send us your letter and we'll see that every one of our members gets a copy." This is not only a help to the missionary, it ties him in more closely with the church in the minds of the people. This is as it should be. Besides, it keeps all the members informed. Where the church supports several missionaries, it sometimes combines their letters in a single issue. A quarterly compilation is very helpful.

D. Magazines

The missionary magazine conveys much more news than the missionary letter, and in a relatively small space.

Each mission has its own magazine. Some are monthly, some bimonthly, some quarterly. Some are well edited, while others are little more than collections of missionary letters. Some have a stated subscription price; others are sent free of charge. But all deal primarily with the work of the mission that publishes them. In every case the mission is glad to send sample copies free on request.

Besides the magazines put out by individual missions or denominations, there are two other types that should interest us. Christian family magazines such as *Moody Monthly* have frequent missionary items. Some are feature articles. Some are in the nature of news reports. In some cases there is a special section of the magazine dedicated to missions. These appeal to the general reader.

More specialized, but still quite readable for those interested in foreign missions, is the *Evangelical Missions Quarterly*. This is jointly sponsored by the Interdenominational Foreign Mission Association and the Evangelical Foreign Missions Association. It is a "must" for those who want to be informed on current trends in evangelical missionary thinking. Invaluable for those who want to be acquainted with the more liberal point of view is the *International Review of Mission,* also a quarterly.

What should the church do about missionary magazines? We recommend three things.

First, the library. The church library should be receiving the regular denominational papers. It should also have at least one Christian magazine of a more general nature in which there will be some coverage of missions. It should regularly receive the mission magazine of each mission in which the church has an interest, plus one of the more technical magazines mentioned above.

Second, promote circulation. The church itself profits when it urges its members to get one or more of these magazines for themselves. An informed church is an active church. The two go together. In some cases the publishers offer a special price if a number of copies are sent to one address. Of course if there is no subscription price the problem is just distributing the magazines. The most economical way is just to announce that they will be available near the door as the congregation leaves a Sunday service. But even when they are available the people are not likely to pick them up unless they are encouraged to do so.

Third, encourage reading. Circulation is not enough if the people don't read what they get. In these days of much printing we skip a great deal in our reading. Very few read a whole magazine. Yet much of what we skip we might read if some friend were to recommend it or stir up our interest in it. So those who lead in the church's missionary program have the responsibility of recommending articles of special interest. But don't just say that they are interesting. Tell why they are important to read. Better still, give a brief excerpt so the people will want to know more. The preacher can do this from the pulpit, or the Sunday school teacher in his class.

26

A CHURCH MISSIONARY PROGRAM—
MISSIONARY SUPPORT

III. Prayer support

It would scarcely seem necessary to say more than we have about the missionary's need for our prayers. Most of us know that he needs prayer and counts heavily on it. Yet we don't take many practical measures to provide it. That is, as a church we don't.

Many are familiar with the story of the missionary who had to leave his field unexpectedly. Reaching his hometown on a Wednesday evening, he decided to drop in on the church prayer meeting. Quietly he took a seat in the rear and listened. During the whole service not a word about missions—not a prayer for the missionaries! Then he knew why the going had been so hard.

This little story highlights the need to pray for missionaries in the prayer meeting. But the need is much broader than that. It is a need for the prayers of the whole church—of all the members who know how to pray. It is a part of the church's ministry, and a part in which every member can take a part.

How to get such prayers? It takes deliberate planning. You can't do it by simply urging everyone to pray, "Lord, bless the missionaries." We pray for people when we know they have a real need. The greater the need, the more likely we are to pray. The problem then is to get the people to see the need.

The missionaries themselves are sometimes at fault here. They don't write when they should. They hesitate to make their needs known. Or sometimes they state them in such general terms you can't be exactly sure of what they do need and why. Not just physical needs; those are usually pretty clear. But all of us are rather shy about revealing our spiritual needs. These may be just as great. We are afraid to talk about them because it may show up our weakness, or the weakness of the work we are doing.

Of course there are many needs that are not purely personal and don't affect the work of just one missionary. The religious persecution of believers, natural calamities such as floods, or the inroads of false cults, all call for prayer. In addition the missionary is not usually hesitant in asking prayer for different ones among his people for whom he is concerned.

The problem is to present the needs in such a way that people will be inclined to pray at home as well as in church. The prayer meeting is the natural place to present the challenge, but it reaches only a small part of the people. A pastoral announcement and prayer on Sunday morning will alert many more. Of course the missionary society should be interested. But why not the Sunday school as well? And you can often get more sincere, unselfish praying in a young people's society than anywhere else.

Sometimes the church issues a missionary prayer list. If it does so the requests should be clear-cut and definite. Give enough information so the people will know why they are being asked to pray. And when the answers come, report them. Nothing encourages prayer as much as the knowledge that prayers are being answered. There need not be many requests. It is far better to concentrate on a few important ones. You will get more cooperation.

The custom that many families have of a missionary bulletin board in the kitchen or dining room is a good one. On it they post the prayer cards with pictures of the missionaries in whom they are specially interested. They

serve as a reminder to pray at mealtime or at other times
during the day.

Prayer is sure to be much more spontaneous and
constant among those who are personally well acquainted
with the missionary and his family. This points up the
importance of personal contact when the missionaries are
at home on furlough.

IV. Material support

We stated that the church should give material support
to missions in as large a measure as possible. Don't ask
how large a measure that is. I don't know. All I can say is
that I never knew a church that was doing all it could.
Yet I have known some very generous ones. The experience
of those churches that have increased their giving year
by year shows that there is always room for improvement.

The measure of a church's giving is not the number
of its members. Some of the largest churches are the
poorest givers. And we may add that some of the wealth-
iest churches are put to shame in their giving by some of
the poorest. The thing is not to measure ourselves by
what others are doing but constantly to improve our own
position.

For this reason we always do well to set an objective.
Make it high enough so that it will not be easy to reach.
It ought to be a challenge. But don't make it so high as
to be unrealistic. If reaching the goal is clearly out of the
question, the people will get discouraged. People are always
stirred to greater efforts when they have a definite, reach-
able goal.

Also let the people know just what they are giving for.
If there is any item on your missionary budget that you
don't want the members to see, it shouldn't be there!
There is no surer way to discourage giving than to keep
part of the budget secret.

A. What missionaries?

Sometimes churches are puzzled to know whether

they ought to support only missionaries who are their own members. The answer is not as hard as some make it seem. Of course you should support your own members first of all. That is, if you have any confidence in the work in which they are engaged. They are your representatives on the mission field in a way in which others could not be. They are a part of you. They are your primary responsibility.

Then if you are able to do more, or if you have no one from your church on the mission field, give to others. Some churches are able to produce more in the way of missionaries, others in the way of money. The really difficult question is whether it is better to give full support to one missionary family or partial support to several. There are advantages both ways. Let the church decide. However, "tokenism" should definitely be ruled out. The church should be able to feel that the missionary is to some significant degree "our missionary," and not someone to whom we give an occasional small contribution.

If the members of the church who go out as missionaries are more than the church can support, the problem becomes a serious one. Even one missionary is more than some churches can fully support. What then? The only possible answer is this. Do what you can. Keep up your support of those already on your list. Take on the support of the newer ones as fast as you are able. Don't drop the ones nor neglect the others. Let the new missionaries needing support be a challenge to greater efforts in giving. But under no conditions drop the older missionaries so as to support the newer ones.

B. Dropping support

Speaking of dropping support, there is a practice that sometimes afflicts independent churches, and even some that are denominational. I saw it first in the experience of one missionary couple a number of years ago. In the middle of their second term of service, their two supporting churches, in different parts of the country, both announced

that they were dropping their support. They had taken on
other interests. There was nothing the missionaries could
do about it. They had to undergo a time of real privation.

Such a thing usually happens when there is a change
of pastor. The new pastor is not acquainted with the
church's missionaries. He has some favorite missionary
projects of his own. So he begins to push his own program
and gets the church to drop the old one. Not so long ago
a large independent church called a new pastor. One of
the missionaries the church was supporting was a young
woman who had grown up in it. For years the church had
been an active supporter of her mission society. When she
decided to go to the field, the church had naturally assumed
her support. But now with the new pastor things changed.
After a time the young woman got notice that the church
was reducing the amount of her support. It was not because
she was getting more than she needed. Nor had the church's
offerings for missions declined. In fact they had been on
the upgrade. It was simply that the church now had some
other plans.

C. Bargain hunting

The preceding fault is not the only one the church
needs to guard against. Another is the temptation to seek
bargains in missions. In a personal interview a young prospective missionary told me that his church would not be
willing to support him in the field to which he believed the
Lord was calling him. The reason? "They told me," he said,
"that if I would go to another field it wouldn't cost so much!"

Maybe not. Maybe we ought to use "good business
sense" and spend all our missionary money where we can
"get the most for it." Maybe we ought to withdraw our
missionaries from the difficult Muhammadan fields and
send them where the results are easier to get. Maybe—but
if we do we are turning our backs on the greatest of all
missionaries, Jesus Christ. Look at what His mission cost
Him! Look at what He paid for our salvation! Dare we
commercialize the dedication of our young people? They

are spending their lives! Are we to count the value of human souls in dollars and cents?

There are no bargains in missions! You get no more than what you pay for by sacrificial effort. "He that soweth sparingly shall reap also sparingly."

D. Support levels

What does it cost to support a missionary? It depends. Better ask the mission. This we can say, though. Many missionary men are receiving less than a bus driver. And many women get less than a stenographer fresh out of high school. Why? Because the church doesn't give more.

"But it doesn't cost so much to live in other countries," some will object.

That's what *you* think. Actually in many places it costs more, *if you try to keep up the same standard of living.* What usually happens is that the missionary learns to do without many of the things we enjoy at home. The fact that the other people around him don't have them either just makes it a little easier to forego them.

E. National workers

The temptation to find bargains in missions makes some take up the idea of supporting national workers. The national can evangelize his own people so much better than the missionary. The missionary himself admits it. And in some cases he can be supported for a fraction of the cost of a missionary. So why not spend our money supporting national workers?

The missionaries themselves started this idea. Now they have to face the consequences. Some are still spreading the idea. But more and more they are coming to realize the weaknesses in the argument. Over and over they have been finding out that what sounds good in theory doesn't always work out in practice.

The first part of the argument certainly is sound. The national *can* evangelize his own people better than the missionary in many cases. Often he *can* be supported for considerably less than the cost of the missionary. But the conclusion doesn't necessarily follow. In most fields, as the national church itself insists, the missionaries are still needed.

Let's put it this way: A certain factory employs two-hundred workmen to manufacture its product. Besides these two-hundred there are a number of supervisors, a large office force and several top officials. One day an agitator gets hold of some of the workers. "Why should those officials. get so much more money than you do?" he shouts. "You're the ones who do the work! What's the use of all those white-collar workers? It's you workmen who produce!"

It sounds right to the workers. But, get rid of those others and what do you have? Only one word can describe it—chaos. Supplies dwindle; finished products pile up in the warehouse with no one to buy them; faulty pieces reach the consumer and break down in use; bills pile up; credit is gone; the factory has to close its doors.

The missionaries will not be needed always. But they will be needed until the time when there are nationals prepared to take over the whole of the work and not just the preaching. We have said that national workers can evangelize their own people better than missionaries. This is not because they are better workers. It is largely because a foreigner always works under a handicap. People always listen more readily to one of themselves, one whose previous life they have known and whose way of speaking has a familiar sound.

But national workers have to be converted first. Then they have to develop and mature in Christian experience, just like our Christian workers at home. And if they are to give full time to Christian work they must get training. All of this means work at the beginning for the mission-ary. But it isn't the end. Workers always need initial direc-tion and supervision in their work. They need to be coun-seled, occasionally rebuked, and sometimes even dismissed. Or would you be willing to hire a worker, sight unseen, and support him regularly in the vague hope that he may do a good work even without supervision? Some churches are actually doing this! Some organizations are even promoting it. And many have come to regret it.

Still this is not what is turning experienced mission leaders away from the idea. It is something deeper, more fundamental. Even though national workers can do a good job of evangelism, this doesn't necessarily mean national workers *hired with foreign funds.* Expecially not today! We Americans are constantly being accused of trying to buy people with our money. So the national worker we hire is at once under suspicion. He is the Americans' hired man, the "running dog of the imperialists," as the Chinese Communists put it.

But let's go a little deeper. The hiring of national workers with American funds once seemed to be a good way of multiplying our ministry. Of course we thought of it as only a temporary measure. Through these workers a church would soon be built up, and then the mission could withdraw its support and the church would take over. It was all very logical. But it didn't work out that way. Two or three generations later the workers were still being supported by American funds. And not too many workers at that. Also the church itself seemed remarkably weak. What was wrong?

Many missionaries have been learning that the so-called "indigenous principles" are the only sound principles on which to build a lasting work. The word *indigenous* means simply native to the land. In its simplest form the idea is that the church should take root among the people and grow spontaneously. The people themselves are expected to spread the gospel and win members for the church. They are to pay all the expenses of the church and they are to run the church. The terms most often used are: self-propagation, self-support and self-government.

We don't need to go into the details of these principles. But we do want to emphasize the fact that the people are supposed to win their fellows. This is the natural and the best way. At the same time notice that they are also supposed to pay the expenses. This means no money from American churches for the support of their normal activities. They grow stronger as they learn to do it for themselves.

This is one compelling reason why missionaries have opposed using American money to support national workers. In the long run it hinders the church. There is no question about it. It has been proved over and over.

One large mission adopted the policy some years ago of refusing to accept gifts for designated national workers. Any contributions for nationals were to be used at the mission's discretion. What they were trying to do was to shift the responsibility for support to the national church itself.

After a few years the mission was able to report that the church was growing faster than ever before in the mission's history. Besides (and this seemed to surprise them), the number of nationals engaged in the work was many times what it had been before. In other words, they got more and better workers when they stopped putting them on the American payroll. Of course it didn't happen overnight. It took time. But the end result justified their procedure.

What place does the missionary have in such a program? Just the place that Paul had in New Testament days. He introduces the gospel and welcomes the first converts. He helps the church get started and begins their instruction in the Word. He counsels and admonishes them and is in constant prayer for them. He shows them how, but theirs is the responsibility for carrying on the work of the church. He trusts that the day will come when he, like Paul, can say, "I have no more room in these parts" (Ro 15:23). As some have said, "The missionary's job is to work himself out of a job."

F. Other material support

When we said the church's objective is "to provide material support" for missions, we didn't mean just money. Money is the most widely useful contribution. But sometimes the church can contribute in other ways.

Some will think immediately of the "missionary barrel." This is something that isn't as much used as it used to be. In former days churches gathered all sorts of items, useful and otherwise, packed them in barrels and shipped them off to missionaries in faraway places. Some things were for the missionary and his family. Others were to be distributed among the people. The arrival of the barrel was always an exciting event. No one could ever foretell what might be in it. Many are the tales missionaries tell of the ridiculous items sometimes included in the vain hope that "maybe the missionaries can use them." Such shipments are no longer welcomed in most fields. So many countries have raised such high tariff barriers that the missionary shudders when he hears that an unsolicited shipment has come for him. He knows that he may have to pay in duty several times what the shipment is worth.

So if you are thinking of sending your missionary a package, big or little, think again. Don't send it until you have checked with him. Then if he approves, follow his instructions. You can't send him a surprise package this way, but better no surprise than one that will cost him dearly. There is no way you can prepay the duty.

However, when the missionary is at home you can readily give him things that will be useful on the field. He will be glad to tell you what he can use. Only remember this: If you are going to buy new items at retail, you might do better to give the missionary the money and let him buy them. He often has access to a supplier who can give him what he needs at wholesale prices. As for used articles, never give them unless they are in tip-top condition.

This brings up the matter of the "missionary closet"

that some churches maintain. It is a place for storing good used clothing and other items that the missionaries might need when they come home on furlough. When properly handled this is a welcome service. Coming from a tropical climate a missionary often needs a warm overcoat, for example, or a wool suit. But don't accept anything for the closet that is well worn or soiled. Some churches insist that any clothing must be washed and ironed, or dry-cleaned and pressed, before it is accepted. In one city a local merchant with a clothing store donates his surplus stock at the end of the season to a church that supports a number of missionaries. He gets a receipt for the market value of the donation, which helps considerably in tax matters. In addition, the missionaries get brand-new merchandise of excellent quality.

Always when giving money or goods, there is one error to avoid. Don't give as if you are dispensing charity. Make sure that the congregation doesn't get that idea either. Give as to a faithful worker who is fully worthy of his hire. He is the Lord's servant. Give as to the Lord Himself.

27

A CHURCH MISSIONARY PROGRAM—
PERSONNEL AND TRAINING

V. Personnel

Most churches are inclined to look at the missionary enterprise as something apart from themselves. This is especially true when we talk about getting missionary candidates. Missionaries have to come from somewhere. They know that. But it hasn't occurred to them that some of their own young people might be missionary material. It hasn't occurred to them because nobody has suggested it. No one has challenged their young people with the need for just what they have to offer—their unselfish devotion and the service of their lives.

The church is really the natural recruiting ground for missions. It is the one place where you will find nearly all of the young people who are interested in Christianity. Some of them have been reared in the church. Some were converted there. But practically all come to church for Christian worship and fellowship. They may not all be truly Christian. They may be there just because it is the proper thing to do. But at least they are susceptible to Christian teaching and they are in the place where they could naturally expect it to be given.

What are you doing with the young people in your church? Do you have any definite aims and program for them? Not just for missions. That will come if your spiritual program is a vital one. But are you paying serious attention to your young people? Do you have goals that you are earnestly trying to help them reach?

We can't have missionaries until we have consecrated young Christians. Yes, and instructed Christians too. The entertainment of our young people is not the church's task, though some seem to think so. Merely to keep them in some sort of association with the church is not enough. A vital program means spiritual guidance. It means bringing them into a living relationship with the Lord and with His Word. It means trying to get them to accept His lordship in deciding the course of their lives, whatever their line of work. And that is not easy. Neither are all ministers willing or capable of doing it.

In recent years young people around the world have become rebellious. It is not a rebellion based primarily on any material injustices they are suffering. Many of them will admit that there has never been such a pampered generation. But what is frustrating them is the apparent meaninglessness of life as they see it around them. What is the purpose of all this? Why are there so many inequities? Isn't there something fundamentally wrong with "the system"? What can one do who doesn't like what he sees? Where is there a cause that is worth dedicating his life to?

The church ought to have the answer. It ought to be providing the challenge. But all too often it doesn't. Rather, even to its own young people, it seems to be a part of "the system" that they deplore. Some churches, in their anxiety to be more "relevant," have plunged into activities that bear little relationship to their fundamental reason for existence. This only adds to the confusion. The church ceases to be the church and becomes just another humanitarian organization aping the practices of the world around it.

The problem of providing personnel for missions is only one phase of the problem of challenging men and women for any sort of distinctively Christian service. It is closely related to the problem of getting candidates for the Christian ministry. If the church cannot demonstrate its relevance to its own young people, much less will they be interested in spreading its gospel abroad. If its ministry is only another form of social service, then why not rather choose the Peace Corps? At least you won't have to sign up for life.

It is not our purpose here to go into the failings of the organized church today. It has never been all that it should be or could be, even in apostolic days. But time and again it has had to be called back to a realization that its true ministry is primarily spiritual. Such a ministry will naturally bring about deep changes in the life of individuals and of society. But the changes themselves are not its essence. They are the outward manifestations of a real faith, where that faith exists.

Is the church a vital spiritual force in the community? Is it "for real?" If so, then the young people will be finding their Saviour there. They will be finding there an avenue for expressing their faith to others. They will be led into a deeper knowledge and experience of Him and of His Word. And from time to time they will face the challenge of dedicating their lives more completely to Him. The regular monthly "consecration meeting" of the Christian Endeavor movement had its basis in this sound scriptural idea.

Don't be misled by the common misunderstanding of what a challenge is. Some people think a challenging message is one with plenty of action, clever turns of phrase and a strong appeal to the emotions. Instead, a real challenge sets before you clearly two courses of action and says, "Make a choice." Whether dramatically or very quietly, it calls you to look at the costs as well as the benefits of each. It asks you to weigh the issues carefully and then, "Choose you this day!"

When young people have accepted the salvation that Jesus Christ offers, then challenge them to a full dedication to Him. This is the first and most basic decision. Now they are Christians. Remind them that they are the ones whom "he hath purchased with his own blood." Tell them that "he died for all, that they which live should not henceforth live unto themselves, but unto him which died for them, and rose again." Show them that the alternative is that very selfish sort of life that they are so ready to condemn in other nominal Christians.

Such full dedication doesn't necessarily lead to "full-time Christian service." But it may. It may even mean foreign missionary service. But we don't stress it for that reason. We stress it because no Christian can be fully effective without it, no matter what his occupation. We stress it because we don't want missionary candidates who are not first of all dedicated wholeheartedly to Christ. They must be first dedicated to Christ and then to missions. Not the other way around.

Then challenge them to look at the world's need and at their own potentialities. The two go together. To know of a need that you can't help meet is simply frustrating. To have a gift, an ability or training for which there is no need is just as frustrating. They won't analyze the world's need perfectly. Who can? And they may put too high or too low a value on their own ability to fill the need. But even such a dim vision will give to life the purpose it needs. We all need to be convinced that what we are doing really matters.

Finally, challenge them to make a definite offer of their lives to the Lord and to get prepared for whatever He has for them. Note that we don't say "to offer their lives for foreign missions." It is much more important that they be ready for anything the Lord has for them. The challenge is to take the risk of letting Him make the choice. Some people are willing to volunteer if they can choose the type and place of service. But what the Lord wants are those who will put themselves in His hands and say, "Use me where You need me most." It may be in foreign missions. But don't be surprised if it is in a line you never thought of. There is no reason why a Christian businessman should not be as sincerely dedicated to the Lord as any minister or missionary.

Note that we said challenge them to get prepared. This is often a weak spot. We appeal to young people to dedicate their lives for Christian service, but we don't tell them at the same time that it takes real dedication to get thoroughly prepared for the job. As a result they are so impatient to "get going" that they slight their preparation or look around for shortcuts. Why don't we tell them that they will have to spend time and work in getting ready for this great ministry? Are we afraid they will get discouraged? They won't if they are the right kind. Instead it is likely to increase their respect for the work.

This ministry of challenging young people to turn their lives over to Jesus Christ is one of the greatest services for missions that a church can perform. Of course it isn't just for missions. The whole church benefits from it, and not the least the young people themselves. Young people are idealists. This in spite of the carping criticism of "the younger generation" by disillusioned middle-agers. They want a cause to which to dedicate themselves. And for what greater cause can you recruit them than that of Jesus Christ? Missions is only one outstanding phase of that cause.

But in your recruiting for missionary service do avoid some of the serious mistakes that are so common today. Let me list five of them.

First is a superficial emotionalism that quickly fades away. We are not discounting emotion. The emotions must be touched. We wouldn't give much for a missionary candidate who didn't feel keenly his obligation to witness for Christ. We want to have those who feel intensely, as Paul did, "Woe is unto me if I preach not the gospel!" But the appeal that reaches the heart springs and has an enduring effect is not the same as the one that merely stirs up the feelings for a night. Decisions made in the warm glow of an exciting meeting are often regretted in the

gray dawn of reality. So don't whip up an artificial enthusiasm that needs a crowd to keep it going. Try to touch
the depths of the soul.

*Second, avoid the glamorizing of missionary life and
work.* Any missionary can tell you how quickly the glamour
vanishes when you reach the field. To some it comes as
a rude shock, for they weren't prepared for the stark
reality. Of course you can't help it that so many think
all strange lands and people are glamorous. Their very
distance from us makes them look romantic. But you can
avoid heightening that impression. Put the emphasis where
it belongs, on the great motives and purpose of missions.
Don't put it on the bizarre, the strange and unusual
features of missionary life. Remember that even horror
can have a romantic attraction. When you tell a missionary story, be careful not to overcolor it.

*Third, don't appeal to a sense of pity for the people
just because of their great physical needs.* Such an appeal
does have a place. But its place is not that of recruiting
young people for the spiritual ministry of missions. Even
the nationals of these other countries have protested
against this sort of appeal. They remind us that we have
paupers and slums in our own country, as well as depraved
criminals. They resent an attitude of condescending pity.
We don't want our missionaries to go to the field with
such an attitude.

*Fourth, there is an unwise tendency to present foreign
missionary work as the highest form of heroic consecration.* Really it isn't. Many a missionary will assure you
that it isn't. Missionaries are often embarrassed by the
unsought and undesired hero worship that is heaped upon
them. Not that there isn't a great deal of heroism exhibited
in many mission fields. And for some young people it
takes a heroic decision to get them out. But for many the
decision to tackle an unromantic job at home is even
harder. In fact, for some the foreign field looks like a way

to escape frustration at home. Actually the highest form of consecration is to deny oneself, to take up one's cross and follow Christ—regardless of where He may lead.

A fifth mistake in recruiting is one that is hardly worthy of our mention. Yet it is quite commonly made. It is the appeal to young people to help enlarge the ministry of their own church, their own denomination, their own mission. This is nothing but selfish ambition masquerading as Christian missions. We are not of those who oppose all denominations. As long as Christianity is a really vital force it is likely to break out in new ways at any time. Regimentation means stagnation. But when any Christian group thinks chiefly of its own perpetuation or enlargement it is getting away from its Christian basis. The shameful competition and overlapping of work in some mission fields is not caused primarily by the fact that we have various denominations. It is caused rather by those who confuse the glory of Christ with the glorification of their own organization. Don't be guilty of inspiring young people to go out with such a vainglorious attitude. Challenge them to preach not themselves but Christ. Try to see that their chief concern is for the honor of Christ and that the world may experience the life of Christ.

But a further word. Don't just challenge. Tell what kinds of missionaries we need. Of course that means that you yourself will need to know. It means that you will have to be interested enough to keep in touch with the missions, though at times you may prefer to have a missionary or mission secretary deal with this subject. But do make it definite. Don't encourage those who have no special ability. Don't say, "You can probably be used somewhere." Could you use them at home? Don't encourage divorced persons, or those who are overage or queer. Or those who are not willing to work hard to prepare. Don't make the mission candidate secretaries do all the weeding out. You know your young people better than they do. Also don't hesitate to encourage some of them individually. They may need just a little encouragement. But don't push. Let the Lord do the compelling.

Provide opportunities for your young people to meet missionaries and missionary candidates personally. Just an invitation for people to speak to the missionary after the service is not enough. Only a few of the more venturesome will do it. Arrange for a discussion group or something similar. Or maybe a small gathering in a home. These personal contacts are extremely valuable. They bring home to your young people, as nothing else could, that missionaries are just ordinary people with an extraordinary devotion to their Saviour.

Again we say, the local church is the natural recruiting ground for missions. Most of our present missionaries got their vision of the work there. Is your church taking advantage of this opportunity? Is it meeting the need?

VI. Training

When we think of the training of missionary candidates, we look immediately to the Bible institutes, seminaries and other such schools. What we don't seem to realize is that they can only do a part of the job. The local church also plays a significant role. We have mentioned before that really the most important part of the preparation of missionaries takes place outside the classroom. In fact, the local church can in some measure provide all four of the indispensables in missionary preparation.

But the local church doesn't need to carry on a separate missionary training program. The preparation of prospective missionaries is just a part of the total program the church ought to have for the training of all its young people. The church can't give the specialized instruction needed for foreign service. That is for the schools. But what it can and should do is train its young people to be good witnesses for Christ wherever they are. This is foundational. The special training they need to serve in other lands can be added elsewhere.

We take it for granted that the church is sincerely

and seriously interested in the development of its young people. It not only wants to see them continue faithful to the church. It desires to help them grow in spirituality and leadership. It hopes to see them make some useful contribution to the work of the church and to the whole cause of Christ. So it should be willing to give special attention to the training of its youth. What then can it do that will be important in missionary training?

Let us mention five things.

First is the matter of personal consecration and the spiritual life. Every pastor recognizes that this is a part of his usual responsibility. Among his Christian young people are some who have been reared in the church. Others have come into it out of nonchristian surroundings through conversion. It makes little difference. In every case they need to be brought to the place of personal dedication. Sometimes those who were brought up in Christian surroundings are the hardest to get to see their need of such dedication. But they cannot know the fullness of the Christian life until they make it.

A single act of dedication is not enough. No more so than the single act of joining the church. It should set the course for our life; but how often we veer away to one side or the other and end up completely off course! We need training in the spiritual life. That is, we need not only to know the principles but to have instruction in applying them to our daily life. We also need to have practice in doing this. We need to learn how to put first in our lives "the kingdom of God and his righteousness."

Second is the matter of systematic Bible study. This too should be a part of the church's usual ministry. Sometimes it is well done. Sometimes any young person who wants to can get in his home church a good foundation in the teachings of Scripture. But more often this is not the case. Especially when most of the Bible teaching is left to the Sunday school with its often haphazard teaching under inexperienced teachers.

This is one of the great values of expository preaching. It is Bible teaching from the pulpit. And since so many never attend any but the preaching services of the church, it is the kind of teaching that helps raise the whole level of Bible instruction in the church. That is, if it is well done.

But when listening to expository sermons, or even to Bible lectures given at the church's midweek service, the young people are passive. They listen and drink in—if they want to. But there is no chance for them to clarify their understanding by asking questions. There is no chance for them to express what they are learning, so as to fix it more firmly in their minds.

It is this purpose that the young people's society should fulfill. It gives the youth of the church a chance to express what they are learning. There is no surer way for them to fix a teaching in their own minds than to try to teach it to others. It encourages them to search the Scriptures for themselves and discuss its teachings among those of similar age and experience. With good counsel the young people's society can be an invaluable training school. Without such counsel it may become just an insipid social club. Or it may turn into just another preaching service where young people are expected to sit and listen.

But besides these things there is still a need for more systematic and consecutive study of the Bible. The Bible class is needed. It may be a part of the Sunday school. It may be held on some weekday evening. Whatever the arrangement, it is a serious and purposeful attempt to get the fullness of Scripture teaching instead of just snatches here and there. Often such a class makes use of a correspondence course such as those offered by Moody Bible Institute. Sometimes examinations are given; sometimes not. Only a minority of the church attends, but it is from this interested minority that the missionary candidates as well as church leaders will probably come.

And when they get to the training schools, the value of this Bible teaching in the home church soon shows up.

A third field in which the local church can provide training is personal evangelism. Perhaps it is more a matter of inspiration and encouragement than it is of instruction. Classes in personal evangelism have their place, but they are not much good without practice. Nothing can take the place of actually talking with men and women about the faith we have in Christ. Many do it spontaneously in the enthusiasm of their newfound faith. But today, when the great majority of our church members have been reared in the faith, this is not the rule. Most young people need to be encouraged to do it, and they need to be shown how.

The subject of personal evangelism is too big for us to deal with it extensively here. But we can make one or two suggestions. People usually do better at first if at least two work together. This is specially valuable when one is experienced and can show the other how. In any case the one encourages the other, and they both learn from their joint experience.

Also, to keep up interest in this personal witnessing, there must be a chance to tell others about it — to share experiences. We have lost more than we realize in dropping the testimony meetings from our churches today. The pleasure people have in any experience is vastly increased by telling someone else about it. If this is true in our personal religious experience, it is doubly so in the matter of witnessing to others.

Fourth, there are opportunities for leadership and Christian service that the local church can provide. This is extremely important in missionary preparation. It is amazing to see how many young people enter missionary training schools without any previous experience in Christian work of any sort. In the case of recent converts to Christianity this is of course understandable. There hasn't been time for them to get such experience. Perhaps we can excuse it, too, on the part of those whose Christianity was largely formal and superficial until shortly before they entered the school. But there are many others who could have performed such service. They may not have lacked initiative. What was lacking was the necessary opportunities and guidance—principally guidance.

It is true that a missionary has to learn to take the initiative. Those who always have to be told what to do don't make good missionaries. But on the other hand, church leaders don't always welcome initiative on the part of the young people. They don't always see the leadership potentialities in many of them. As we have said before, leadership is not merely a matter of natural talent. Even where that talent exists, it needs encouragement and guidance.

The wise church deliberately gives responsibility to its young people. We don't mean just the responsibility for running their own young people's society. Every bit of Christian service that they can perform will help in their training. This is specially true of jobs that call for leadership of others. In every church there are many services in which young people could take a part. They often teach Sunday school classes, though they usually need more instruction and counsel for the task than they get. High school boys can develop into very acceptable ushers with supervision. Games at the Sunday school picnic, and even other parts of the program, can be turned over to the young people. Older young people can sponsor still younger groups, sometimes with better understanding and greater success than adults would have. Some churches have found it worthwhile to turn over an occasional evening service to the young people, letting them plan and direct it all *except the sermon*. Others have encouraged the formation of "gospel teams" and other such groups to carry the witness to neglected places, to jails, missions, and even occasionally other churches. Some are encouraging their young people to go help out the home missions during their vacations from school. We could extend the list indefinitely.

The important thing is that two principles be kept constantly in mind. One is that the work should profit. It shouldn't be just "a lark" for the young people. The other is that they should have competent supervision. Only so can they get proper training.

Our fifth suggestion has to do with schools. When a young volunteer offers his life for missionary service, he usually knows that he will need special training. But being young and enthusiastic, he doesn't want to spend any longer getting that training than he has to.

It is at this point that his pastor can render a real missionary service. If the pastor has the young person's confidence he can direct him to those schools and courses of training that will best meet his need. He can see to it that he doesn't try to shortcut his preparation. He can tell him where to get the special advice that the pastor himself may not be able to give. He can encourage him to go ahead in spite of difficulties.

One major difficulty that faces many prospective candidates is the financing of their training. Even in those few schools where no tuition is charged, the student still has many other expenses. Should the church help him? Especially since he is going to be a missionary?

Some do. Some churches include in their budget a certain amount to be used in helping their young people get training for Christian service. They believe it is a sound investment of the Lord's money. And that can be very true.

But there are problems. There are always some who begin their training and never complete it. There are others who finish their training but never enter the service they intended. How is the church going to feel about these young people? Will it condemn them for accepting its help and then not carrying through? Will it make them feel like debtors?

Again, there are some whose choice of a mission board is not what the home church would prefer. Because the church has given them some financial help in their train-

274 AN INTRODUCTION TO CHRISTIAN MISSIONS

ing, they may feel obligated to accept the choice of the church or the pastor. Or if they don't, they are afraid they will offend the people of their church. Should young people be tied down with financial strings to the choices others make for them?

Such problems can be solved. But we need to face them frankly in order to solve them. Let us do this. Let us urge our young people to follow the Lord's guidance. Then let us show our confidence in Him and in them by offering our help with no strings attached. Let them be responsible to Him, not to us, even as we also are responsible to Him. Let His gospel and the glory of His name be our chief concern, and not our own interests. Only so can we fulfill our missionary obligation.

28

A CHURCH MISSIONARY PROGRAM— ORGANIZATION

WE HAVE WRITTEN rather extensively about the objectives of a church missionary program. We have also given a number of practical suggestions for the carrying out of those objectives. The pastor's own part in the program we naturally dealt with in some detail.

But how should the church in general be organized for the carrying out of such a program? No program is self-implementing. Neither can the pastor alone do all that is needed. Even when the pastor has the backing of various individuals in the congregation, he may have a hard time making the program effective.

Essentially we must give missions a clearly assigned place within the organizational structure of the church. There must be persons, whether elected or appointed, who have the missionary program as their primary responsibility. These persons must have authority to act, not as individual members but as representatives of the church.

THE MISSIONARY COMMITTEE

Most churches today that are seriously interested in missions have a missionary committee. It is a committee chosen in the same way as other committees that carry on the normal operations of the church. It is not a separate society like the women's missionary society. It is chosen by the church and it represents the whole church in missionary matters. Its ultimate responsibility is to the congregation as a whole.

The duties of such a committee need to be carefully

275

spelled out. They may vary from church to church. But a few major items are usually a part of its responsibility. This committee, for example, draws up the annual missionary budget for the church, subject to the church's approval. The committee also authorizes disbursements from the missionary funds of the church. It has the responsibility for planning the missionary conference and any other special missionary events.

When prospective missionaries seek the approval and support of the church, they approach the missionary committee first. Some committees actually take it in hand to counsel missionary volunteers in their preparation for service. Others merely pass on their qualifications after they have secured their training and are under appointment.

What the committee is able to accomplish depends in large measure on its personnel. For this reason it is important that every member should be a warm supporter of missions. But in addition they need to be knowledgeable in the field and willing to spend time and effort in carrying out the committee's objectives. A consistent program also requires a minimum of turnover in the committee. The chairman, at least, should continue in office for several years.

POLICY STATEMENT

Even a good missionary committee needs guidelines. Sometimes the church decides on them. More often the committee itself draws up a set of principles for its own operation. In either case it needs to have them in writing so anyone can refer to them.

The value of these guidelines shows up when the committee has to make a possibly touchy decision. For example, an influential member of the church presents the name of a friend of his who needs support. However, this friend is going to the field independent of any mission board. The committee doesn't want to offend the church member. Yet it questions the advisability of taking on a candidate they are not personally acquainted with under these conditions. What should it do?

If there is a policy statement covering the matter the answer is easy. The committee can say, "We are sorry, but if you will read our policy statement you will see that we can approve only those who go out under recognized mission societies." The church member then has no ground for thinking that anything personal is involved.

What should go into a policy statement? No one pattern will fit all churches. There are too many differences in the problems they are likely to face.

A church near a missionary training school, for example, has a special problem. Many of the young people attend that church during their school days. Some even become members in the hope that the church will support them when they go to the field. Yet the church obviously cannot take on the support of all of them. It may not even be enough to state that the church will take on the support only of those who are members. In some cases it is wise to specify that the prospect must have been a member for a reasonable length of time before application, and that he must have taken an active part in the church's work.

Some churches see more of their members go into missionary service than they can fully support. Then it is necessary for the committee to specify how they determine the amount of support they will assign to each. Many other churches, however, are able to support far more than their own members. Their committees must then determine on what basis they will select the additional ones for support. A church in Canada, for example, specifies that the candidates must be Canadian. Denominational churches sometimes will support only those who serve with their denominational board. Independent churches sometimes accept only those whose mission holds membership in the Interdenominational Foreign Mission Association.

Policy statements also deal with such things as the support of missionaries during normal furlough, allowances for children up to a certain age or point in their schooling, special grants for outfit and passage, any provisions for retirement and the conditions under which the support of a missionary may be dropped.

Some churches have a policy of requiring their missionaries on furlough to serve the home church for a short time, particularly in visitation. This serves a double purpose. It of course helps the church in its ministry. But at the same time it is a blessing to the missionary and to the church members. It provides an exceptional opportunity for getting acquainted—or reacquainted—and it draws them closer together.

It is sound policy for the missionary committee to concern itself with the total missionary program of the church. It need not in any way interfere with the special interests of such organizations as the Sunday school or the young people's society. Yet it should seek out ways of coordinating their efforts with the church's overall plan.

An individual missionary is no less supported by the church when his support is underwritten by the Bible class to which he belonged. Nor is there any good reason why the primary department should not enjoy the privilege of specifying their missionary gifts for the support of missionary children. It will certainly stimulate more interest. The different organizations in the church, like the different parts of the body, need to work together to accomplish the one task, each one contributing his own special part. This is scriptural.

The "Faith Promise" Plan of Financing

There is a plan of financing missionary work that has come into increasing use among the churches in recent years. It is called the "Faith Promise" plan.* The plan

*See Norman Lewis, *Triumphant Missionary Ministry in the Local Church* (Lincoln, Nebr.: Good News Broadcasting Assn., 1960).

has yielded such spectacular results in some churches that it deserved a brief treatment here.

Essentially the idea is that people need a definite stimulus as well as a clear-cut objective in their giving. If we depend on the momentary inspiration that a stirring missionary speaker may bring, we get a good offering for that once. If we remind the people periodically through a monthly missionary offering, we get only what the donors happen to have in their pockets at the time. But to carry on effectively missions need a steady, sustained flow of contributions from dedicated givers.

Churches often have used a system of pledges, but with less than satisfactory results. Some object to the legalistic nature of the pledge. Others hesitate to pledge for fear they may not be able to fulfill their pledge.

The "Faith Promise" plan is different. The faith promise is not considered a pledge. It is merely a statement of intention. At the time of the annual missionary conference, when missionary interest is at its peak, people are urged to decide on what they will try to do during the coming year. Trusting in the Lord to provide the means to do so, they declare their purpose to give for missionary work a certain regular amount. The matter is primarily between the giver and his Lord. No one else will hold him accountable if the promise is more than he can fulfill.

Yet, so the church can have some basis on which to estimate its probable receipts for the coming year, the donor is asked to record the amount of his faith promise on a card to be turned in. The names of those who promise are not revealed, but sometimes the total is calculated as the cards come in. Then at the final service of the conference the grand total is announced. If it reaches the goal set for that year, there is of course a great deal of rejoicing.

Of course these are only promises, and some will not be paid. Yet the giving often exceeds the promises. Many churches using this plan have multiplied their missionary giving. It is systematic, not depending on the impulse of the moment. It calls for a definite objective, which is always helpful. It is linked with anticipated blessing from the Lord. And it has scriptural warrant in the instructions Paul gave to the church at Corinth: "Upon the first day of the week let every one of you lay by him in store, an God hath prospered him, that there be no gatherings when I come" (1 Co 16:2).

ORGANIZATIONS WITHIN THE CHURCH

Every church has two or more organizations within the overall structure of the church itself. Some of the most common are the Sunday school (often with an organization of the individual classes), the young people's society, the women's society and the men's fellowship. In the larger churches the women's society may be divided into a number of subsidiary "circles."

These and other organizations in the church all have historic reasons for their beginning. Some, such as the Sunday school, are under fire today by those who think they are not "relevant" to current needs. However, most of us will agree that they do perform useful functions in the work of the church.

How should these organizations be related to the missionary program of the church? The answer is twofold.

First, if missions is the task of the whole church, then clearly the organizations must in some definite way be related to that program. *Second,* the part they have in the program must be determined by their own special nature and objectives. It would be a mistake to think of them as just so many different channels for raising funds for missions.

THE SUNDAY SCHOOL

The Sunday school is primarily designed to be a teaching agency. Its part in the total missionary program should be that of teaching missions. Yet many Sunday schools seldom if ever teach a missionary lesson except those that have to do with missions in ancient times.

One Sunday school, however, came up with an imaginative plan for both teaching missions and increasing Sunday school attendance. The church had six missionary families on its list. It was decided to divide the Sunday school classes into six groups, with one missionary family assigned to each group. Then the Sunday school announced a six-week contest for attendance and new members.

Each Sunday of the contest featured one missionary family. Someone gave a brief talk about the missionary's work, illustrating it with slides the missionary sent. Every student present that day got a postage stamp from the country where the missionary was serving. It was pasted in his special-attendance folder.

Classes that recorded 100 percent attendance were awarded one dollar each week to be sent to their missionary family. At the end of the contest an additional three dollars would go to those who maintained at least 80 percent attendance for all the Sundays. These awards went to the missionaries.

There was also a special award in each group that went personally to the pupil bringing the most new members or visitors. This award was a trophy or curio contributed by the missionary. Each pupil of course was allowed to keep his attendance folder with the foreign stamps for each Sunday he attended.

The plan called for careful planning long ahead of time. It took time for the missionaries to send in the slides, the stamps and the prize curio. The church assured them that it would cover whatever expenses they incurred. Thus the missionaries were out only the small amount of time and effort they expended. On the other hand they profited financially and in the increased interest in their work.

THE YOUNG PEOPLE'S SOCIETY

The young people's society offers the channel for

religious expression of the younger people in the church. These are the ones who have their careers yet before them. Certainly here of all places is the opportunity for open discussion of missions and all that such a ministry involves.

Only a few of the young people will themselves become missionaries. But all of them certainly should have the opportunity of finding out what it is all about. The future of missions in the church depends on it. So at regular intervals, or whenever a qualified person is available, they do well to schedule a missions forum. Their own leaders should of course be in charge. There should of course be complete freedom to bring up any questions that trouble them about missions.

But young people are not satisfied with talk. They also want to be active. Here the missionary committee can help out. It can suggest the channeling of that activity into various types of assistance to missions. Even such tasks as the packing of records for Gospel Recordings, or the packaging of pills for Medical Assistance Programs, can be an adventure to the young people. There are also city missions and other home missions that can sometimes make good use of their help during vacations.

SPECIAL WOMEN'S AND MEN'S SOCIETIES

Every church seems to have its special women's society. Special men's societies are not so universal. The basic reasoning for such societies seems to be that there are certain phases of the church's ministry that are of particular concern to the women, while others involve principally the men.

However, it has happened in many churches that the women's society has become the women's missionary society, while the men's society, if it exists, has undergone no such transformation. Men's missionary societies are few and far between. Unfortunately this has tended to create the impression that missions is primarily a women's concern.

There are two ways of meeting this problem. One is to seek out a plan for giving missions an important part in the men's program. It certainly should have it. Many of the missions' most pressing needs today are for men. Even when they appeal for short-term workers, as they are increasingly doing, their great emphasis is on men, such as builders, doctors and engineers.

But there is another way. Why can't the church make missions more central in its whole program? After all, we know that this is the one great task the Saviour committed to His church. Would it not be possible to have one midweek service per month dedicated to missions under the charge of the missionary committee? I am sure it would revitalize the midweek service. We often use this meeting for the church's business affairs as well as for prayer. Why not deal here with the missionary business of the church? Why not concentrate on prayer for the missionary outreach?

CONCLUSION

In all of our treatment of the church's missionary program we have considered that the expansion of the faith is a primary concern of the church. We realize that there are some who disagree. There are some who are not really concerned about winning converts to the Christian faith. They believe that the church's task is to make the "Christian presence" felt in the world, particularly in its secular affairs.

Those who hold to such a belief are also those who have a low view of the Scriptures. That is, they do not believe the Bible to be the very Word of God and authoritative for all those who profess to belong to Jesus Christ.

For those who do believe the Bible, it seems to us there can be no question. The propagation of faith in Jesus Christ, the Son of God and our Saviour, is at the very heart of the church's ministry in the world.

INDEX

Abraham, 54, 60
Adaptation, 110
Africa, 92, 100, 140-41, 143, 186, 190, 198-99
Age of missionaries, 110-11
Aims of missions, 65, 69-70, 134
Alexandria, 47
American Baptist Foreign Mission Society, 96
American Board of Commissioners for Foreign Missions, 97-98
Antioch, 37-39, 43, 45, 47, 72, 81-82, 84, 154
Apostles as missionaries, 43-44
Arabia, 21
Aramaic language, 47
Asia, province of, 41
Audiovisuals, 200, 230, 232-34, 242-43
Aviation, 149, 151, 200-01

Barnabas, 37-40, 45-46, 72, 81-83, 153
Bentley, Holman, 192, 217
Bible institutes & seminaries, 77, 117, 131, 135, 140, 146, 206, 212-14, 268
Bible study, 130, 134-35, 211-12, 269-71
Bible translation, 49, 119, 140, 218-19
Bolivia, 201
Bookkeeping, 146
Bookstores, 220
Brazil, Protestants in, 21
Buddhism, 21
Building, 149
Bulletin board, 244, 246
Burma, 96
Business training, 146

Cain, 59
Call, missionary, 78-101, 173; definition of, 101; examples of, 92-101; false ideas of, 80-85; general, 86-87; Macedonian, 83; needed, 85, 89; special, 80-81, 88-91, 173, 180
Camp Wycliffe. *See* Summer Institute of Linguistics
Candidates, 77, 102-51, 158, 161, 163, 224, 228-29, 261-74; age, 109-11; Christian life & experience of, 121-22, 135-37; education, 113-17, 128; engagement & marriage, 122-26;

handicaps, 113; health, 111-13, 124; personality, 118-21; training, 117, 127-51
Carey, William, 16, 89, 225
Central America, missions in, 10, 138
Chalmers, James, 95-96, 101
China, missionaries in, 66, 93, 100, 164, 173, 193, 205
China Inland Mission. *See* Overseas Missionary Fellowship
Christian experience, 121-22, 130-32, 137
Christian service, 135-36
Christianity; exclusive claims, 21-22; missionary nature, 19-27; view of mankind, 22-27
Church missionary program, 8-9, 71-77, 153-77, 222-83; creating interest, 222-23, 225-43; financial support through, 250-60; keeping informed, 244-49; objectives of, 223-25; organization of, 275-83; providing personnel, 261-68; training in, 268-74
Church establishment, 69, 110, 182-83, 204
Church Missionary Society, 99-101
Colportage, 220
Conference, missionary. *See* Missionary conference
Constancy, 107
Corinth, 84
Cornelius, 36-37, 40, 154
Cost of living, 254-55
Counseling, 132, 137, 202-4
Covenant, Abrahamic, 54, 60
Crawford, Dan, 186
Cyprus, 45-46, 82, 84

Debts, 161, 165
Democracy, 205-6
Denominations and missions, 70, 73, 117, 160-63, 170-72, 238
Devotion, 103, 122, 131, 264
Discernment, 106-7
Discussion periods, 241-42
Doctrinal standards, 174

East Africa, 100
Education for missions, 73, 77, 113-

17, 157, 164, 172
Egypt, 44, 47
Engagement. *See* Marriage.
Ephesus, 41, 44, 84
Ethiopia, 44
Ethiopian eunuch, 35-36
Europe, Paul enters, 41-42, 82-83
Evangelical Foreign Missions Association, 228, 248
Evangelical Missions Quarterly, 248
Evangelism, 69, 150, 172, 197-202, 204-5, 225; personal, 132, 199, 271
Exclusiveness of Christianity, 16-17, 21-24
Experience in pagan religion, 132
Expression, oral, 136-37

Faith missions, 117, 155, 162-69, 204-5
Faith promise plan, 278-80
Family, missionary, 123-26
Fellowship in a mission, 176
Finances, 39, 75-76, 155-59, 161-69, 174-75, 224, 230, 243, 252-58, 273-74, 278-80
Freedom, religious. *See* Religious freedom.
French language, 140-41, 217

General fund, 167-68
Gentiles, 29-30, 36-43
God, missionary message about, 52-54
Goths, 49
Great Commission, 30-32, 67-68, 72, 73-74, 86, 101, 153
Greece, 42, 44-45, 84
Greek language, 47, 140
Greek religion, 52, 57
Gutzlaff, Karl, 93

Health, 111-13, 124, 144
Heathenism. *See* Paganism.
Holy Spirit: and missions, 33-42; in the call, 72, 88; in organization, 153, 154; in preparation, 137
Home missions defined, 11. *See also* Missions, home vs. foreign.
Hyper-Calvinism, 16

Illiteracy. *See* Literacy.
Image of God in man, 54-55
Independent missionaries. *See* Missionaries, independent.
Independent missions, 160, 162-77
India, 21, 44, 97-99, 100, 190, 199-200
Indians, 55, 138, 200
Indigenous principles, 257
Indispensables in missionary preparation, 128-37
Individual support plans, 167-69

Indonesia, 21
Information, missionary, 157, 169, 223-24, 244-49
Innovation, 159
Interdenominational Foreign Mission Association, 176, 228, 248
International Review of Mission, 248
Interpretation, 189-90
Islam, 21, 22, 53, 186

Jacob, 54, 60
Japan, 21, 80, 188, 193
Jerusalem: church in, 38, 72, 81, 154; council, 39-41, 43-44
Jesus Christ: character of life, 28-29; and the Jews, 29-30; and missions, 28-32; objective of ministry, 29-30; purpose of coming, 28
Jews, 21, 29-30, 35-43, 47, 51, 52, 56, 57, 60, 61-63
John, 28, 44
Jonah, 63
Judaism, 40
Judson, Adoniram, 96-97, 101

Keys, Peter's use of, 37
Korea, 15-16, 93, 208, 226
Koreans, 15

Ladies' Missionary Society, 73, 75
Language learning, 102, 110, 115, 123-25, 139-44, 188-93, 214-15
Language reduction, 217-18
Latin America, 20-21, 55, 140, 190, 220
Leadership, 108, 115, 132-35, 204
Leadership training, 209-14, 271-73
Letters, missionary. *See* Missionary letters.
Liberalism, 16-17, 66-67, 170-71, 236
Library, missionary. *See* Missionary library.
Literacy, 134-35, 218
Literary work, 113, 149-50, 182, 214-20
Literature for missions, 76, 159, 182, 213-20
Livingstone, David, 92-93, 100, 188
London Missionary Society, 93, 100
Lostness of man, 24-27
Love, 104-5
Luke, 46-47

Macedonian vision (call), 41-42, 82-85
Mackay, Alexander M., 99-101
Madagascar, 100
Magazines, missionary, 247-49
Man, missionary message about, 22-27, 54-57
Maps, 245
Mark, 46, 84

Marriage, 122-26
Matthew, 44
Maturity, 110-11, 130, 204
Medical instruction, 138, 144-45
Medical missionaries, 110-12, 127, 144-45, 148-51
Mental balance, 112
Methodist Episcopal Church, 98
Mexico, 10
Mills, Samuel J., 96
Mission boards: 39, 102, 108, 109, 117, 152-77, 180-81; denominational, 160-62; how to choose, 170-77; independent, 162-69; interdenominational (faith), 163-69; opposition to, 152-54, 158-59; values of, 155-58
Missionaries: false, 47; held to be spies, 63; independent, 8, 71, 178-86, problems of, 179-83; selected, 9-10, 39; support of, 75-76, 252-58, 276-78; types, 178-79, unnamed, 46-47
Missionary: call (see Call, missionary); closet, 259-60; committee, 275-76; conference, 238-43, 279; letters, 157, 245-47; library, 234-37, 248; life, 114, 125, 194-96; magazines, 247-49; nature of Christianity, 19; packages, 259; policy statement, 276-78; preparation (see Preparation, missionary); qualifications (see Qualifications, missionary); speakers, 227-32, 238, 242-43; turnover, 177
Missionary as ambassador, 28-29, 71, 86
Missionary work, 187-221; church establishment, 204-8; counseling, 202-4; evangelism, 197-202; just living, 194-96; knowing the people, 193-94; language study, 188-93; leadership training, 209-14; literature 214-21
Missions: definition of, 8-10; home vs. foreign, 10-12, 74, 80, 81, 88-91, 266; opposition to, 12-17; responsibility for, 51, 59, 64
Missions and the church. See Church missionary program.
Missions and mission, 17, 156-57
Moffat, Robert, 93
Mohammedanism. See Islam.
Moral courage, 105
Motion pictures, 157, 232-33
Motives for missions, 13, 65-69, 238 n., 266-68
Muhammad. See Islam.

National workers, 255-58
New Guinea, 80, 95

New Hebrides, 94
New Testament and missions, 18-48
Nigeria, 139
Nonprofessional missionaries, 179, 183-86

Old Testament and missions: 49-64; activity, 63-64; message, 51-58; purpose, 59
Opium War, 93
Organizations in the church, 280-83
Overseas Missionary Fellowship, 164-65, 190

Paganism, 53, 56-57, 132
Papuans, 15
Pastor & missions, 222-27, 246, 254
Paton, John G., 94-95, 101
Paul, 22, 25, 28, 37-47, 52, 59, 68, 72, 78, 81-85, 153, 205, 258
Peace Corps, 69, 263
Pentecost, Day of, 35, 37, 64, 226
People, study of, 150, 193-94, 213, 215
Personality, 118-21
Personnel for missions, 224, 261-74, 276
Peter, 22, 36-37, 40, 43-44, 47, 133-34
Pharisees, 64
Philip, 35-36, 72, 81, 154
Phonetics, 143-44, 217
Pictures & projectors, 232-34, 242
Policy statement, missionary, 276-78
Polygamy, 50
Pooling plan, 166-67
Portuguese language, 140-41
Prayer for missions, 75, 224, 250-52
Preaching, 70, 197-99, 204
Preparation of missionaries: 39, 127-51, 224, 265, 268-74; Bible, 134-35; controlling factors in, 127-28; experience in, 135-37, 149-50; indispensables in, 128-37; language, 139-44; medical, 144-45; social, 132-34; specialized, 147-51; spiritual, 130-32; teacher training, 145-46
Printing, 149
Proof-text method, 18, 50
Proselytism, 9, 13, 36, 64
Protestantism, 20, 73
Purpose, 106, 264

Qualifications: 68, 78, 102-26, 172, 179-80, 212-16; educational, 113-17; essential, 102-8; personality, 118-22; physical, 109-13

Race in the Bible, 55-56

Radio, 149, 200
Reformed Church in America, 97
Religion a matter of country or race,
    20-21
Religion a private concern, 19-21
Religious freedom, 20
Reputation of missions, 176-77
Responsibility for missions, 71-91;
    church, 72-77; individual, 78-91
Romans, 21, 56-57
Rome, church in, 41-42, 44, 84-85

Salary, missionary, 76, 161, 165
Samaria, 29-30, 72, 81, 154
Saul. *See* Paul.
Schools, missionary training, 127-51
    passim, 268, 273-74
Schweitzer, Albert, 217
Scriptures, 21, 134
Scudder, John, 97-98, 101
Service support, 168-69
Shintoism, 21
Short-term missionaries, 68
Silas, 46
Sin: in New Testament, 21-27; in Old
    Testament, 56-57
Social action, 9, 17, 69-70, 208, 263
South America, 200
South Pacific, 15, 94-96
Spain, 19-20, 46, 85
Spanish language, 140, 192, 216-17
Specialists, 110, 113, 117, 129, 134,
    147-51
Spirituality, 103-4; 113-15, 122, 129-32,
    269
Stevenson, Robert Louis, 95
Summer Institute of Linguistics, 144
Support of missionaries. *See* mission-
    aries, support of.

Syrian Christians of India, 44
Syrians, 20

Tarsus, 38, 45, 81-82
Tax rulings, 168
Taylor, J. Hudson, 164-65, 225
Teaching, 69-70, 113, 117, 145-46, 148,
    150-51, 204, 212-13
Theology and missions, 16-17, 174, 176
Thoburn, James M., 98-99, 101
Thomas in India, 44
Timothy, 46, 154
Titus, 46, 154
Toronto Institute of Linguistics, 144
Training nationals, 182-83, 210-14,
    256-57
Training of missionaries. *See* Prep-
    aration.
Translation, 216-17. *See also* Bible
    translation.
Traveling, 199-201
Troas, 41, 85
Trust, 104

Uganda, 99-101
Ulfilas, 49
Unity of human race, 55

Venezuela, 198, 202
Visitation, 201-2

West Indies, 93
World War II and missions, 16, 123,
    188, 205

Zeal, 107